CU00956359

THE
CAMBRIDGE
BOOK
OF
DAYS

ROSEMARY ZANDERS

For Ed, without whom not

First published 2011

The History Press
The Mill, Brimscombe Port
Stroud, Gloucestershire, GL5 2QG
www.thehistorypress.co.uk

British Library Cataloguing in Publication Data.
A catalogue record for this book is available from the British
Library.

ISBN 978 0 7524 5953 0

Typesetting and origination by The History Press
Manufacturing managed by Jellyfish Print Solutions Ltd.
Printed in India

January 1st

1631: On this day, the carrier Thomas Hobson died, prompting the young poet John Milton from Christ's College to write a verse, beginning with:

Here lies old Hobson. Death hath broke his girt,
And here, alas! hath laid him in the dirt.

Though hardly the most reverential of epitaphs, it was unique in being written by Milton about someone outside his usual university circles. Described variously as 'shrewd, industrious, successful and unpretentious', Hobson was the city's undisputed transport king, running a thriving business behind the George Hotel; today, Hobson's Building in St Catharine's College marks the site. Hobson had wagons which conveyed both goods and passengers to the Bull Inn in London; he also hired out individual horses, on a strict rota basis, only offering the horse which was next in turn for work. This system gave birth to the phrase 'Hobson's Choice', meaning no choice at all. Hobson was buried in the chancel of St Bene't's Church in Cambridge, but although he was survived by a widow, two daughters and six grandchildren, no memorial was erected in his memory. (Bushell, W.D., *Hobson's Conduit*, CUP: 1938)

January 2nd

1300: On this day, the 'brethren and sisters' of St Mary's Gild celebrated a solemn mass for their deceased members at the Church of St Mary by the market. The 'congregation' of the Gild of St Mary met on a very irregular basis, usually in order to agree on procedures and to elect officers. Just half a century later, in 1352, the Gild of St Mary was permitted by Royal Charter, on 'account of poverty', to merge with the Gild of Corpus Christi, which was attached to the Church of St Benedict. The main purpose of this alliance appears to have been the foundation of a college, established primarily to train priests, who were in short supply after the ravages of the Black Death in 1348. Thus was born Corpus Christi College, which has the distinction of being the only college in either Oxford or Cambridge to be founded neither by royalty nor by wealthy individuals, but by its citizens. The Gild archives are still in the College's possession, along with a drinking-horn of similar vintage, taken from an aurochs (a now-extinct animal); students still drink from it today when it is passed around the table at College feasts. (Stanley, L.T., *The Cambridge Year*, Chatto & Windus: 1960 / Cambridge Society Magazine: 2002)

January 3rd

1873: On this day, Josiah Chater made the following entry in his diary, a sad reflection on the stigma associated with illegitimate births in Victorian times: 'The poor girl assistant in Jackson's in the Cury [Petty Cury today], was found in the river this morning just below the Great Bridge. An inquest was held this morning. M. [the father, a well-known wine merchant in Cambridge] was summoned but did not appear; she left a note stating that if he had done as he ought to have done he would not now be answerable for her death and that friends were to apply to him to bury her'. At the adjourned inquest a week later, a verdict of 'found drowned in an unsound mind caused by her seducer' was given. M., the man whom the girl had accused in her letter, was present in the court and was named by one of the jury. 'He had a fearful reception,' wrote Josiah. An earlier diary entry tells of a Cambridge servant who had given birth to an illegitimate child, suffocated the baby and then put it in a drawer where it was found the following day by her mistress, who 'vowed that she was completely ignorant of the girl's condition'. (Porter, E., *Josiah Chater's Diaries*, Phillimore: 1975)

January 4th

1852: On this day, Captain Davies, accompanied by about sixty of his 'fine and powerful' men, attended an inaugural service in Chesterton Church, Cambridge, for the newly-formed Cambridgeshire police force. The new police officers were earnestly exhorted to perform 'their duty to God and man' and were reminded in the vicar's sermon that 'rulers are not a terror to good works but evil'. The police uniform was supplied by Messrs Hibbert & Co. and included truncheons, handcuffs, lanterns, capes and even a small supply of leg-irons. The use of handcuffs was questioned in court after a policeman was 'hooted' for leading a detainee through Cambridge in 'bracelets', but this was overridden. At night time, officers could wear their own clothes in order to save wear and tear on the uniform, but this of course made the officers harder to identify. In 1855, PC Peake was reported missing in the early hours of the morning, wearing 'a brown straw hat, a brown overcoat and Wellington boots'. In the same year, the county constabulary mooted a 'moustache movement', which was approved and recommended by the authorities. (Watts, P., *The Formation of the Cambridgeshire Constabulary*, Cambridgeshire Local History Society Review: 2001)

January 5th

1970: On this day, Roberto Gerhard, Spanish Catalan avant-garde composer, scholar, writer and broadcaster, died in Cambridge following a stroke and was subsequently buried in the romantically atmospheric Ascension Burial Ground, alongside such Cambridge luminaries as G.E. Moore and Ludwig Wittgenstein. A staunch Republican supporter during the Spanish Civil War, Gerhard left his homeland after the Republican defeat in 1938, never to return except for holidays; his music, with its strong Catalan sympathies, was virtually banned in Spain during the Franco regime. After short stays in Paris, Vienna and Berlin, Gerhard was offered a research scholarship at King's College in Cambridge, a city in which he was to reside for the rest of his life, not only becoming a British citizen and 'a virtuoso master of the English language' but also being awarded the CBE for his services to music. Gerhard was a very prolific composer and one of the first to master electronic composition; his incidental music for the 1955 Stratford performance of *King Lear* has the distinction of being the first electronic score for the British stage. Gerhard's archive, including most of his musical manuscripts, over a thousand letters plus photographs and other documents, is kept in the Cambridge University Library. (*The Times* / CUL)

January 6th

1973: On this day, at the beginning of its 500th anniversary year, work began in St Catharine's College to excavate the area below the east end of the chapel. Records show that only four people had been buried in the main chapel since its consecration in 1704 and a handful of others, including John Addenbrooke (after whom the Cambridge hospital is named), in the antechapel. Several of these graves had been located when central heating was installed in the mid-1950s, but the east end remained a mystery. In 1970 the original altar was moved, revealing a heavy stone slab; it was decided to remove this and replace it with black and white marble squares, to match the surrounding floor. Brickwork was revealed just 2 inches below the stone slab; further investigation showed this to be a brick arch, beneath which was a vault, approximately 6ft deep, containing two coffins, soon identified as containing Archbishop Sir William Dawes, Master of St Catharine's College, and his wife. Lady Dawes had died at the age of twenty-nine in 1705 and her distraught husband buried her here, placing an elaborate monument to her memory, now removed to the antechapel. (Aston, S.C., *St Catharine's College Society Magazine*: 1973)

January 7th

1780: On this day, an inquest opened into the death of a newborn child whose body had been discovered in the river behind Trinity College. Local surgeon Mr Bond carried out a post-mortem examination, recording: 'The head swelled and bruised, the skull fractured in several places', concluding that in his opinion the child had been born alive and 'received its death by the wounds in the head.' The mother of the baby was found to be Elizabeth Butchill, a young bed-maker at Trinity College, who, it was suspected, had had an affair with one of the undergraduates. Described as a 'fair young maiden', she was also uneducated and naive; as soon as her newborn baby started crying, the terrified girl, still weak after giving birth, took her baby outside. She reached the 'bogs' (toilets near the River Cam) and threw the infant down one of the holes which opened into the river. She buried the placenta and other evidence of the birth in a nearby dunghill. Convicted of 'wilful murder', poor Elizabeth was sent to the prison in Cambridge Castle, whence to the gallows to hang 'for her crime'. (Bell, J., *More Cambridgeshire Crimes*, Popular Publications: 1995)

January 8th

1880: On this day, 'the great baking powder case', a Victorian dispute over food additives, was heard at the Cambridge Borough Sessions and aroused a lot of interest, especially among housewives and shopkeepers. Local grocery shops were accused of selling baking powder consisting of ground rice, alum and soda bicarbonate. Despite being on the market for forty years, it was claimed that the alum was 'injurious to health' and should be removed. The conviction was quashed, but debates over food additives were of course only just beginning ... (Porter, E., *Josiah Chater's Diaries*, Phillimore: 1975)

———— ◆ ————

2001: On this day, bells rang out across Cambridge, celebrating the sealing of Cambridge's first royal charter by King John 800 years ago to the day. The charter gave the city more control over its finances, kick-started the local economy and helped create the conditions which led to the birth of Cambridge University just eight years later. To celebrate the octocentenary the City Council joined forces with Cambridge universities, churches, colleges and businesses to organise a year-long programme of special events. (*Cambridge Evening News*)

January 9th

1756: On this day, poet Thomas Gray wrote from Peterhouse to his friend Dr Wharton asking for a rope-ladder, 'for my neighbours every day make a great progress in drunkenness, which gives me reason to look about me'. Gray gave very specific instructions: 'It must be full 36 foot long ... but as light and manageable as it may be, easy to unroll, and not likely to entangle ... it must have strong hooks ... to throw over an iron bar to be fix'd withinside of my window'. The rope ladder was duly delivered and an iron bar installed outside his college window from which to hang it; Gray must have enjoyed a moment of peace, knowing that he could make a hasty emergency exit in the event of fire or another tragedy. He was of course opening himself up to derision, and Viscount Percival and friends, rising early to go hunting, roared out 'Fire! Fire!', hoping to see Gray descend the ladder in his nightcap. Gray was indeed very agitated, but spotted the perpetrators in time. His complaints to the College fell on deaf ears and within two months Gray had decamped to Pembroke College, taking with him his 'rope-ladder and firebags'. The iron bar remains in position to this day. (Chainey, G., *A Literary History of Cambridge*, Pevensey Press: 1985)

January 10th

1985: On this day, Cambridge computer pioneer Clive Sinclair launched his iconic, battery-powered, one-seater tricycle, the C5. Sinclair, who had invented the slim-line pocket calculator and Spectrum computers in the 1970s and '80s, was convinced that C5s would sell in their millions, but the reality was rather different. Although the novelty value of the C5 meant that sales got off to a quick start, they soon dwindled and production was eventually discontinued. The vehicle had a maximum speed of 15mph and required pedal power for starting and for travelling uphill. There were other problems; it had a very limited range, its cockpit was exposed to the elements and its drivers were very vulnerable on open roads. Worse, no driving license was required, even fourteen year olds were allowed to drive it and helmets were not compulsory. In Cambridge, a C5 was seen 'weaving among pedestrians' on Parker's Piece, prompting a debate as to whether it was a car or a tricycle. Some were worried that it seemed to have 'a licence to go anywhere, posing a threat to people'. The whole project had a disastrous effect on Sinclair's finances. Facing losses of up to £7m, he sold his computer business to Alan Sugar's Amstrad. (*Cambridge Evening News*)

January 11th

1584: On this day, the charter of Queen Elizabeth I authorising Sir Walter Mildmay, for many years her Chancellor of the Exchequer, to found Emmanuel College was sealed. From the outset, Emmanuel College was well known as a Puritan establishment and the statutes made clear that it was to be a 'school of prophets', to train learned and devoted ministers of the Church of England. By the reign of Charles I, the high church was having a revival under William Laud and a number of Emmanuel graduates decided to emigrate to America, taking their Protestant faith with them. Of the first hundred university graduates who settled in New England, no fewer than one third were from Emmanuel College in Cambridge. The best known of these was John Harvard, who died young in 1638, leaving his books and half his estate to found a new university which still bears his name today. A Victorian representation of John Harvard can be seen in the chapel windows; in the background of the window is a sailing ship, such as that in which he would have crossed the Atlantic, along with the monument on the site of Harvard's supposed grave at Charlestown. (Stubbings, F., *Emmanuel College: An Historical Guide*: 1996)

January 12th

1567: On this day, the Vice-Chancellor of the University of Cambridge made Joan Fan atone for her misdemeanours; she was ordered to kneel at the porch of St Giles' Church while the bells tolled, then when the curate said the Ash Wednesday penitential prayers she was brought into the middle of the church, told to kneel there throughout the service, and 'after the commandments said, she should turning to the people acknowledge her fault and pray the people to pray for her amendment'. There is no mention of what misdemeanour had warranted this very public punishment. (Oosthuizen, S., *A Woman's Guide to Cambridge*, Woody Press: 1983)

———◆———

1825: On this day, a son was born to botany lecturer Frederick Brooke Westcott and his wife Sarah. Brooke Foss Westcott's home life was simple, frugal and solitary, but it was during his time at Trinity College in Cambridge that he established the ascetic lifestyle for which he was later renowned, rising early, eating very little and working until after midnight. As Regius Professor of Divinity, Westcott helped to set up the clergy training school in Jesus Lane which now bears his name, Westcott House. (*Ely Ensign / Dictionary of National Biography*)

January 13th

1998: On this day, forty-five years after his arrival as an undergraduate, leading Indian economist Professor Amartya Sen became the thirty-sixth Master of Trinity College. His initiation as Master did not, however, go totally according to plan. Tradition dictates that the Master-to-be should hand a letter from the Queen to the Head Porter, confirming his new appointment. The Fellows, gathered in the Chapel, then examine its authenticity whilst the new incumbent waits outside the Great Gate. Amartya Sen left this important letter in the room where he changed after lunch. He locked the door and put the key in his coat pocket; when he returned later to retrieve the letter, he realised that he had left his jacket, along with the crucial key, somewhere else. The investiture was due to start in nine minutes and the Porters' master-key was staircase specific. Desperate measures were called for and it was decided to kick the door down; Sen grabbed the letter with just one minute to spare. Probably no one else realised what had happened, but Sen later described his entry as being 'more like King Kong than the Master of Trinity College'. Eleven months after his installation at Trinity, Amartya Sen was awarded the Nobel Prize in Economic Sciences. (*Cambridge Evening News*)

January 14th

2004: On this day, the *Cambridge Evening News* showed a photograph of Ian Whittle unveiling a plaque to his father Sir Frank Whittle, who through his invention of the jet engine had 'made the world a smaller place'. The plaque was erected this week on the gatepost of the University's Engineering Department in Trumpington Street. Frank Whittle came to Cambridge in 1934 as a mature student and completed a three-year mechanical science course in just two before inventing the jet engine a year later. Sir Frank had begun his research into the engine while he was in the RAF in 1929, although his early proposals were rejected by the Air Ministry as 'quite impracticable'. After completing his studies, the RAF assigned Sir Frank full time to the development of the jet engine and the first run of the experimental model was achieved in 1937. The first flight of his jet engine took place in May 1941, when an E-28-39 aircraft made a seventeen minute flight, marking the start of a new age of air transport and travel. In 1972, his contribution to jet propulsion was commemorated by the opening of the Whittle Laboratory in West Cambridge, still active today in the research of compressors and turbines. (*Cambridge Evening News*)

January 15th

1350: On this day, William Bateman, Bishop of Norwich, founded 'The Hall of the Holy Trinity of Norwich' to replenish the numbers of lawyers and priests who had been lost to the plague and in particular to educate students in canon and civil law. Trinity Hall, as the college is known today, is still often called the Lawyers' College. Bishop Bateman was an absentee founder, spending much of his time at Avignon, home of the Popes in the fourteenth century; Bateman had been sent there in an attempt to end the Hundred Years' War. Several of the early colleges were initially called Hall and later changed their title to College, but Trinity Hall was unable to do this after Henry VIII founded Trinity College, a completely separate entity, just down the road in 1546. Nestling between its larger neighbours of King's, Clare and Trinity, Trinity Hall is a very attractive college, with gardens leading down to the River Cam. Novelist Henry James commented: 'If I were called upon to mention the prettiest corner of the world, I should draw a thoughtful sigh and point the way to the gardens of Trinity Hall.' (Crawley, C., *Trinity Hall: The History of a Cambridge College*, Trinity Hall: 1976)

January 16th

1999: On this day, Dadie Rylands, Shakespearean director and former Dean and Bursar of King's College in Cambridge, died in his college rooms aged ninety-six. After a glittering undergraduate career, Dadie Rylands – the name was an infant attempt to lisp 'baby' – was elected as a Fellow of King's and given a set of rooms which looked over the great lawn to the river and Clare College beyond. Rylands was much influenced by members of the Bloomsbury Group; the view from his rooms was painted by Dora Carrington and Douglas Davidson and during the inter-war years became a centre of artistic and intellectual life in Cambridge. It was here that he hosted the lunch party described by Virginia Wolf in *A Room of One's Own*: 'How good life seemed … how trivial this grudge or that grievance … as, lighting a good cigarette, one sunk among the cushions in the window seat.' Rylands went on to be a leader of the artistic avant-garde, prominent as both performer and producer at several Cambridge theatres. In his last years he felt he had outlived his time and complained that he was unable to see, read, hear or walk properly. He was unmarried and lived right to the end in the college rooms which he had made his home. (*The Times*)

January 17th

2009: Today marked the launch of the celebrations for the 800th anniversary of the foundation of the University of Cambridge. At 7.15 p.m. churches in central Cambridge, including the University Church of Great St Mary's, rang touches of eight hundred changes especially composed for the occasion by Clare College alumnus Phil Earis. Additionally, a light show was projected onto Senate House and Old Schools; this spectacular show, orchestrated to music, was produced by world-renowned light artist Ross Ashton. It traced 800 years of Cambridge's history and included specially produced drawings of two of the University's most famous alumni, Isaac Newton and Charles Darwin, by renowned illustrator and Downing College alumnus Quentin Blake. Charles Darwin was portrayed chasing a butterfly whilst riding a giant beetle, whilst Newton examined a prism of light. Around 7,000 people gathered to witness the launch. Professor Jeremy Sanders, chairman of the University's 800 anniversary committee, said: 'We are doing things that Cambridge has never done before. We want to open Cambridge University up to people who wouldn't normally think about it.' Ross Ashton is well known for his large-scale projections across enormous surfaces; these have included a mountain in Oman, the Edinburgh Tattoo and the Queen's Golden Jubilee at Buckingham Palace. (University of Cambridge Press Office)

January 18th

1766: On this day, a note was written to the effect that a small case had been sent 'by the Cambridge Waggon' to Dr Elliston, Master of Sidney Sussex College. The note went on to say that the case contained a portrait, which the Master and Fellows of Sidney Sussex 'are *requested* to accept'. The case in question duly arrived, together with the following communication: 'An Englishman, an Assertor of Liberty, Citizen of the World, is desirous of having the honor [*sic*] to present an original Portrait in Crayons of the Head of O. Cromwell, Protector, drawn by Cooper, to Sydney Sussex College in Cambridge'. It was requested that the portrait should be placed so as to 'receive the light from left to right ... and to be free of sunshine'. The portrait of Cromwell (who had been an undergraduate in the college) was hung in the Hall, protected from sunlight by a small curtain, but the identity of the donor remained unknown for fourteen years, until one Thomas Hollis died; a reference to the gift was found in his memoirs. A generous benefactor, Hollis had also sent four copies of Milton's *Paradise Lost* (two of them first editions) to Christ's College and a portrait of Isaac Newton to Trinity College. (Scott-Giles, C.W., *Sidney Sussex College: A Short History*, CUP: 1951)

January 19th

1964: On this day, a highly controversial debate took place in the Cambridge Union debating chamber, on the topic 'This House deplores the Labour Party's hypocritical attitude towards immigration policy.' The main speaker was Peter Griffiths, who had just notoriously unseated the new Foreign Secretary Patrick Gordon-Walker. Following a successful career in opposition, Gordon-Walker had been destined to become Foreign Secretary in the hotly anticipated Harold Wilson government. At a time when voters in most parts of the country were swinging towards Labour, the constituency of Smethwick in the West Midlands went the opposite way as Gordon-Walker's Conservative opponent Peter Griffiths fought a racist campaign, exploiting local inhabitants' fears about large numbers of immigrants moving into the area. The most notorious slogan in Griffiths' campaign was 'If you want a nigger for your neighbour, vote Labour.' Harold Wilson was so appalled by the result that he stated that Griffiths should 'serve his term here as a parliamentary leper'. So the Cambridge debate was both highly topical and highly controversial. There was a large demonstration against Griffiths outside the Union building; there were around 200 protesters with banners and placards and forty policemen holding back the crowds. (Parkinson, S., *Arena of Ambition*, Icon Books: 2009)

January 20th

1511: On this day, an important step in the foundation of St John's College Cambridge was taken when the executors of Lady Margaret Beaufort, mother of King Henry VII, were given possession of St John's Hospital. This hospital had catered for the poor and the sick (with the exception of pregnant women, lepers, cripples and the insane) since 1200 and also housed a number of 'corrodians', lodgers who received board and lodging in return for gifts of land or property. Those admitted had originally been well looked after, but the Black Death had taken its toll and the hospital acquired on this day was dilapidated, with few brethren left to run it. On 12 March the last surviving monks 'departed from Cambridge towards Ely... at four of the clock at afternoon by water.' In April, Robert Shorton was installed as the first Master and St John's College was born. The hospital chapel served as the chapel for the new college until 1868, when it was replaced by a neo-Gothic extravaganza designed by George Gilbert Scott. Foundations and tombs from the old chapel can still be clearly seen in the First Court of the College. (Haigh, D., *The Religious Houses of Cambridgeshire*, Cambridgeshire County Council: 1988 / Miller, E., *Portrait of a College*, Silent Books: 1961)

January 21st

1495: On this day, Thomas Barowe, eminent Doctor of Laws in the University of Cambridge and former Fellow of King's Hall, gave £240, a considerable sum at the time, 'for the restoration of the university chest and the building of the church of the blessed Virgin of our university [now known as Great St Mary's]'. Barowe already had a good track record as a University benefactor, having been described in 1483 as 'to his mother the university a great and faithful lover'. Part of Barowe's gift was to go towards perpetuating the names of both King Richard (died 1485) and himself, after his death, as benefactors. The University declared that 'the names of Richard III and Thomas Barowe, our benefactors, will be recited openly and publicly'. To this day, an annual service is held in Great St Mary's for the commemoration of benefactors. For a considerable period, King Richard's name disappeared from the list of benefactors, but it has been restored in recent generations by a modern antiquary, who had studied the document of 1495. Barowe is no longer mentioned. (Binns, J. and Meadows, P., *Great St Mary's*, GSM: 2000)

January 22nd

1831: On this day, the *Cambridge Chronicle* listed one Charles Darwin as tenth out of 178 BA candidates. Darwin later recalled: 'By answering well the examination questions, by doing Euclid well and by not failing miserably in Classics, I gained a good place'. Darwin had not yet however resided the required number of terms in order to be awarded his degree, which resulted in him spending his last two terms at Christ's College without any examination pressures. These few months turned out to be some of the most important he spent in Cambridge. Some years later Darwin described this time: 'During these months lived much with Professor Henslow, often dining with him and walking with. Became slightly acquainted with several of the learned men in Cambridge, which much quickened the … zeal … In the Spring … talked over an excursion to Tenerife'. His trip to Tenerife never materialised but it was Professor Henslow who later that year invited Darwin to travel on board HMS *Beagle* as a naturalist, an opportunity which would change his life forever. Darwin embarked on the *Beagle* in December 1831, not to set foot again on British soil for another five years. (Van Wyhe, J., *Darwin in Cambridge*, Christ's College: 2009)

January 23rd

1898: On this day, John Selwyn, Master of Selwyn College Cambridge and the son of Bishop Selwyn, after whom the college is named, attended college chapel for the last time. Bronchial and gastric problems, coupled with chronic rheumatism, were taking their toll and two days later Selwyn left with his family for Pau in southern France; everyone hoped that the warmer climate would do him good, but he died within two weeks of his arrival. Selwyn's rheumatic problems and bad legs meant that he had never been able to stand for the college's loyal toast to the Sovereign; the Fellows, out of courtesy and sympathy, would also remain seated, thus starting what was to become a long-established college tradition. In 1976 the Master of Selwyn College wrote to the Queen explaining the history of this custom and asked, more than three quarters of a century later, for her approval, adding that one outcome was that they probably drank her health more frequently than elsewhere. Her Majesty graciously replied that she was 'fascinated to hear of the custom, that she had no objection to its continuance … but she felt her formal approval would not be appropriate'. (Brock, W. and Cooper, P., *Selwyn College: A History*, Pentland Press: 1994)

January 24th

1999: Today, security guards and police were out in force when former Israeli Prime Minister Shimon Peres visited Robinson College in order to address the Cambridge University Jewish Society. The politician arrived at the college in Grange Road amid tight security and a heavy police presence and was greeted by a protest vigil by members of the University's Palestinian Society. (*Cambridge Evening News*)

2000: Today, an exhibition at Cambridge art gallery Kettle's Yard attracted a lot of press interest. The exhibition contained images of the world's smallest picture, on a grain of salt, and the world's largest picture, taken by reflecting an image on to a satellite in space. Centre-stage was taken however by half of the brain of nineteenth-century Cambridge mathematician and computer pioneer Charles Babbage. The half-brain, contained in a bell-jar, is normally kept at the Royal College of Surgeons in London. The part displayed here was the right lobe, since both lobes are not allowed to be displayed in the same place at the same time. (*Cambridge Evening News*)

January 25th

2006: On this day, forty-two-year-old Nick Flynn, a visitor to the Fitzwilliam Museum in Cambridge, tripped on his shoelaces and tumbled down a marble staircase, smashing on his way three seventeenth-century Chinese Qing dynasty porcelain vases. The vases had been standing on a windowsill and were estimated to be worth hundreds of thousands of pounds. Flynn was later arrested on suspicion of criminal damage but then released without charge. Meanwhile, the vases were meticulously pieced back together by specialist ceramic conservator Penny Bendall, who described the project as 'the ultimate jigsaw puzzle'. The first vase to be restored was the highlight of an exhibition at the Fitzwilliam entitled *Mission Impossible*, exploring ethics and choice in conservation. On close inspection, small cracks can still be seen in the vases, a conscious decision by conservators who wanted the vases to tell their own story, 'maintaining the integrity … while preserving … beauty'. The accident made headline news around the world. In the run-up to Christmas 2006, a popular item on sale in the museum's gift shop was a small jigsaw puzzle representing one of the vases, to be broken up and then put back together again. (*Cambridge Evening News*)

January 26th

1895: Today, Professor Arthur Cayley, described in his obituary as 'England's greatest mathematician', died at his home, the Garden House, in Cambridge. Twenty-seven years later, the house and the neighbouring mill workers' cottages were converted to create a hotel of the same name. Cosmologist Stephen Hawking and his wife Jane celebrated their civil wedding in the Garden House Hotel, often later returning for anniversary dinners. In 1972 the original hotel burned down, to be replaced by a modern version. (*The Times*)

1983: On this day, Australia Day, the highlight of the term was *An Evening with Dame Edna Everage*, assisted by her alter ego Sir Les Patterson, who was presented with an 'honorary degree' by the Cambridge Union Society for 'services to Australian culture'. A glowing citation was read out in both Latin and English, followed by a much briefer Australian version: 'Good on yer, Les!' (Parkinson, S., *Arena of Ambition*, Icon Books: 2009)

January 27th

1791: On this day, William Wordsworth was awarded a very average pass degree, without honours. This result came as no great surprise to the University of Cambridge, as he had spent much of his last year of 'studies' on an extended walking tour holiday of France and Switzerland; he returned just in time to complete the statutory residence requirements, but then spent the week before his exam reading Samuel Richardson's *Clarissa* rather than studying for his exams. Wordsworth already called himself a poet, but had made no effort to make himself known as such to the authorities; for example, when the Master of St John's died in 1789, the coffin had as usual been adorned with verses by members of the college, but young Wordsworth had not contributed. Wordsworth's undergraduate rooms, which he called his 'nook obscure', near the kitchens which he said 'made a humming sound, less tuneable than bees, with shrill notes of sharp command and scolding intermixed', are today used for special functions and dinners; still situated next to the college kitchens, they are however apparently much more peaceful today. (Chainey, G., *A Literary History of Cambridge*, Pevensey Press: 1985)

January 28th

1933: On this day, a young Muslim student called Choudhary Rahmat Ali issued, from his house in Humberstone Road, Cambridge, a pamphlet entitled 'Now or Never: are we to live or perish forever?' In it, Ali was the first to coin the name Pakistan, proposing this as the name for a separate Muslim homeland in South Asia. 'Pak' means 'spiritually pure' in Urdu (Ali expected Pakistanis to become known as Paks) and 'stan' means land. The name was also a near acronym from the words Punjab, Afghania, Kashmir, Iran, Sindh, Tukharistan, Afghanistan and Balochistan. In 1947 India and Pakistan became separate countries as a result of partition, overseen by Mountbatten. But when Ali visited Pakistan in 1948, his reputation foundered and he was ordered to leave the country. In an obituary, one of his Cambridge tutors, Edward Wellbourne, said: 'Ali's invention was seized upon by men of perhaps greater political gifts'. Back in England, Ali worked as a lawyer and returned to Cambridge, where he died in the 1951 flu epidemic. As there was no one to take responsibility for his funeral, the Master of Emmanuel College, who had been Rahmat Ali's tutor, arranged for him to be buried in the Newmarket Road Cemetery in Cambridge. (*Sunday Times*)

January 29th

1969: On this day, eighty students wandered into one of the lecture rooms in Mill Lane, Cambridge, declaring the event a 'token of solidarity with their oppressed comrades' who were then occupying the London School of Economics. The Cambridge students wanted Sir Eric Ashby, University Vice-Chancellor, to state publicly that he did not approve of the threatened closure of the LSE. The demonstration quickly escalated as, according to student publication *Varsity,* 'the mob then followed a handful of leaders and marched on the Senate House'. Finding the Senate House being used by the Purcell Society for a rehearsal, the demonstrators instead occupied the Council Room of the Old Schools next door, marching in to shouts of 'Is there an Ashby in the house?' As news of the sit-in spread through the colleges, the building began to fill up with an 'anarchic crowd of sympathisers, sight-seers and trouble-makers'. These actions resulted, by the end of term, in twenty-three of the twenty-four student council representatives resigning their positions; elections followed throughout the University. (Weatherall, M., *From our Cambridge Correspondent*, Varsity Publications: 1995)

January 30th

1854: On this day, Joseph Romilly, having been disturbed at his Cambridge home by the dance that his neighbours, the Fosters, had organised for their servants (an annual custom, described by Romilly as 'rather a nuisance' because of the noise) dined at 6.30 p.m. in more peaceful surroundings and in very distinguished company. One of the guests, Henry Philpott, had been Vice-Chancellor of Cambridge University when Prince Albert had been installed as Chancellor in 1847; he had received the Prince and Queen Victoria on that occasion and from this time on Philpott was in close touch with the Court. At the dinner this evening, Romilly was curious to get some inside information about court life, saying that he 'pumped Philpott a good deal' on the subject. Romilly learned that 'the Queen and the Prince breakfast and lunch by themselves and (unless a special audience is vouchsafed) are not seen till 8 o'clock at dinner: the Queen leaves the Saloon at 11 and everybody retires to their own room.' Philpott went on to become Bishop of Worcester but eventually retired to Cambridge, where he died in 1892. (Bury, M. and Pickles, J., *Romilly's Cambridge Diary*, Cambridge Records Society: 2000 / *Dictionary of National Biography*)

January 31st

1980: On this day, *New Scientist* magazine published some recollections written by Austrian-born Cambridge scientist Max Perutz. Perutz recalled: 'One morning in March 1938, a friend walked past my window at the Cavendish [Laboratory] and told me that Hitler had invaded Austria … The threat to Austria, which I loved, had not been uppermost in my mind when I decided to come to Britain; I came for scientific reasons, but I should have taken the threat more seriously. The invasion changed my status overnight, from a guest to a refugee. My father's money was soon exhausted and as a foreigner I was not allowed to earn any, not even by College supervision … ' Perutz eventually plucked up the courage to discuss the matter with Sir Lawrence Bragg, the Director of the Cavendish Laboratory, and showed him his X-ray pictures of haemoglobin. Bragg instantly realised the potential of Perutz's research and obtained a grant from the Rockefeller Foundation to appoint him as his assistant. Perutz concluded: 'Bragg's effective action saved my scientific career and enabled me to bring my parents to England, so that they escaped the holocaust.' In 1962, Max Perutz and his Cambridge colleague John Kendrew were jointly awarded the Nobel Prize for Chemistry for their work on the structure of proteins. (*New Scientist*: 1980)

February 1st

1903: On this day, physicist Sir George Gabriel Stokes died at Lensfield, his Cambridge home. Although born and brought up in Ireland, Stokes had spent most of his working life in Cambridge, becoming Master of Pembroke College, Lucasian Professor of Mathematics and even, at one stage, MP for Cambridge University. There is a memorial brass to Stokes in St Paul's Church, Hills Road, where he was a regular worshipper and churchwarden for over thirty years. (*Ely Ensign*)

1999: On this day, American philanthropist, art collector and racehorse owner Paul Mellon died in his Virginia home at the age of ninety-one, leaving $15m to Cambridge institutions Clare College, Clare Hall and the Fitzwilliam Museum. Mellon had studied at Clare College in the 1930s; friends there introduced him to racing at Newmarket, which he always considered the most beautiful race-course in the world. Mellon was once quoted as saying that his aim in life was to give away a fortune wisely. (*The Times*)

February 2nd

1891: On this day, a seventeen-year-old girl called Jane Elsden was arrested by the University Proctor, charged with being a prostitute, and committed to the Spinning House (the Cambridge gaol for prostitutes) for seven days. University authorities had the power to arrest girls on suspicion of prostitution and the Proctors kept a logbook listing the 'loose ladies of the town'. Two days after Jane's release she was back on her beat in Petty Cury, only to be arrested again by the University Bulldogs {University officials in charge of discipline}. Jane was sent back to the Spinning House, this time managing to escape through a window and return to her home village of Dullingham near Newmarket. The Vice-Chancellor, Dr H. Butler, had her arrested by police on a charge of prison-breaking and the charge was heard this time not in the Vice-Chancellor's Court but at the Assizes. This turned out to be an unwise move, as the Vice-Chancellor's right to arrest the girl was challenged, and the issue gathered momentum on a national scale, with the Home Secretary eventually intervening to have Jane released. Jane, quite unwittingly, had become a symbol and a martyr, though hardly a saint. (Parker, R., *Town and Gown*, Patrick Stephens: 1983 / *Magdalene College Magazine 2002-2003*)

February 3rd

1933: On this day, the Mond Laboratory, part of the renowned Cavendish Laboratory, was opened in Cambridge by Stanley Baldwin, Conservative politician and Chancellor of the University. It was an august occasion, starting with a large luncheon party at Corpus Christi College, followed by a procession, everyone in academic dress, to the Arts School, where a number of speeches were made. For the actual opening ceremony, a gilded key in the shape of a crocodile was produced, reflecting the carving by Eric Gill of a crocodile (Rutherford's nickname), on the outside of the building. Baldwin's opening speech caused some puzzled amusement, since much of it was almost identical with what Lord Rutherford, then Director of the Cavendish Laboratory, had said earlier in the proceedings; it seems that Rutherford had quite forgotten that he had previously briefed Baldwin as to what to say, using the same remarks. The building was erected with money from Ludwig Mond, a co-founder of ICI and a generous benefactor. The original roof was very flimsy, since their work on low temperature physics was so hazardous that there could have been an explosion at any time, a fact often used to 'wind up' nervous visitors to the Mond Laboratory. (Boag, J.W., *Kapitza in Cambridge and Moscow*, Elsevier: 1990)

February 4th

1901: On this day, *Granta,* the Cambridge magazine for 'student literary enterprise', was the first to publish verses written by Alan Alexander Milne, better known in his later years as A.A. Milne, creator of *Winnie the Pooh.* The magazine editor was later to say: 'I remember how I rejected – how arrogant we were! – his first contributions, telling him to persevere and that he might one day learn to write'. By the time Milne was in his second year at Trinity College, he was himself editor of *Granta,* fulfilling a childhood ambition. Milne came up to Trinity College from Westminster School in 1900; his rooms on P staircase in Whewell's Court were later inherited by his son Christopher Robin Milne, whose teddy bear inspired the story *The House at Pooh Corner.* Milne was to bequeath the manuscripts of *Winnie the Pooh* and *The House at Pooh Corner* to his old college, where they are still kept today, in the Wren Library. The Winnie the Pooh Society has become one of the most famous in Cambridge, with several television appearances to its credit and a membership that includes Her Majesty the Queen. (Thwaite, A., *A.A. Milne,* Faber: 1990 / Chainey, G., *A Literary History of Cambridge,* Pevensey Press: 1985)

February 5th

1818: On this day, Trinity undergraduate Lawrence Dundas dined with friends at a lodging house in Bridge Street. The wine flowed and by the time he wended his way home, he was very much the worse for wear. Lawrence fell into a ditch, from which, according to Winstanley, 'he vainly endeavoured to extricate himself. Frenzied with drink and perhaps hoping to gain great freedom of movement, he divested himself of most of his clothes and as the night was cold, he was found on the following morning dead where he had fallen, having perished from exposure.' The coroner's jury reached the verdict that 'the said Lawrence Dundas ... came by his death in consequence of being exposed all night to the severity of the weather in a naked state in a wet ditch and that it was the fatal and melancholy result of having been intoxicated.' More publicity was given to this case by Francis Maberly, 'an eccentric and unbalanced evangelical clergyman' who wrote a pamphlet entitled *The Melancholy and Awful Death of Lawrence Dundas Esq*, taking up the cause of better supervision in student accommodation. And all this at least 150 years before the term 'binge drinking' was coined ... (Winstanley, D.A., *Early Victorian Cambridge*, CUP: 1940)

February 6th

1557: On this day, two coffins containing the remains of Protestant reformers Martin Bucer and Paul Fagius were taken out of Great St Mary's and St Michael's churches and bound to a stake which had been erected on Market Hill. They were burned, along with a number of books which were considered heretical by Queen Mary and her followers. It was written that 'the dead bodies being bound with ropes and layd upon men's shoulders … were borne into the middle of ye market sted with a great trayne of people following them … .as soon as it began to flame round about, a great sort of books that were condemned with them, were caste into the same. There was that day gathered into the town a great multitude of country folk (for it was market day) … who partly detested and abhorred the extreme cruelty … toward the rotten carcasses … ' Just three years later, in the reign of Queen Elizabeth I, the University rescinded its previous condemnation of the reformers and Bucer was honoured with a second funeral in Great St Mary's. A brass plate in the chancel commemorates this event. (Bushell, W.D., *The Church of St Mary the Great*, Bowes & Bowes: 1948 / Waterlow, S., *In Praise of Cambridge*, Constable & Co.: 1912)

February 7th

1800: On this day, Dr Robert Glynn, a wealthy, unconventional and famous Cambridge doctor, died and was later buried by torchlight in King's College Chapel. The following Sunday, the Vice-Chancellor William Mansel led some seventy members of the University to pay their respects to his memory, an act of mourning which was, according to the *Cambridge Chronicle*, as 'uncommon and unprecedented' as Glynn himself had been. Although Glynn had never held an official University appointment, he had been for decades the most influential figure in Cambridge medicine. The speedy appearance of this familiar figure in his scarlet cloak, three-cornered hat and gold-topped cane was much appreciated by generations of sick Cambridge people who had called on his services. One of his more famous patients was William Pitt the Younger, whom he treated while the latter was an undergraduate at Pembroke College; Pitt went on to become, at the tender age of twenty-four, the youngest ever Prime Minister. Glynn later declined the Regius Professorship of Physic which Pitt offered him in 1793. In many ways Glynn's death marked the passing of the old order of Cambridge medicine, to be followed by what Weatherall calls 'the darker side of [Cambridge] traditions: the privilege, exclusivity, politicking, patronage and outright jobbery'. (Weatherall, M., *Gentlemen, Scientists and Doctors*, Boydell Press: 2000)

February 8th

1901: Today saw a fatal accident on the Cambridge street tramways, when Florence Foreman Ebbon, aged twelve, died after falling from one of the horse-drawn tramcars. The inquest decided that the driver had applied the brake, but the child had jumped or fallen off the tram before the car had actually come to a halt. Death was due to blood poisoning from a large, lacerated wound. The accident prompted a spate of letters in the local press advocating much tighter safety measures on the trams. (Swingle, S.L., *Cambridge Street Tramways*, Oakwood Press: 1972)

1949: On this day, a flamboyant nineteen-year-old undergraduate called Norman St John Stevas was expelled from the Cambridge Union Chamber, the culmination of a long-standing dispute between him and the Union President, George Pattison. A staunch Roman Catholic and fervent Conservative supporter, Stevas became Union President himself the following year, before moving to Oxford to join yet more student debates, most famously with future broadcaster Robin Day. Many years later, Stevas returned to Cambridge as Master of Emmanuel College, where his portrait now hangs in the Hall. (Parkinson, S., *Arena of Ambition*, Icon Books: 2009)

February 9th

1685: On this day, trumpets sounded and bells rang as James II, following the death of his brother Charles II, was proclaimed as the new King at the Market Cross in Cambridge. Five days later, in their loyal address, the townsmen declared that all their lives and fortunes were his Majesty's and that they would be 'daily employed to preserve him in his royal seat'. A convert to Catholicism, James II was keen to increase the number of Catholics in positions of authority. In April 1688 orders were sent to remove the Mayor of Cambridge, along with five aldermen, twelve councillors and the town clerk, and replace them with nominees of the King. The following month, the new corporation voted an obsequious address of thanks to the King, praising the greatness of the royal mind; even the 'mean and inconsiderable dissenters' acknowledged the King's 'moderation and tenderness'. The tensions underlying this public façade of support were short-lived; by the end of 1688 James II, discouraged by defection and desertion, fled, eventually joining his Queen and son in France. The people of Cambridge were ready to welcome their next monarch. (Gray, A., *The Town of Cambridge*, Heffer & Sons: 1925)

February 10th

1799: On this bitterly cold day, the curiosity of a young farmer called William Muncey was aroused when he saw a red handkerchief tied to a twig, protruding from a wall of snow and ice. Closer inspection revealed Elizabeth Woodcock, who, one week earlier, had set off on horseback from her home in Histon on her weekly shopping trip to Cambridge. Shopping done and several gins later, Elizabeth set off back home, but the weather conditions had worsened; it was getting dark and the snow was falling thickly. Half-blinded by the falling flakes, she was within a mile and a half of her cottage when her frightened horse suddenly reared up and raced off. Stranded in the snowstorm, Elizabeth collapsed, exhausted, under the shelter of a hedge. The snow piled up around her, forming a sort of cave; on her fourth day she managed to push a twig through the ice, tying her red handkerchief on the end. When William Muncey rescued her, Elizabeth had survived in her ice cave for a whole week. She lived only until the following July, suffering greatly from the frostbite which caused her fingers and toes to turn gangrenous and eventually drop off. (Porter, E., *Josiah Chater's Diaries*, Phillimore: 1975)

February 11th

1957: On this day, Gwen Raverat, wood-engraving artist, author of the classic Cambridge book *Period Piece* and granddaughter of naturalist Charles Darwin, died at her Cambridge home, the Old Granary. Gwen had become increasingly incapacitated and could not even get out of a chair without assistance. The night before her suicide, her children, Elisabeth, Sophie and Mark, had dined with her at the Old Granary and it was Mark who discovered her the next morning, deeply unconscious, with a note under the bed: 'My dearest loves, Liz, Mark, Sophie and Eddi, this seems to be the simplest plan for everyone. I've had it planned for a long time. Thank you and everyone else for your boundless kindness to me.' Gwen remained unconscious for three days and died on 11 February from bronchial pneumonia which set in soon after the overdose. She lies buried in Trumpington where her gravestone contains four lines from Shakespeare's *Cymbeline*: 'Fear no more the heat of the sun, Nor the furious winter's rages; Thou thy worldly task hast done, Home art gone, and ta'en thy wages.' Gwen's house has now been incorporated into Darwin College, where a block of student rooms bears her name. (Spalding, F., *Gwen Raverat*, The Harvill Press: 2001)

February 12th

2009: On this day, HRH the Duke of Edinburgh visited Christ's College in Cambridge to unveil a new statue of Charles Darwin, 200 years to the day since the naturalist was born. Unlike his more usual portrayal as an elderly 'éminence grise', this statue shows Darwin in 1831 as a fresh-faced young man, on the cusp of a life-changing experience; six months later he was to board the *Beagle* on an epic five-year journey through the southern seas. The bronze statue was made by Anthony Smith, young zoology graduate turned sculptor, who was given a studio in Christ's College for the duration of his work. Hours after the unveiling, a special and rather expensive dinner was held in the college Dining Hall. The dinner cost £5,000 per head, most of which went to fund a new collaboration between Christ's College and the Galapagos Conservation Trust. After-dinner speakers included film-maker and naturalist Sir David Attenborough and broadcaster Andrew Marr, who famously championed Darwin in the 2002 poll to decide the greatest Briton. Darwin's statue stands today in front of New Court in Christ's College, surrounded by a garden planted with specimens he would have encountered on his *Beagle* journey. (*Cambridge Evening News*)

February 13th

1970: Today's announcement on the back page of the *Shilling Paper* (the journal of the Socialist Society in Cambridge), stated: 'Greek Fascists hold a propaganda party, all invited, 7.30 p.m. Friday 13th, Garden House Hotel. Cut out this poster, put it on a banner and bring it to the demo.' The 'party' was in fact an evening of Greek-themed food and music, the culmination of a Greek Week in Cambridge; the proposed demonstration was directed against the right-wing régime of colonels who made up the Greek government at the time. Around 400 students answered the call that evening, intending initially just to stop people attending the dinner. The demonstration started to escalate however, with some protestors drumming on the hotel windows and others climbing on to the roof. Eventually the protestors poured into the room where the dinner itself was taking place. To shouts of 'Down with Fascism!' tables were overturned, curtains torn down and windows broken as the event turned into a full-scale riot. Several arrests were made and in April thirteen students and one don were charged, resulting in prison sentences for some and criminal records for all. Four years later, democracy returned to Greece. (Weatherall, M., *From our Cambridge Correspondent*, Varsity Publications: 1995 / Fowler, L. and H., *Cambridge Commemorated*, CUP: 1984)

February 14th

1807: On this day, Lord Byron wrote to his tutor, the Revd Thomas Jones at Trinity College: 'I certainly do not feel that predilection for Mathematics which may pervade the Inclinations of men destined for a clerical, or collegiate life … ' concluding: 'I have other Reasons for not residing at Cambridge, I dislike it; I was originally intended for Oxford.' From the outset, Byron had felt 'wretched at going to Cambridge instead of Oxford', where most of his school friends had gone, but where Christ Church, 'the only college acceptable to him had not found him acceptable to it'. And so Byron left Cambridge, writing: 'The Cam will not be much increased by my tears on the occasion', only to return in the summer term, after threats that his allowance would be discontinued. As a nobleman, Byron led a privileged lifestyle in college, dining at High Table and wearing a richly embroidered gown with gold-tasselled mortar board. By Christmas, Byron left Cambridge for good, returning only the following July to be awarded, with some reluctance on the part of the University, his MA degree, not earned or worked for, but a privilege of the nobility. (Fowler, L. and H., *Cambridge Commemorated*, CUP: 1984 / Chainey, G., *A Literary History of Cambridge*, Pevensey Press: 1985)

February 15th

1865: On this day, St John's College in Cambridge appointed a committee to 'consider the question of painted windows for the new chapel, with respect to the selection of an artist and to the general character of the windows'. The committee worked long and hard at their project over the coming months, consulting Sir George Gilbert Scott (architect of the new chapel) and examining works in painted glass from all over the country and overseas. It was not until December that the committee was able to submit its report, concluding: 'that, of living artists, English are to be preferred to foreign ... that Messrs Clayton and Bell, of London, and Messrs Hardman and Co., of Birmingham, are to be preferred to other artists.' It was Clayton and Bell who were responsible for the imposing west window, portraying the last judgement. This window was paid for with money raised by former junior college members; the College guidebook points out that immediately under the image of the damned being shovelled into the flames of Hell are the words '*Juniores Collegii Alumni*', a rather unfortunate juxtaposition. (Crook, A., *From the Foundation to Gilbert Scott*, St John's College: 1980 / *St John's College*, Rawle Associates)

February 16th

1765: Today, Dr Samuel Johnson, compiler of the first English dictionary, arrived at the Rose Inn for what was to be his first and last visit to Cambridge. Johnson was at the height of his fame and strove for a low profile, 'studious to preserve a strict incognito'. Staying for three nights at the Rose, Johnson was not only able to meet his various literary contacts but also drank 'sixteen dishes of tea' after supper at Sidney Sussex before he 'rolled or waddled' through various other colleges. (Chainey, G., *A Literary History of Cambridge*, Pevensey Press: 1985)

1875: On this day, sixteen pioneering pupils arrived at the newly founded Leys School in Cambridge, to be accommodated in buildings which were barely built. The dormitories were not yet completed so the pupils slept in the headmaster's house. The school was formally opened four weeks later; the boys had moved in to their dormitory just the night before and decorated it with flags and garlands to welcome the guests. (Houghton, G. and P., *Well-regulated Minds and Improper Moments*, The Leys School: 2000)

February 17th

1967: On this day, a local psychedelic rock band called Pink Floyd played in Cambridge at the St Catharine's College Valentine's Ball. The group was on the cusp of fame, having two weeks previously recorded their first single *Arnold Layne*, allegedly based on a Cambridge transvestite whose favourite pastime was to steal women's clothes and underwear from washing lines. *Arnold Layne* was released on March 11 1967 and catapulted iconic front-man Syd Barrett and his band members on to the national, then international stage; they went on to become one of the world's most successful music acts, selling over 200 million albums. The 1967 Valentine's Ball took place not in St Catharine's College itself, but in another venue, officially called the Dorothy Restaurant and Banqueting Suites but popularly known as 'The Dot'. During the 1960s, the Dot was famous for its rather genteel afternoon tea dances for the older generation, but would transform in the evenings into a rock and pop venue, hosting such big-name headline acts as The Who, The Kinks and even the legendary Jimi Hendrix. Today the same building houses Waterstone's bookshop. (Worden, M. and Marziano, A., *A Pink Floyd Fan's Illustrated Guide to Cambridge*, Damned Publishing: 2007 / *Cambridge Evening News*)

February 18th

1914: On this day, Cambridge lost the horse-trams which had been such a prominent feature of Cambridge street life for the last thirty-four years. Times were changing rapidly and throughout the country motor buses were taking over from trams as a faster and more effective form of transport. The trams were crowded for their last day in service; one group of undergraduates even held a mock funeral service, wearing surplices and chanting a dirge. The last tram left the station at 6.25 p.m., driven by Mr Ephraim Skinner, a driver for the company for thirty-four years. When interviewed he said that he had never had a hot dinner on working days all his life, but had had a 'hot-cold' dinner. When asked to explain, he replied: 'It's a pint of beer and a strong onion!' On the following Friday, everything belonging to the tram company, from horses to harnesses and tram cars, was put up for auction. An imaginative sales catalogue said that the cars could easily be adapted as 'seaside bungalows, summerhouses or houseboat bodies', but many were happy just to buy small souvenirs. One undergraduate paid 1s 6d for 'three lengths of tram tubing', a gas fire and a hand-clipper. (Swingle, S.L., *Cambridge Street Tramways*, Oakwood Press: 1972)

February 19th

1848: On this day, Cambridge resident Josiah Chater wrote in his diary: 'The gownsmen [from the University] have become as bad as they were when Tom Thumb was here, for last night they marched about the town in regiments of about two or three hundred, with pokers and all kinds of weapons of both offence and defence. This evening they have been as bad. I saw one poor Fellow pulled to safety into Mr Barrett's – he looked almost dead – there were about sixty townsmen after him. One gownsman last night got his leg broken and many others were very much hurt.' Josiah's mention of Tom Thumb refers to the famous dwarf, called General Tom Thumb, who locals could, for a shilling apiece, watch perform various feats. Tom Thumb's performances of March 1846 were however disrupted by numerous noisy undergraduates who stormed into the hall and started fights which then spilled over on to the streets outside. Since the first students arrived in Cambridge from Oxford in 1209 there had been sporadic tension between the townspeople of Cambridge and the academics and students of the University, often referred to as 'town versus gown'. Between 9 and 21 February 1848 there were riots nearly every evening between town and gown. (Porter, E., *Josiah Chater's Diaries*, Phillimore: 1975)

February 20th

1818: On this day, controversial, flamboyant poet Lord Byron, never one to shrink from criticising his contemporaries, wrote the following words to Mr John Murray: 'I remember to have seen Porson at Cambridge … and I never can recollect him except as drunk or brutal and generally both … I have seen him in a private party of undergraduates, many of them freshmen and strangers, take up a poker to one of them and heard him use language as blackguard as his action.' Warming to his subject Byron continued: 'Of all the most disgusting brutes, sulky, abusive and intolerable, Porson was the most bestial … I saw him once go away in a rage, because nobody knew the name of the "Cobbler of Messina", insulting their ignorance with the most vulgar terms of reprobation. He used to recite, or rather vomit pages of all languages and could hiccup Greek like a Helot; and certainly Sparta never shocked her children with a grosser exhibition than this man's intoxication.' The victim of Byron's wrath and despising was satirist and Trinity Fellow Richard Porson; Porson had died in London in 1808 and was buried near the statue of Isaac Newton in Trinity College Chapel. (Waterlow, S., *In Praise of Cambridge*, Constable & Co.: 1912)

February 21st

1846: On this day, in the early hours of the morning, many locals helped to fight back the flames from a fire on Market Hill in central Cambridge. Local resident Josiah Chater wrote in his diary: 'We had not been in bed last night half an hour when we heard the alarm of fire … at Headly's Iron Foundry. It was not three yards from Simpson and Basham's, but they soon got their great warehouse cleared by carrying the goods over to the Red Lion. I carried the books, but happily the premises did not catch…..After we had done all we could, William and I walked behind the Hall and had a glass of lemonade each. I went to bed about three o'clock … ' Miraculously, the flames were blown towards Holy Trinity Church, where there was 'a vacant space with no houses'. If the wind had come from the north then the whole of Petty Cury could have been destroyed. For the next few days, the local press was full of recriminations, not least because the factory had been sited right next to a shop 'filled with tallow, fat … gunpowder…and all sorts of combustibles.' Relocation to a more suitable site was inevitable and the following year a new factory was built in Mill Road. (Porter, E., *Josiah Chater's Diaries*, Phillimore: 1975)

February 22nd

1850: On this day, a grim tale worthy of any Victorian melodrama began to unfold when young Susan Lucas died after eating gruel containing arsenic. Susan's husband, Elias Lucas, was convicted of the crime, along with the victim's twenty-year-old sister Mary Reader, with whom he had allegedly been conducting an adulterous affair. They both eventually confessed to their crime, although Mary declared that she alone had administered the poison. Mary and Elias were both hanged at the gaol on Castle Hill in Cambridge. The execution took place in public and although Josiah Chater did not witness the event, he wrote in his diary: 'I went up at nine o'clock this morning to see the gallows prepared for the two poor souls condemned to die at twelve ... thousands of people were there to witness the sight. The town has been full all day and hundreds have been rolling about Market Street drunk, proving what a demoralising effect public executions have upon the people.' The last public hanging in Cambridge was in 1864, but even after that date large crowds would gather on an execution day, hoping to see the hoisting of the black flag or the solemn tolling of the execution bell. (Porter, E., *Josiah Chater's Diaries*, Phillimore: 1975)

February 23rd

1674: On this day, work began on the complete rebuilding of St Catharine's College in Cambridge. Founded in 1473 by Robert Woodelark, Provost of nearby King's College, the original buildings had by now fallen into a bad state of disrepair. Various attempts had been made to patch up the old buildings until it was realised that the only solution was to pull down the old and begin again from scratch. Lightfoot was the elderly Master, frail but living long enough to see the Hall and Butteries completed at Whitsuntide 1675; £119 14s 11d was spent at the opening. The stone laid to mark the start of work on the Hall in May 1674 was later discovered when removing the steps leading to it; this stone initially found a new use as the support of the scraper at the door of the Master's Lodge, but in 1936 it was repositioned, rather discreetly, on the south exterior wall of the Hall. As the college expanded, a new Dining Hall, with a much greater capacity, was opened in 1967. The original seventeenth-century Hall has now become the Fellows' Senior Combination Room. (Jones, W., *A History of St Catharine's College*, CUP: 1936)

February 24th

1941: On this day, Shrove Tuesday, German bombers flew in low over Cambridge, making a concentrated attack on the section of Hills Road between the Catholic church and the war memorial, leaving ten dead. One bomb exploded on the roof of the sacristy of the Catholic church, blowing a 6ft hole in the roof and damaging many of the windows. After the war all the damage was made good and most of the stained-glass windows were replaced to the original designs by the original makers. The intended target of this bomb attack was probably the railway sidings where, under cover of darkness, an important consignment of tanks was being unloaded that night. This carefully targeted attack, though missing its aim, fuelled rumours and speculation that some assistance was being given to the bombers from the ground and the episode has come to be linked with the notorious German agent Jan Ter Braak, who was known to have been operating in Cambridge at that time, before ending his life in an air-raid shelter on Christ's Pieces on April 1 1941. (Rogers, N., *Catholics in Cambridge*, Gracewing: 2003)

February 25th

1956: This is the day that British poet Ted Hughes first met American poet Sylvia Plath; she was twenty-three and he was twenty-five years old. They met at a Cambridge party held in Falcon Yard for the poetry magazine *St Botolph's Review.* Hughes was as well-known as a womaniser as he was as a poet. Clive James, his contemporary at Pembroke College, said that Hughes invited women not only to stay the night but to advertise their presence by hanging stockings to dry outside his window, overlooking the Old Court. In her journal, Sylvia describes her first impressions of Hughes as 'big, dark and hunky, the only boy in the room huge enough for her'. Their relationship started as violently as it was later to end; they shouted at each other rather than conversing and he eventually ripped off her hairband, then kissed her first on the mouth and then on the neck. She responded by biting him 'long and hard' on the cheek, making blood pour down his face. Two days after meeting Hughes, Sylvia wrote a poem called *Pursuit*, which she described as 'a poem about the dark forces of lust'. It was almost inevitably going to end in tears … (Hayman, R., *The Death and Life of Sylvia Plath*, Heinemann: 1991)

February 26th

1880: On this day, the Prince of Wales, future King Edward VII, came to Cambridge to attend a full day of celebrations for the Silver Jubilee of the University's Amateur Dramatic Club, better known by its acronym ADC. Starting with a banquet at the Guildhall for 200 people (exclusively past and present members of the ADC), His Royal Highness went on to the ADC Theatre in Park Street where two pieces, *First Night* and *Ticklish Times*, were performed for him. (Colthorpe, M., *Royal Cambridge*, Cambridge City Council: 1977)

1922: On this day, a group of Cambridge undergraduates travelled to London and by various devious means stole Phineas, the prized mascot of University College London. Back in Cambridge, Phineas, the dummy of a kilted Scottish highlander, was paraded with great pride through the Gate of Honour at Gonville and Caius, to reappear later in the underground toilets in Market Square, which had been restyled for Rag Week as the tomb of 'Toot-and-kum-in'. Various other quirky objects had been produced from this 'tomb' but Phineas was the undoubted highlight. (Reeve, F., *Varsity Rags and Hoaxes*, Oleander Press: 1977)

February 27th

1973: On this day, a simple notice was posted in *Varsity*: 'In Memoriam. *Varsity*, the Cambridge University newspaper, died suddenly today, aged 26 years. Mourned by generations. No flowers please'. Despite high journalistic standards under the editorship of future television journalist Jeremy Paxman, *Varsity* was haemorrhaging funds at an alarming rate and expected to end that year £4,000 in the red. There was no option but to close it down; soon re-forming with its rival as *Stop Press with Varsity*, it reverted to its original name in October 1987. (Weatherall, M., *From our Cambridge Correspondent*, Varsity Publications: 1995)

———◆———

2003: On this day, the sixth-century Canterbury Gospels were not in their usual home of the Parker Library in Corpus Christi College, Cambridge, but in Canterbury Cathedral for the enthronement of Dr Rowan Williams as Archbishop. Dr Williams had close links with Cambridge in his own right, having studied at Christ's College and later returning as a University lecturer; during his six years of teaching he also served as curate in Chesterton and later as Dean of Clare College. (*Ely Ensign*)

February 28th

1953: On this day, two scientists, Francis Crick and James Watson, raced into their local pub, the Eagle in Bene't Street, and announced that they had just discovered 'the secret of life'. Most of those present were no doubt rather underwhelmed by the announcement, but in fact the pair had just made one of the most important scientific discoveries of the twentieth century: that the structure of DNA was the shape of a double helix, explaining how genes are passed down through the generations. Crick and Watson were part of a small biological section of the Physics Department, quite an oddball group by all accounts. Crick was a British physicist and Watson had originally been an ornithologist in America before switching disciplines; Crick himself was later to say that the whole discovery process had been a 'chapter of accidents'. Their discovery spawned the whole new science of molecular biology and made DNA a household name. Two plaques in the Eagle pub commemorate Crick and Watson's historic announcement: one outside the pub, near the main entrance and one in the bar where they would regularly drink on Saturday lunch-times. (*Cambridge Evening News / The Times*)

February 29th

1896: On this day, physicist Ernest Rutherford wrote to his future wife May Newton. Rutherford had only recently arrived in England thanks to a science research scholarship which enabled him to work at the Cavendish Laboratory in Cambridge. He was soon working on wireless waves and wrote in today's letter: 'When I left off last time I had just been out on the Common trying to detect waves at long distance. The next day I tried and got an effect from the Lab. to Townsend's diggings, a distance of over half a mile through solid stone houses all the way. The Professor [J.J. Thomson, Director of the Cavendish Laboratory] is extremely interested in the results, and I am at present very useful when he is writing to various scientific pots as he can mention what his students are doing at the Lab.' In a short time Rutherford had broken the world record for distance transmission, but soon moved on to the study of X-rays. Just twelve years later, at the age of thirty-seven, Rutherford was awarded the Nobel Prize in Chemistry for his work on explaining radioactivity. In his native New Zealand, Rutherford is acclaimed as 'our Kiwi genius'. (Eve, A., *Rutherford*, CUP: 1939 / Smith, P., *Rutherford*, Educational Solutions: 2000)

March 1st

1958: On this day, large crowds gathered outside the Cambridge Guildhall, hoping to gain admission to a special celebrity match of … tiddlywinks. The recently formed Cambridge University Tiddlywinks Club (CUTwC) had responded to an article in *The Spectator* entitled 'Does Prince Philip cheat at tiddlywinks?' by inviting Prince Philip to defend his honour by nominating Royal Champions to represent him in a match. The chosen representatives were, by royal command, the popular group of comedians called the Goons; by chance, the club had already invited them to a match 'at their convenience', to which Spike Milligan replied that 'their convenience was too small'. Today's event attracted huge publicity and was covered by several news networks; the Goons, trying to avoid the cameras, were smuggled into the Guildhall using a secret subterranean passage from the public library. After the event, a helicopter whisked Harry Secombe away to the pantomime in which he was performing that evening in Coventry. The Goons lost the tiddlywinks match and sadly by the time a fiftieth anniversary event was arranged in 2008, all of them had passed on. The club did however receive a goodwill message from Eric Sykes, one of their scriptwriters. (Barrie, P., *Emmanuel College Magazine 2007-2008*)

March 2nd

1613: On this day, twelve year old Prince Charles, the future King Charles I, along with his sixteen-year-old German brother-in-law, Prince Frederick, rode with a large entourage from Newmarket to Cambridge. An unidentified source from Gonville and Caius College wrote a detailed description of the day's events, starting with their arrival, when 'loud music was placed upon the top of Jesus College' and the Vice-Chancellor welcomed the two princes with a speech in Latin. As they progressed through the city, more trumpeters were heard from the tower of St John's College and at Trinity they were welcomed by the Master, Dr Thomas Nevile, who had invested so much money in magnificent new college buildings that this was the obvious place for the royal guests to stay. But first the princes had a walking tour of the colleges, taking in Gonville and Caius with its three symbolic gates and also King's College Chapel, where they were taken on to the roof to enjoy the wide-ranging view. Any visitor to Trinity College today can view in Great Court the statue of a young Prince Charles, alongside his parents King James I and Queen Anne of Denmark. (Colthorpe, M., *Royal Cambridge*, Cambridge City Council: 1977)

March 3rd

1920: On this day, future cartoonist and illustrator Ronald Searle was born in Newmarket Road in Cambridge. His parents, William (a porter at the city's railway station) and Nellie were not well-off and so at the age of fifteen Ronald started packing parcels at his local Co-op in order to pay for classes at the Cambridge School of Art. His art lessons overlooked the Cambridge High School for Girls and Searle confessed in later life that the schoolgirls there were the inspiration for his most famous characters, the girls of St Trinian's. During the Second World War, Searle was captured by the Japanese and while a prisoner of war he made numerous cartoons – hiding them under the mattresses of prisoners suffering from cholera. Returning to Cambridge after the war, Searle had his first printed collection *40 Drawings* published by Cambridge University Press. Searle was highly active in the 1950s, turning his St Trinian's cartoons, detailing the misadventures of, in his own words, a group of 'sadistic, cunning, dissolute, crooked and sordid schoolgirls' into a best-selling series of books. The subsequent films have recently been revived and are as popular as ever, the latest version featuring Rupert Everett and various members of the Girls Aloud pop band. (*Cambridge Evening News*)

March 4th

1910: On this day, James Hancock of Water Street in Chesterton was so incensed with his brother-in-law for taking out his horse and cart without permission that he drew a knife across his throat, slicing through the jugular vein; the doctor concluded that death would have occurred quickly and was due, perhaps not surprisingly, to loss of blood. Hancock told the policeman who arrested him: 'I hope he is dead, I hit him hard anyhow … I don't care. I shall get three weeks before I shall get my neck stretched then I can have some beer. He went out with my horse and cart and I won't let anyone go out with that.' In court, it took just twenty-three minutes to find Hancock guilty. On June 14, Hancock was woken at 6 a.m. and given a pint of beer for breakfast and a pipe with some tobacco. Just before 8 a.m. he was led to the gallows. The executioner, Mr Pierpont, fastened Hancock's legs with a strap before placing a hood over his head. He placed the noose around the neck before stepping aside and pulling the lever. James Hancock dropped 7ft 3in and died instantly. (Bell, J., *More Cambridgeshire Crimes*, Popular Books: 1995)

March 5th

1651: On this day, Samuel Pepys, according to a later diary entry, first put on his academic gown and 'went to reside in Magdalene College Cambridge'. College numbers were low at the time because of the war; there were only thirty in residence in the college and Pepys was one of only eleven freshmen. Each had put in £5 5s a year towards their 'commons' (shared provisions) and paid twelve shillings a year for washing and ten shillings for a bed-maker, who had to be either a man or an old woman, since young women were forbidden entry to any college. Relatively little is known about Pepys' student days in Cambridge, but a month after donning that first gown he was awarded a 'Spendluffe' scholarship and two years after that a Smith scholarship, solid evidence of his academic achievements. But perhaps these achievements went to his head, quite literally, since just two weeks after his second scholarship award there is another entry in the college register: 'Peapys [*sic*] and Hind were solemnly admonished by myself and Mr Hill for having been scandalously overseen in drink the night before.' (Chainey, G., *A Literary History of Cambridge*, Cambridge University Press: 1995 / Tomalin, C., *Samuel Pepys*, Viking: 2002)

March 6th

1846: On this day, a significant 'disturbance' took place at the Town Hall in Cambridge, where General Tom Thumb was putting on a show. Tom Thumb, only a couple of feet tall, had earlier in the day amused the crowds by driving about town in a tiny coach; the coachman and footman were two little boys wearing wigs and the 'horses' were small ponies. But as the day wore on, the jovial atmosphere soured and fights broke out in central Cambridge in what was later to be called the Tom Thumb Riot. Even one of the police constables was arrested in the process; 'Fierce Freestone' was so forceful in his attacks on undergraduates that he was dismissed from the force and sentenced to fourteen days' imprisonment. While all this mayhem was occurring on the streets of Cambridge, Trinity Fellow Joseph Romilly was dining with friends. He wrote in his diary that it was 'a most magnificent dinner with real turtle and *buffalo hump*; this last is worthless, being like very coarse stringy over-salted beef.' Romilly went on to say that he had never come across buffalo hump before and was therefore 'much pleased at tasting it'. (Whibley, C., *In Cap and Gown*, Heinemann: 1898 / Bury, M. and Pickles, J., *Romilly's Cambridge Diary*, Cambridge Records Society: 1994)

March 7th

1615: On this day, King James I arrived in Cambridge from Newmarket, accompanied by his son Prince Charles (later King Charles I) but not the Queen, who had apparently not been invited. The Recorder of Cambridge was there to meet the royal pair and to present them with 'our poor present', a rather modest description for two silver cups valued at £56, a significant amount in 1615. The weather was 'hard' and the ways 'foul', but the King made his entry with 'much solemnity'. The royal couple were lodged at Trinity College, where plays were put on for them in the Great Hall, which was arranged in such a way that 2,000 people could be accommodated. During the visit, the royal pair found plenty of time for sightseeing, as John Chamberlain recorded: 'He visited all the Colleges save two or three, and commends them beyond Oxford'. The King declared that were he at the University he would choose 'to pray at King's, to dine at Trinity and to study and sleep at Jesus.' During the visit, poet John Donne was made Doctor of Divinity and Ben Jonson was asked to 'pen a ditty'. (Colthorpe, M., *Royal Cambridge*, Cambridge City Council: 1977)

March 8th

1959: On this day, Mervyn Stockwood, one of the most colourful, outspoken, controversial priests of a generation and also one of the most popular and successful, delivered his farewell sermon to a packed congregation at Great St Mary's Church in Cambridge. He had been vicar here for the last four years and was now moving on to become Bishop of Southwark. In his sermons, Stockwood would famously consider both sides of an argument and then come to a firm and clear conclusion, based on Christian principals. He was adamant that the sermons should not outrun their allotted time, saying, 'Nobody could make out whether I was High Church or Low Church but they did know that I was not "long" church. I could not stand any service that went on for more than one hour'. As his services grew in fame and popularity, sometimes the congregation numbered well over a thousand; there would be one queue down King's Parade to Corpus Christi and another round the Market Place. Stockwood also claimed that he never took a day off during term-time and was always present at every service. (Binns, J. and Meadows, P., *Great St Mary's*, University Press, Cambridge: 2000)

March 9th

1846: On this day, there was an outbreak of violence in Cambridge city centre, yet another example of ongoing tension between undergraduates and townspeople. The previous evening, four students had been arrested, one of them carrying a poker. Josiah Chater wrote in his diary today: 'The four University men were tried this morning at the Town Hall … There were a great many people on the Market Hill and the University men vow vengeance to the police tonight. About half-past eight the gowns-men assembled in the Rose Crescent to the amount of, as near as I could guess, 300 … they began to kick up a row; they had tremendous cudgels'. Chater went on to say that this was the beginning of the worst 'row' he had seen for many years: 'The gownsmen threw glass bottles on to the townsmen's heads and water and stones, which so enraged the townsmen that they went to all the colleges and smashed the windows to pieces. Christ's have got it worst. There are above 80 panes broken'. On the following day, the Vice-Chancellor issued a statement to the effect that whenever more than four University men are found 'assembled together' they will be 'rusticated or expelled'. (Porter, E., *Josiah Chater's Diaries*, Phillimore: 1975)

March 10th

1627: On this day, the Duke of Buckingham, Chancellor of the University of Cambridge, was taken on to the roof of King's College Chapel. It was customary for visitors to have the shape of their foot set in the leads of the roof, but Buckingham refused. Later that year the antiquary Sir Simonds d'Ewes visited Cambridge with his new thirteen-year-old bride and wrote: 'we went both up to the top of King's College Chapel … upon the leads, my wife's foot was set, being one of the least in England (her age and statue considered)'. (Chainey, G., *In Celebration of King's College Chapel*, The Pevensey Press: 1987)

1952: On this day, Douglas Hurd was elected as the President of the Cambridge Union Debating Society, hoping to breathe some new life into debates which he found were becoming too contrived. Two years previously, Hurd had likened the Union to 'the Assembly of the United Nations in its ignorance and unrepresentative nature'. Hurd went on to a successful political career, playing a leading role in Margaret Thatcher's government. (Parkinson, S., *Arena of Ambition*, Icon Books: 2009)

March 11th

1929: On this day, a dinner took place in Cambridge to mark the retirement of Charles Heycock, the pioneer of phase-diagram determination, an important branch of physical chemistry. Heycock's main area of interest was metallurgy and the names (but hopefully not the contents) of items on the menu for his special dinner tonight incorporated metallurgical terms, for example 'tortue d'alau' followed by 'agneau bronzé Heycock et Neville' (Neville was Heycock's principal collaborator), 'haricots malachite', ending eventually with 'flux', no doubt to the great amusement of the gathered chemists. Heycock's original work on metals attracted the attention of the Goldsmiths' Company, who endowed a readership in metallurgy at Cambridge; he was appointed to this office in 1908 and held it right up until his retirement. One of his duties had been to oversee the extension of the Department of Physical Chemistry into the old engineering laboratories in Free School Lane and the name of his department can still be seen today, inscribed on the outside wall above the entrance to the Whipple Museum. Sadly, Heycock did not enjoy a long retirement, dying aged seventy-three in 1931. (Charles, J. and Greer, A., *Light Blue Materials*, Maney: 2005 / *Nature*)

March 12th

1448: On this day, King Henry VI wrote his 'will and intent' for King's College Chapel, laying out his requirements for its foundation and building. Henry was to live for another twenty years, but this was an important and influential document even within his lifetime. In this document Henry called for simplicity of decoration and insisted on the absence of any 'superfluity of too great curious works of entail and busy moulding'. According to Carola Hicks, 'For him, the monumental scale and proportions of the building were enough to create beauty through perfect design and execution'. But the building and decoration of King's College Chapel was completed not by Henry VI but by the Tudors, nearly a century later, and simplicity was not their hallmark. Hicks continued: 'What the sculptors produced was outstanding and eye-catching, an exuberant profusion of the symbols of monarchy, obsessively repeated through the interior of the antechapel'. The pinnacle of the stone-carving is the fan-vaulted ceiling, a far cry from the simplicity requested by Henry VI, but today hailed as one of the iconic images of Cambridge and admired by visitors from around the globe. (Gray, A., *Cambridge and Its Story*, Methuen: 1912 / Hicks, C., *The King's Glass*, Chatto & Windus: 2007)

March 13th

1920: On this day, music scholar and benefactor Sedley Taylor died, soon to be buried in Trinity College Chapel, where a Latin plaque commemorates him. Enjoying a private income, Taylor lived for most of his adult life in Trinity College, without holding a university or college position (apart from one year as librarian of Trinity). He remained unmarried, was a great raconteur and had a distinctive appearance, with a thick and spreading black beard, prompting his contemporary Alfred Marshall to refer to him as 'that owl in the ivy bush'. Taylor was also a generous benefactor and in recognition of this he was given the freedom of the city of Cambridge. Fascinated by both music and physics, he conducted numerous experiments on sound waves in the Cavendish Laboratory and was a leading figure in the Cambridge University Musical Club. One of his inventions, the 'phoneidoscope', was patented; the device showed the effect of sound upon soap bubbles. Towards the end of his life his considerable powers began to fail and it was written in his *Times* obituary: 'Defective eyesight and increasing loneliness produced mental depression and this he was never able to shake off'. Sedley Taylor Road in Cambridge is named after him. (*The Times*)

March 14th

1946: On this day, Major Blank of the US army hosted a farewell dinner, a feast of southern fried chicken, to which the great and the good of Cambridge were invited. The dinner marked the end of Bull College, founded just six months previously for the education of selected American servicemen, many of whom were 'rationed and quartered at the Bull Hotel, under the supervision of the American Red Cross'. It was the eccentric Provost of King's College, John T. Sheppard, who oversaw the transformation of the Bull Hotel into an academic house, saying in his welcoming address: 'As the word "hotel" sounds so very undignified, I will just call you simply "Bull College". And you, Major Blank, I refer to as the Big Bull.' The name was enthusiastically adopted by the GIs, who soon also had their own colours, tie and a coat of arms and were taught by such Cambridge luminaries as the philosopher Bertrand Russell. They did not want to leave, prompting such headlines as 'Keep us at Bull, say Yanks' and 'truants in reverse, the boys who would sooner stay at school than go home'. In the autumn of 1946, the Bull Hotel was taken over by neighbouring St Catharine's College to house the influx of undergraduates demobbed from UK forces. (CAM 59)

March 15th

1858: On this day, great excitement was spreading through most of Britain, as a rare eclipse of the sun took place and people were urged to take out their opera glasses and view the sun through various pieces of coloured glass. In Cambridge, Josiah Chater made the following observations: 'All excitement, everybody procuring coloured glass to view the Eclipse. It was predicted to commence at 11.42 a.m. and sure enough, just at that time, the moon began quietly to creep on to the face of the sun and put out his light. Alex Macintosh, Mr Buxton and I went on to Madingley Hill where we had a good view, and a pretty sight it was. The greatest obscuration was at one o'clock and just then it was tolerably clear so we had an excellent opportunity of witnessing the various changes assumed by the sun. I did not perceive a perfect ring but I saw quite ¾. The atmosphere was quite dull, not approaching to darkness, and all at once got very cold, as cold as just before sunrise.' (Porter, E., *Josiah Chater's Diaries*, Phillimore: 1975)

March 16th

1875: On this day, the following rather laconic entry appeared in the Order Book of Pembroke College: 'It was agreed that Mr Waterhouse be authorised to pull down the College Hall.' Despite protests from past Pembroke students and a spirited correspondence in *The Times* the order was carried out and architect Alfred Waterhouse built a grand new Dining Hall on the site of the old one which had latterly worn 'a singularly forlorn and desolate aspect'. Luckily, the architect's plans to demolish and rebuild the College Chapel (designed by Christopher Wren) were not approved. (Attwater, A. and Roberts, S., *Pembroke College Cambridge: A Short History*, CUP: 2010)

2009: On this day, the ADC (Amateur Dramatic Club) Theatre in Cambridge hosted a gala event, part of the University of Cambridge 800th anniversary celebrations. Guest of honour was HRH Prince Edward, who unveiled a plaque in the bar to mark the occasion. Current undergraduates performed scenes from some of their most successful shows, but were almost eclipsed by the star-studded audience, which included Griff Rhys-Jones, Richard Stilgoe, Trevor Nunn, Germaine Greer and Margaret Drabble. (*The Cambridge Student*)

March 17th

1868: On this day, an order from St John's College in Cambridge stated: 'Agreed that the Old Chapel be dismantled for the purpose of removing whatever materials are to be used, either in the New Chapel or in the College Hall, immediately after the conclusion of the College General Examination in June next, and that the Old Chapel be therefore put into a fitting temporary condition for the celebration of Divine Service until the sixth of May 1869 when it is intended that the New Chapel shall be consecrated.' The 'Old Chapel' predated even the college, having belonged originally to the Hospital of St John, an Augustinian house on the same site; the foundations of this chapel, containing several graves and memorial slabs, can still clearly be seen in the First Court of St John's College. By the 1860s the original chapel had become too cramped and with increased student numbers attending compulsory services, it was decided to build a new, larger one. Eminent Victorian architect Sir George Gilbert Scott was selected as the man for the job; inspired by the Sainte-Chapelle in Paris, the Chapel is a prime example of high Victorian neo-Gothicism. (Crook, A., *From the Foundation to Gilbert Scott*, St John's College: 1980 / Tim Rawle Associates: *St John's College Cambridge*)

March 18th

1869: On this day, author Charles Dickens paid his third visit to Cambridge, part of a long farewell tour based partly in London and partly in the provinces. He had been on the road since his first performance of the tour in London some five months previously. The readings in the Cambridge Guildhall included extracts from *Martin Chuzzlewit* and *Holly Tree Inn*. Josiah Chater wrote in his diaries that he went to the performance with his father, who had come over from Saffron Walden for the day. His comment was brief and to the point: 'I liked it very much.' It is likely that Dickens' son, Henry Fielding Dickens, was in the audience. Charles had been very proud of his son for winning a scholarship at Trinity Hall. In his first term at Cambridge, Charles Dickens had sent his son an impressive 'three dozen sherry, two dozen port and three dozen light claret' and warned him 'now, observe attentively. We must have no shadow of debt. Square up everything whatsoever that it has been necessary to buy. Let not a farthing be outstanding on my account.' Dickens Senior died the following year. (Chainey, G., *A Literary History of Cambridge*, Cambridge University Press: 1995 / Porter, E., *Josiah Chater's Diaries*, Phillimore: 1975)

March 19th

1632: On this day, a play called *The Rival Friends* was performed in Trinity College for King Charles I and his wife Henrietta Maria. The play, a laboured and lengthy satire, was not a success, to the chagrin of the Vice-Chancellor Dr Henry Butts who had not only promoted the play but also had a small part in it himself. Desperately affected by the bad reviews, Butts later hanged himself in the Master's Lodge at Corpus Christi, where his ghost is still said to appear. (Colthorpe, M., *Royal Cambridge*, Cambridge City Council: 1977)

———◆———

1963: On this day, a little-known band named the Beatles played at the Regal Cinema in Cambridge, to unenthusiastic reviews: 'The fast-moving show was not the best Cambridge audiences have seen.' It was a different story when the Beatles returned to Cambridge just eight months later and 'Beatlemania' was in full flow. The queue for tickets stretched round the block, the Red Cross were on hand to revive swooning female fans and police were out in force to control the crowds. (*Cambridge Evening News*)

March 20th

1738: On this day, as his time as an undergraduate was nearing an end, twenty-one-year-old Thomas Gray wrote to Horace Walpole, an old school friend from Eton College: 'I don't know how it is, I have a sort of reluctance to leave this place, unamiable as it may seem; 'tis true Cambridge is very ugly, she is very dirty and very dull; but I'm like a cabbage, where I'm stuck, I love to grow.' But after his graduation Gray did indeed leave Cambridge, moving initially to his father's house in London, with a view to becoming a lawyer. Bored with that, he set off the following year to Italy, where he undertook the grand tour with his friend Horace Walpole; after two years away, strong personality differences were apparent between the 'introverted, scholarly Gray' and the 'extrovert, socialising Walpole'. And so Gray found himself back in Cambridge, living first at Peterhouse and then moving over the road to Pembroke College. By the time Thomas Gray died, in his college rooms at Pembroke, he was the dominant poetic figure of the time; his poem *An Elegy Written in a Country Churchyard* remains one of England's best loved poems. (Chainey, G., *A Literary History of Cambridge*, Pevensey Press: 1985)

March 21st

1941: On this day, buildings at Pembroke College Cambridge were on fire. Opinions diverged as to the cause of the fire; the occupants reckoned it was due to a fault in the electrical wiring, but the college authorities put it down to their 'frivolity with cigarette ends'. Whatever the cause, Pembroke's new buildings on Downing Street were left roofless for about eighty yards; luckily, the older college buildings were not affected. Ironically, the chairman of the University ARP (Air Raid Precautions) Committee at the time was also the Master of Pembroke College. Even though Cambridge was relatively little affected by bombing raids during the Second World War, this was a time when the college authorities and townspeople had to be highly vigilant. Important buildings were sand-bagged and air-raid wardens were posted around town, some on the top of St John's College tower, watching out for approaching enemy fire. Classicist A.S.F. Gow described the Pembroke fire in his diaries, where he also recalled a conversation between W.E. Heitland and his wife on seeing from afar a fire at Fulbourn: '*Mrs H.:* "Oh, I *do* hope it isn't the Asylum". *Mr H.:* "What would you prefer, my dear?"' (Gow, A.S.F., *Letters from Cambridge*, Jonathan Cape: 1945)

March 22nd

1933: On this day, renowned stone-carver Eric Gill wrote a letter to Russian scientist Peter Kapitza, then working at the brand new Mond Laboratory in Cambridge. Eric Gill had carved a crocodile on the outside of this building, which met with general approval, unlike his plaque showing the face in profile of the laboratory's director, Lord Rutherford, on the wall just inside the building. There was pressure to have the carving removed or modified to give the nose a less Jewish appearance, while some of the younger researchers talked of hacking it to pieces secretly, at night. In his letter today, Gill explained that it was more a Roman than a Jewish nose and that the 'classical people' in Cambridge ought to appreciate that, summing up by saying 'what a lot of frightful balls it all is.' The noise about the carving gradually died down and the plaque was eventually accepted as a 'correct impression' of Lord Rutherford. Decades later, the plaque can still be seen on the wall just inside the entrance of the Mond Building, appreciated mostly by visitors to the Centre of African Studies which is housed in the building today. (Oliphant, M., *Rutherford: Recollections of the Cambridge Days*, Elsevier: 1972)

March 23rd

1613: On this day, after negotiations lasting sixty-six years, involving many different interested parties, a deed was drawn up between Thomas Nevile, Master of Trinity College, and Edward Cropley, Mayor of Cambridge, to make an official exchange of land. Trinity College received several acres of land adjoining the River Cam. The town, in return, received £50, a farm in St Andrew's parish and various pieces of land, the most important being a plot of twenty-five acres; this plot became known as Parker's Piece, because it had previously been leased to Edward Parker, a Cambridge cook. For the next 200 years Parker's Piece was enclosed by a hedge, divided by a ditch and many shrubs, trees, waterways and hedges. After the land's levelling in 1813, Parker's Piece became famous for cricket. The weathervane on the pavilion today shows a cricketer and stumps, commemorating the famous Edwardian cricketer Jack Hobbs who, as a teenager, would practise cricket here every morning at 6 a.m. before his rounds as a baker's errand boy. Hobbs later described Parker's Piece as 'the finest cricket ground in the world'. (Mitchell, E., *Notes on the History of Parker's Piece Cambridge*, Mitchell: 1984)

March 24th

1995: On this day, Joseph Needham, ninety-four-year-old biochemist and chronicler of the history of science in China, breathed his last. Needham was at his home in Cambridge, just next to the Institute which he had created. He had been working right up till the day before his death, when, looking very frail and weak, it had been suggested, for the first time in memory, that he should take the day off. Earlier today two nurses had arrived and someone told Joseph he was lucky to have two beautiful young girls looking after him. Always one to have eyes for a pretty girl, Simon Winchester says that 'he grinned wickedly, impishly, happily'. A friend and neighbour called to see him and said goodbye, saying that she would be back to see him soon. And with that 'Noel Joseph Terence Montgomery Needham, CH, FRS, FBA, sighed once, very slightly – there was no pain, no gasping, no more than a weary acceptance of the inevitable – and died'. Written in elegant calligraphy by the fireplace in Needham's old college room is the famous Chinese aphorism: 'The Man departs – there remains his shadow'. His ashes were later scattered in the garden of the Needham Institute in Cambridge. (Winchester, S., *Bomb, Book and Compass*, Penguin: 2009)

March 25th

1960: On this day, a most unusual burial service took place in the antechapel of Sidney Sussex College in Cambridge. The Master, Dr David Thomson, and seven others watched as the embalmed head of Oliver Cromwell, transfixed by a metal spike on a wooden pole, was lowered into its new resting place. Admired by some and despised by others, Cromwell had as a young man cut short his studies at Sidney Sussex in order to pursue a political career, eventually establishing himself as Lord Protector. When Cromwell died he was buried in Westminster Abbey with full pomp and circumstance, surrounded by the kings and queens of medieval England. Revenge came when King Charles II ordered Cromwell's embalmed body to be exhumed, hanged publicly at Tyburn (where Marble Arch stands today) and decapitated. Cromwell's head was exposed on a spike outside the Palace of Westminster until it was supposedly blown down in a storm and taken home by a soldier. From then on the head had a curious history, moving from one owner to another until, in 1960, it was offered to Cromwell's old college in Cambridge. The exact location is unmarked and known only to a few. (Beales and Nisbet, *Sidney Sussex College: Historical Essays*, Boydell and Brewer: 1996)

March 26th

2001: Today, a headline in the *Cambridge Evening News* read: 'Ancient elk back in pride of place after repairs'. The elk skeleton, described as 'one of the museum's best-loved specimens', is nearly 2 metres tall and has an antler span of 2.5 metres. The 12,000-year-old elk had been a prized specimen at the museum for over sixty years until 1996, when its head and antlers had to be removed for vital repairs as they were beginning to fall apart. The elk was found preserved in a peat bog in Enniscorthy, Ireland; the museum's founder, Adam Sedgwick, bought the specimen in 1834 for £140. Seven years after its re-installation the elk (in fact more strictly speaking, a kind of extinct giant deer) was on the move again, this time to free up space for the *Darwin the Geologist* exhibition, part of the 2009 anniversary celebrations. The elk this time benefits from a striking new position right opposite the famous hippo which had been found in the chalk pits in Barrington near Cambridge, suggesting that East Anglia was once a much warmer place than today. (*Cambridge Evening News*)

March 27th

1841: On this day, Joseph Romilly, Fellow of Trinity College, wrote in his diary: 'We met to enquire into that sad affair of John Wilson having drunk wine in an undergraduate's rooms …, having been taken thence by the young men in a state of stupefaction down stairs and laid on the grass, conveyed in a barrow to the station house where he was bled, thence to the hospital where he was again bled and all usual means of restoration applied but died in twenty-four hours. The coroner's inquest yesterday pronounced a verdict of "died by excessive drinking".' Romilly and his colleagues read the witness statements of all involved and were able to piece together a picture of Wilson's final hours. Wilson hailed originally from Carlisle and went to an undergraduate's rooms in order to meet up with others from that area. Port, then wine, was passed round in tumblers, other students started to arrive and more wine was poured. Just fifteen minutes after his first tumbler of port Wilson became 'insensible'. The verdict from the Fellows of Trinity was that the seven undergraduates involved would be 'had up' the following Monday to be 'reprimanded by the Vice-Master.' (Bury, M. and Pickles, J., *Romilly's Cambridge Diary*, CUP: 1967)

March 28th

1801: On this day, a chimneysweep by the name of Grimshaw was hanged in Cambridge. He had been accused of stealing and his house on Newmarket Road was pulled down in the search for stolen articles. According to a letter sent to Arthur Young, Grimshaw had been visited regularly in gaol by evangelical preacher Charles Simeon, who had reportedly said 'that he found Grimshaw's conversation delightful; that he had grace to die; and that the sooner he was executed the better, for fear this grace should evaporate.' Simeon was a regular visitor to prisoners on death row and not only in local gaols, paying no fewer than nine visits to Newgate Prison in London in order to preach to its inmates. On another occasion Simeon attended the hanging of a man who had been condemned to death merely for stealing a watch. The young Charles Simeon stood next to the criminal on the gallows, the latter humbling himself and exulting Christ and the former commending his soul into the hands of Jesus. The whole of this spectacle was watched, after the custom of the day, by all who had come to stare at the latest public execution. (Hopkins, H., *Charles Simeon of Cambridge*, Hodder & Stoughton: 1977)

March 29th

1662: On this day, John Strype was admitted to Jesus College in Cambridge. His stay there was brief; following his tutor's expulsion on religious grounds, Strype's Protestant refugee family, originally from the Spanish Netherlands, thought that Jesus College was 'too superstishus' and moved him to Catharine Hall just one year later. Soon after his arrival at Jesus College, Strype wrote a letter to his mother, giving an extremely interesting insight into student life at the time: 'We have roast meat, dinner and supper, throughout the week; and such meat as you know I had not use to care for; and that is veal; but now I have learned to eat it. As yet, I am in a chamber that doth not at all please me. I have thoughts of … a very handsome one … that looketh into the Master's garden. The price is but 20s. per annum … We go twice a day to Chapel; in the morning about 7 and in the evening about 5. After we come from Chapel in the morning … we go to the Butteries for breakfast … ; an half penny loaf and buter [*sic*], and a cize of beer. But sometimes I go to an honest house near the college and have a pint of milk boiled for my breakfast.' (Gray, A., *A History of Jesus College*, Heinemann: 1960)

March 30th

1865: On this day, Henry Hoare, alumnus and benefactor of St John's College in Cambridge, was severely injured in a railway accident on the Great Eastern Railway, dying the following year on April 16. Hoare had been keen for the new chapel at his old college to have a tower, going against the preferences of the architect Sir George Gilbert Scott, who favoured a 'flèche' or short spire. Money won the day, with Hoare offering £2,000 as a down-payment and £1,000 a year after that until the work was completed. At the time of his early and unexpected death, only £2,000 had been contributed and despite the advice of the Bursar, the College had not insured his life. Following his father's death, Henry Hoare Junior wrote a letter to the Master of St John's College offering to pay for the building of the rest of the tower, in return for the opportunity to buy some college land which adjoined his property in Kent. The Master was adamant that he would not enter into such a deal, declining gracefully. And so the tower was eventually built according to Hoare's wishes, but financed mostly by the College and not by the Hoare family. (Crook, A., *From the Foundation to Gilbert Scott*, St John's College: 1980)

March 31st

2010: On this day, Princess Anne visited Cambridge for the official opening of the new £7m Cambridge Central Library. This was the Princess Royal's first official visit to Cambridge since opening the Lion Yard shopping centre in 1977 and she remarked on the area's transformation since then. In the children's section, she spoke to pupils from Park Street Primary School, who said that they were very pleased to have met a 'real princess' and that she was 'very pretty'. After unveiling a plaque, the Princess gave a speech, thanking the local council for their 'investment in the library system not just here but around the county.' The library was originally scheduled to open in May 2008, but the project was delayed due to serious structural problems in the original 1970s building. The new library quickly established itself in the Cambridge community, welcoming 17,000 visitors in its first week of opening alone. 'Not all about books', the new facility offers a huge range of services such as free access to computers, online newspapers and e-books, story-time sessions for toddlers, IT courses for the over fifties, talks by guests speakers, not to mention the wonderful resource of the Cambridgeshire Collection, much visited for the production of this book. (*Cambridge News*)

April 1st

1632: On this day, Dr Henry Butts, Master of Corpus Christi College and Vice-Chancellor of the University of Cambridge, was found dead in his rooms, hanged by a 'kerchief' (a sort of scarf used to cover the head). At this time of plague, many of his colleagues had forsaken Cambridge for the relative safety of the countryside, but Butts heroically stayed put, saying: 'Myself I am alone, a destitute and forsaken man, not a scholar with me in the college, not a scholar seen by me without.' Just weeks before his untimely death, Butts had been badly affected by the poor reviews given to a play which he had produced for King Charles I and his wife Henrietta Maria on their visit to Cambridge. As Vice-Chancellor he also faced criticism for the high number of rather lucrative honorary degrees which were conferred that day, many to 'unworthy graduates'. The shame was too great and Butts took his own life. Since that date, there have been repeated sightings of his ghost, sometimes with the kerchief still around his neck; in the twenty-first century, Butts has become one of the stars of Cambridge ghost walks. (Halliday, R. and Murdie, A., *The Cambridge Ghost Book*, Fern House: 2000 / Colthorpe, M., *Royal Cambridge*, Cambridge City Council: 1977)

April 2nd

1441: On this day, Passion Sunday, the nineteen-year-old King Henry VI laid the foundation stone of the Old Court of King's College in Cambridge. His plans were modest: a college comprising a rector and twelve scholars (the number of apostles), occupying a small court where the Old Schools, the central offices of the University's administration, now stand. Only the lower part of the gatehouse of the original college still survives, just opposite Clare College. The foundation stone was laid at the base of the right-hand turret of the gate tower. In the event, Henry's gate tower and the nearby west range of the college were only half finished when work began on the new great court in 1446 and it seemed that the Old Court would no longer be needed, so the original buildings were roughly finished off and temporary buildings erected nearby. Yet, as it turned out, this makeshift college was in continuous use for nearly four centuries. Until 1724, when Gibbs' Fellows' Building was erected, it housed both Fellows and Scholars and served as the home of the Scholars of King's College until 1828. (Morris, C., *King's College, A Short History*, King's College: 1989 / Saltmarsh, J., *King's College and its Chapel*, Jarrold & Sons: 1969)

April 3rd

1542: On this day, Thomas Lord Audley, who as Lord Chancellor had presided over the trials of Sir Thomas More and Anne Boleyn and helped Henry VIII rid himself of two other wives, re-founded Buckingham College as the College of St Mary Magdalene. He was at the peak of his career and the name of his new college was no doubt very appealing to him, as Magdalene was pronounced (then, as now) 'maudlin', a pun on his own name Audley. He unfortunately died just twelve years later, at the age of fifty-six, leaving his college inadequately endowed; financial problems were to beset the college over the next few centuries. However, one of the most remarkable legacies to Magdalene was made in 1703, when writer and diarist Samuel Pepys bequeathed his library to his old college, including the famous diaries with his handwritten accounts of life in the seventeenth century, amongst which was an eyewitness account of the Great Fire of London in 1666. Today these diaries can be viewed, along with other books from his collection, in the Pepys Library, which was purpose-built at Magdalene College to contain these books after his death. (Cunich, P., Hoyle, D., Duffy, E. and Hyam R., *History of Magdalene College*, Magdalene College: 1994 / Anon., *Magdalene Described*, Crampton: 1982)

April 4th

1617: On this day, James Shirley received his Cambridge BA degree. Later becoming a playwright and poet of some repute, two lines from one of his poems: 'Some ring the bell, 'twill raise the court' were inscribed in 1994 on a stone in his old college, St Catharine's. The stone was placed, appropriately, under a bell inscribed 'De Catharina 1772'. The bell has no connection with the college other than its name; it was probably used as a plantation bell for slaves in British Guiana. The bell is still in daily use and is sounded by electrical means from a switch in the nearby Porters' Lodge. (*St Catharine's College Society Magazine / Dictionary of National Biography*)

———— • ◆ • ————

2010: Today, Pink Floyd fans entered Cambridge along the River Cam, having spent three days walking from London. The fans were following in the footsteps of Syd Barrett, the Cambridge-born, charismatic front-man of rock band Pink Floyd, who thirty years ago decided to leave London for good and just carried on walking until he reached his home town of Cambridge. He lived here alone until his death in 2006, at the age of sixty. (*Cambridge News*)

April 5th

1855: On this day, in the Baptist Chapel in Cambridge, the marriage took place between engineer Charles Todd and his cousin, eighteen year old Alice Bell of 3 Free School Lane, Cambridge. They were soon to set sail for Adelaide in Australia, where Todd's new position would be Government Astronomer and Superintendent of Telegraphs for South Australia. In his wedding speech, Charles commended his new wife, adding that one day he would like to see a telegraphic string stretching round the world, like the necklace of pearls around Alice's throat. It was Todd who greatly contributed to this plan, the precursor of today's telecommunications and the internet. Todd and his team braved disease, extremes of climate and natural disaster to lay the wire across the Australian continent from Adelaide to Darwin, where it linked up with the undersea cable to Java and then ultimately to London. Along the way, Todd and his 400 men named places after both themselves and their nearest and dearest; this is how Todd River was named, and of course Alice Springs, named after his wife, so far away from her original home of Free School Lane in Cambridge. (Thomson, A., *The Singing Line*, Chatto & Windus: 1999)

April 6th

1855: On this day, Charles Spurgeon, the renowned evangelical preacher from London, preached to a packed congregation in St Andrew's Street Baptist Chapel in Cambridge. Stocky, clumsy and with coarse features, Spurgeon was often caricatured as vulgar, sensational and irreverent, but despite or perhaps even because of this, he was the celebrity preacher of his day, developing a talent for making the congregation feel that his message was directed at them personally. Spurgeon had strong links with Cambridge, having moved there at the age of sixteen, soon giving Sunday school addresses at the Baptist Chapel. He was tricked into giving his first sermon in a small cottage in Teversham, near Cambridge at the age of seventeen, being under the impression that a companion had been assigned the task; his totally impromptu sermon, with no notes, held the small audience spellbound. When Spurgeon was dying in 1892, daily bulletins on the state of his health were published in *The Times*. Thousands then attended memorial services around the country and an estimated 60,000 people queued to view his coffin. Today his name lives on in Spurgeon's Tabernacle, just by the Elephant and Castle in London, where the tradition of evangelical preaching continues. (Porter, E., *Josiah Chater's Diaries*, Phillimore: 1975 / *Dictionary of National Biography*)

April 7th

1747: On this day, Cambridge physician Dr Heberden delivered the first lecture in a course of thirty-one; the series ended on May 22, missing just one week between the tenth and eleventh lecture for his beloved horse races at Newmarket. In his lectures, Heberden conducted a course of experiments on locally sourced plants in order to show their uses in medicine, at the same time lamenting the fact that there was no public garden in Cambridge which was 'furnished with sufficient variety of plants for making the like experiments'. Some fifteen years later, when Richard Walker, Vice-Master of Trinity College, gave land to the University 'for the purpose of a Botanic Garden', he quoted Heberden's comments and made it clear that the aim of the garden was to provide plants for 'the benefit of mankind'; flowers and fruits were to be looked on 'as amusements only'. Heberden went on to become a very eminent physician; he was the first to differentiate chickenpox from smallpox and the nodes seen on the fingers in osteoarthritis are named after him. His medical cabinet, used in the course of his Cambridge lectures, still survives in St John's College. (Walters, S., *The Shaping of Cambridge Botany*, CUP: 1981)

April 8th

2008: On this day, a complete set of ornate iron gates was discovered in a gardener's storeroom in the grounds of Gonville and Caius College. The gates had been languishing there for fifty years; before that, they had been for another twenty years at least in a bicycle shed in Tree Court. The storeroom was being cleared to make room for the new Stephen Hawking building which was about to be built on the site. The chance discovery of these gates led to their identification by a college member who had been researching college locations for a possible memorial to Francis Crick, co-discoverer of the structure of DNA and Honorary College Fellow. One mooted location had been the archway under the Great Gate, facing King's Parade. College records and photographs showed ornate gates here; these were the very gates which had been found in the shed, designed by distinguished Victorian architect Alfred Waterhouse as part of an overall scheme for new college buildings. The gates were duly cleaned, restored and reinstated in their original position, where they open up, during the day, an attractive view from the street outside into Tree Court, a view of the college that has not been available for over 100 years. (Howell, J., *Once a Caian …*: 2009)

April 9th

1511: On this day, the seals of the executors to the estate of Lady Margaret Beaufort were affixed to the charter for the foundation of St John's College in Cambridge. Lady Margaret, having already founded Christ's College in Cambridge, had been persuaded by her confessor, John Fisher, to found a further college. Consent was acquired from the Bishop of Ely to dissolve the dilapidated St John's Hospital, proposed site of the new college, but before the legal documents could be obtained, both King Henry VII and his mother Lady Margaret Beaufort died, within weeks of each other. There ensued a lengthy battle between Fisher and the courts, which Fisher eventually won, and the four remaining monks were sent packing, leaving by boat for Ely just two weeks before today's charter was signed. According to Thomas Baker, 'the master of the house was forced to hide his head and the brethren were dispersed'. The original foundation of St John's was not wealthy, but Fisher bequeathed land and other benefactions began to pour in, so the new college 'did not suffer from financial stringency'. (Crook, A., *From the Foundation to Gilbert Scott*, St John's College: 1980)

April 10th

2009: On this day, an announcement was made in the *Cambridge News* that an egg collected by naturalist Charles Darwin on his five-year journey on HMS *Beagle* had been re-discovered by an octogenarian volunteer at Cambridge University's Zoology Museum. The chocolate brown egg, one of sixteen collected on Darwin's epic journey, was one of many items being catalogued by the museum. Volunteer Liz Wetton carefully recorded that the specimen had C. Darwin written on it, without at first realising that no one knew of its existence. Further research revealed that the egg had been donated to the museum by Alfred Newton, a zoology professor in the late nineteenth century who was a friend of Charles Darwin and his son Frank. Newton recorded in his notebook: 'One egg, received through Frank Darwin, having been sent to me by his father who said he got it at Maldonado and that it belonged to the common Tinamou of those parts'. The newly discovered egg has been given its own display case in the museum, alongside press cuttings about the story from around the world. Liz Wetton's discovery was, by pure chance, perfectly timed to coincide with the 2009 celebrations for the 200th anniversary of the birth of Charles Darwin. (*Cambridge News* / *The Guardian*)

April 14th

1794: On this day, Samuel Taylor Coleridge returned to Cambridge in order to resume his studies at Jesus College. Coleridge had previously led a dissolute lifestyle at Cambridge, running up huge debts, writing less than flattering poems about his environment and, according to Chainey, 'dissipating himself with harlots, opium ... and notions of suicide.' His first published poem, in 1893, was called 'To Fortune: On buying a ticket in the Irish lottery' but the lottery ticket did not produce the winning funds he needed to pay off his debts and so he bolted, signing up for the 15th Regiment of Dragoon Guards under the assumed name of Silas Tomkyn Comberbache. Months later he was discharged from military duties, 'insane', and returned to Cambridge on this day in 1794. Coleridge was full of good intentions; he would now study hard, contend 'for all the prizes' and sell his verse in order to pay off debts. The college's reprimand was a month's gating (being confined to college) and ninety pages of Greek translation ('dry and utterly intransferable to *modern* use'). Coleridge 'played the part of a penitent' and was outwardly resolute but he would never again settle down at the University; his dreams were elsewhere. (Holmes, R., *Coleridge*, Hodder & Stoughton: 1989 / Chainey, G., *A Literary History of Cambridge*, Pevensey Press: 1985)

April 12th

1758: On this day, Elzimar Smith, the greatly mourned sister of Robert Smith, Master of Trinity College, died at the age of seventy-four. A stone marks her burial place in the antechapel of Trinity College; amongst the myriad commemorative stones and plaques contained here, this is allegedly the only one dedicated to a female. Her name has in fact been mis-spelt on the plaque as Elizmar; furthermore, unusually for a woman who never married, her coat of arms is not contained within a lozenge. Elzimar lived in the Master's Lodge at Trinity College with her unmarried brother Robert Smith, mathematician and Master of the College. Her brother, though often portrayed as somewhat of a recluse, was in fact quite sociable at times. In later life both his academic work and social life were affected by ill health, particularly gout, and he died aged seventy-nine in the Master's Lodge ten years after his sister. For many years, Robert Smith's name lived on through his bequest to found the Smith's prizes, which were awarded annually to the two junior students who had made the greatest progress in mathematics and natural philosophy. These prizes were awarded annually from 1779 to 1998. (*Dictionary of National Biography*)

April 13th

1816: On this day, two wagons arrived in Cambridge, loaded with items bequeathed to the University by the 7th Viscount Fitzwilliam of Merrion. Fitzwilliam had studied at Trinity Hall in Cambridge and was well-read, cultivated and musical. He collected musical manuscripts, studied the harpsichord in Paris and was also a great art collector, having inherited many important works of art from his parents. Most of the Dutch paintings in the founder's collection in the Fitzwilliam Museum today had originally belonged to Fitzwilliam's grandfather, a wealthy Flemish financier and art collector. Childless and unmarried, when Fitzwilliam himself died, the viscountcy lapsed and he was buried in the parish church of Richmond upon Thames in Surrey. His closest relative, the Earl of Pembroke, inherited the bulk of Fitzwilliam's estate including the house on Richmond Green, which was well known for its musical soirées and well attended by French émigrés living in London. The original house no longer exists, but Pembroke Villas mark the spot. More important for Cambridge, Fitzwilliam left his art collections to his alma mater, the University of Cambridge, and these now lie at the heart of the University Museum which bears his name. (Pasmore, S., Richmond Local History Society)

April 14th

1932: On this day, excitement mounted as Cambridge scientists Cockcroft and Walton, along with Lord Rutherford, crouched uncomfortably in their home-made box and observed large numbers of alpha particle flashes, clearly indicating that they had not only penetrated the nucleus of lithium but had split it in two. Rutherford had compared the nucleus to a fly in a cathedral, his biographer Cathcart saying: 'the more he had learned ... about that tiny fly buzzing about in the huge, empty cathedral of the atom the more tantalising it had become. He had weighed it, measured it, prodded it and chipped it but he had never had the means to get inside it to see how it worked.' Popular legend later had it that Cockcroft went skipping down King's Parade shouting, 'We've split the atom! We've split the atom!' In reality, Rutherford, aware of the huge impact their discovery was to have on the global scientific community, swore the two men to secrecy, allowing them to work night and day in their laboratory before submitting a paper to the scientific journal *Nature* with their ground-breaking discovery. Cockcroft and Walton received the Nobel Prize in Physics in 1951. (Cathcart, B., *The Fly in the Cathedral*, Viking: 2004 / Oliphant, M., *Rutherford: Recollections of the Cambridge Days*, Elsevier: 1972)

April 15th

1905: On this day, bus wars broke out in Cambridge when two rival motorised omnibus services were launched on the same day, both offering the same service between the station and the post office. The Cambridge Motor Omnibus Company used two dark-blue single-deckers whilst the Cambridge Town and University Omnibus Company ran a light-blue double-decker which knocked down a lamppost on its very first day. Both buses were full on the first day, but their huge popularity did not last and as the novelty value wore off, the safety of these buses was questioned. The double-decker was only in service for six months, having had many accidents. On one occasion the bus conductor fell from his open 'footplate' on to the road and was run over by the bus. On another occasion a bus filled the streets with black smoke and was ordered off the road for 'not consuming its own exhaust'. All the buses damaged kerbstones and shop awnings, to the extent that by the end of 1906, just eighteen months after their launch, all motor bus operations came to an end for safety reasons and the slow, safe, reliable trams reigned supreme once more … at least for the time being. (Seal, M., *Cambridge Buses*, Oleander Press: 1978)

April 16th

1705: On this day, Queen Anne visited Cambridge and both the town and the University were determined to entertain her in style. The Vice-Chancellor had issued orders to all students to line the streets in central Cambridge and 'that as Her Majesty passeth by they all kneel down and say with loud and audible voice *Vivat Regina!* ... that none be seen in any college or in the town but in his gown and cap ... ; and all demean themselves with such modesty, civility and decency as may be to the honour of the University.' The Queen went straight to Trinity College, where she was welcomed by the Master, Dr Richard Bentley. The *London Gazette* reported that, 'Her Majesty was pleased to confer the honour of knighthood upon ... Isaac Newton Esquire, formerly Mathematick Professor and Fellow of that College. Then about three hundred ladies and gentlewomen were admitted to kiss Her Majesty's hand. She was later entertained at dinner in Hall, on a throne erected five foot high for that purpose.' After a visit to St John's College, Her Majesty proceeded to Newmarket, 'very well satisfied with all the marks of obedience and loyalty which she had met with.' (Colthorpe, M., *Royal Cambridge*, Cambridge City Council: 1977)

April 17th

1997: On this day, at 9.30 in the evening, two butlers from Peterhouse, Cambridge's oldest college, went into the dimly lit, oak-panelled Combination Room to collect some plates. Casually chatting, they were stopped in their tracks when they both saw something move slowly across the room, a white hooded figure, hovering about one foot off the ground. The ghost is thought to have been the tortured soul of one William Dawes, who hanged himself from a nearby bell rope in 1789. There was much scepticism about this story in college but a few months later the much respected Senior Bursar heard a repetitive knocking in the same room and felt a sudden chill, even though a large fire was burning in the fireplace. The college was sufficiently concerned to contact the diocese of Ely, requesting a requiem mass to exorcise the spirit; such a mass required all forty-five Fellows to be present and in the Senior Bursar's words, 'They are a cynical lot!' Word spread quickly about the Peterhouse ghost and by December 1997 the story was splashed across national papers, including *The Times*. Today the story is a highlight of Cambridge guided ghost walks. (Halliday, R. and Murdie, A., *The Cambridge Ghost Book*, Fern House: 2000 / *The Times*)

April 18th

2001: On this day, the results of some important Cambridge research in the Department of Materials Science and Metallurgy were announced in the press: the best way to eat spaghetti without splattering. The research was commissioned by supermarket chain Tesco, after studies suggested that UK pasta consumption had risen 560 per cent in the last five years. A team of researchers were instructed to test different techniques in a bid to calculate the 'kinetic energy, centrifugal forces and co-efficient of friction' for each method. Findings showed that the most common error is to hold the spoon vertically at right-angles to the fork, as this fails to shield both the eater and fellow diners. It was also concluded that if not using a spoon then it is crucial not to rotate the fork too many times or splatter will result. While long pasta is the most dangerous, the safest method is to hold the spoon parallel to the plate, with fork perpendicular to both plate and spoon. As the Cambridge professor directing this crucial research said: 'in terms of human advancement, it could undoubtedly benefit millions of people all over the world.' (*Cambridge Evening News*)

April 19th

1947: Today saw the launch of Cambridge University student newspaper *Varsity* and, carefully marketed, all 5,000 copies had sold out by lunchtime. The newspaper, according to its American first editor Harry Newman, 'began over a bottle of sherry in St John's, matured over a bottle of port in Caius and blossomed with a firkin of ale over the Victoria Cinema …' The editorial team put this first edition together on trestle tables in the Victoria Cinema, but by its third issue the newspaper had found its own home in a second-floor room above the Scotch Hoose, a restaurant in the Market Square. There was a mix of news, reports of debates and speaker meetings and reviews of shows, plays etc. It also contained feature articles; it was rumoured that the first of these had in fact been a sub-editor's essay hastily requisitioned when it was realised that there was not enough copy to fill all twelve pages. Harry Newman was later credited personally for the huge success of this publication; he went on to a successful career as a publisher in London and his native California. (Weatherall, M., *From our Cambridge Correspondent*, Varsity Publications: 1995)

April 20th

1954: On this day, the Association of New Hall was incorporated and registered as the 'third foundation' for women students at Cambridge University, at a time when Cambridge had the lowest proportion of women undergraduates of any university in the UK. The question of the name of this new college had been the subject of much discussion; many had favoured the name Darwin College, but the Darwin family was unwilling. Many other suggestions were made, ranging from a locality such as Mount Pleasant (corresponding to 'Girton' and 'Newnham') to a figure from history such as Erasmus. Eventually, the name of New Hall was chosen as being the name which had the most (albeit unenthusiastic) support. It left the way open for a benefactor to have the college named after him or her; it was to be fifty-four years before the college was re-named Murray Edwards College in 2008, following a gift from New Hall alumna Ros Smith and her husband Steve Edwards. Their £30m endowment was the largest in the history of the University and it was decided to name the college jointly after Ros Edwards and Dame Rosemary Murray (the first President of the College). (Murray, R., *New Hall 1954-1972*, New Hall: 1980 / Murray Edwards College website)

April 21st

1850: On this day, Joseph Romilly, Fellow of Trinity College, went to hear his friend William Carus, College Dean and Minister at the Holy Trinity Church in Cambridge, preach his sermon. Romilly was not impressed, writing in his diary: 'Carus preached on the character of Apollos. It was a horrid low church sermon which rather offended even me ... Carus said that Ministers might profit by the example of Apollos, and as he learned from Priscilla and Aquila so might they also learn from laymen! I think however that Carus would look upon anybody (whether lay or clerical) who offered to instruct him in theology [as] ridiculously impertinent'. Carus is frequently mentioned in Romilly's extensive diaries and usually shown in a much more positive light. In June 1844, the King of Saxony, on his visit to Trinity College, was accompanied by his physician, also called Carus. Romilly said that it was 'comical' for Carus to meet a namesake, a 'cousin German, as he called him' and apparently the King called him 'carissimus' when presented. William Carus had also been a very eligible bachelor, breaking the hearts of several Cambridge ladies when he eventually announced his engagement to Maria Selwyn in 1847. (Bury, M. and Pickles, J., *Romilly's Cambridge Diary*, Cambridge Records Society: 1994 and 2000)

April 22nd

1581: On this day, a Sunday, the Vice-Chancellor sent several University officials to Chesterton in order to investigate reports of bear-baiting in 'sermon-time', in other words between 1 and 2 p.m. They arrived to find a large crowd gathered in the yard of Jackson's Inn, all watching a bear chained to a stake, with huge dogs lunging at him. Richard Parish, the bear-keeper, refused to be arrested by the University's Esquire Bedell and a scuffle ensued, during which the Bedell was 'violently thrust and shoved upon the Beare, in such sort that he could hardly keepe himself from hurt.' Parish claimed that he had the authority of his patron, Lord Vaux, to carry out bear baiting, but the University officials cited the five mile rule of jurisdiction and eventually managed to arrest Parish, taking him off to the prison at Westminster Gatehouse in London, where he was detained for nearly a month before being sent back to Cambridge. Chesterton in the sixteenth century bore approximately the same relationship to Cambridge that Southwark had to London; according to Nelson, it was 'a site of often dubious activity which the university tried, with only limited success, to regulate.' (Gray, A., *The Town of Cambridge*, Heffer & Sons: 1925 / Nelson, A.H., *Early Cambridge Theatres*, CUP: 1994)

April 23rd

1616: On this day, the same day on which William Shakespeare died, Oliver Cromwell entered Sidney Sussex College in Cambridge. Thomas Carlyle has been much quoted on the subject: 'Whilst Oliver Cromwell was entering himself of Sidney Sussex College, William Shakespeare was taking his farewell of this world … Oliver's father saw Oliver write in the album at Cambridge; at Stratford, Shakespeare's Anne Hathaway was weeping over his bed … They have their exits and their entrances and one people in time plays many parts.' Tradition has it that Oliver lived in rooms overlooking Sidney Street, in the north-west corner of the college. His father died about a year after his son's arrival in Cambridge and Oliver was obliged then to leave college and return home. There is a 'forceful' portrait of Cromwell in the college Dining Hall, presented to the Master of Sidney Sussex by Thomas Hollis in 1766. Two years later, when Christian VII, King of Denmark, visited Cambridge, he 'contemplated the picture with attention' and remarked: '*Il me fait peur*' (he scares me). Oliver Cromwell's head is buried in a secret location, somewhere in the antechapel of Sidney Sussex College. (Stokes, H.P., *The Cambridge Scene*, Bowes & Bowes: 1921)

April 24th

1972: On this day, just before 6 a.m., a fire broke out at the heart of Cambridge's Garden House Hotel. Nine fire appliances and fifty firemen fought the blaze, which was all over within twenty minutes of their arrival. Two lady hotel guests died in the fire; one of them, Miss Allen, refused to follow her friend who had jumped from a first floor window to safety. Her body was discovered by firemen three hours later. Other guests were rescued by hero-of-the-day James Badenoch, who had the foresight to grab the builders' ladders, propped up against the new hotel extension (still under construction) and was able to help several elderly people escape from the first floor. Two middle-aged ladies, originally thought missing, had in fact escaped the hotel in their nightclothes and were rescued by a milkman who took them on his milk-float to the home of friends. Due to the extensive damage it was decided to demolish the old building completely and build a new first-class hotel. Despite the best efforts of the police, fire service and forensic experts, the cause of the fire remained a mystery. (Reynolds, D., *Growing Up with the Garden House Hotel*, Reynolds: 2007 / *Cambridge Evening News*)

April 25th

2003: Despite the rain, hundreds of well-wishers turned out to the Eagle pub in Bene't Street today to watch Nobel laureate James Watson unveil a blue plaque on the front wall of the pub where he and his colleague Francis Crick had spent 'many happy hours'. This pub used to be the 'local' for scientists working at the nearby Cavendish Laboratory, so in 1953 was the natural place for Crick and Watson, having determined the double helical structure of DNA, to announce to a rather under-whelmed and bemused group of customers that they had discovered 'the secret of life'. The date chosen to unveil this plaque was the fiftieth anniversary, to the day, of the publication of Crick and Watson's paper in science journal *Nature,* beginning with the words 'We wish to suggest a structure for the salt of deoxyribose nucleic acid (DNA). This structure has novel features which are of considerable biological interest.' And the rest is history. During the fiftieth anniversary celebrations Dr Watson was presented with a 2lb gold DNA commemorative coin by Prince Philip, the Chancellor of Cambridge University, at a conference attended by 500 leading international scientists. (*Cambridge Evening News / Nature*)

April 26th

1969: On this day, the Chapel of Jesus College was filled to capacity for the memorial service of well-known Cambridge don Dr Frederick (Freddy) Brittain. Just a few weeks earlier, on March 9, Brittain had gone to an undergraduate sherry party then come back to his college rooms saying, 'Gosh! I *did* enjoy that party.' But he had picked up a virulent infection and died in his rooms on March 15, the last day of term. Brittain's ashes were divided into two parts as he had wished, one half being buried in his parents' grave at South Mymms and the other half outside the east end of Jesus College Chapel. The simple inscription 'FB 1893-1969' is cut into the Chapel wall. Today's eulogy, given by the Archdeacon of Wells, painted the picture of a scholarly, Christian gentleman 'sitting in an upright chair at his desk, busy and interested about some aspect of life, though never too busy to put down his pen and give his attention to a visitor.' Brittain's published books clearly show the huge range of his interests, from a book about Latin in Church to light-hearted publications about rowing and the Roosters (Jesus College dining club). (Brittain, M., *The Diaries of Frederick Brittain*, Muriel Brittain: 2001)

April 27th

1951: On this day, daffodils on the Backs greeted King George VI and his wife Queen Elizabeth as they drove across the River Cam and right up to the doors of the world-famous King's College Chapel, where their twenty-year-old daughter Margaret was waiting for them. This was to be a day of celebration, beginning with a meeting with the Cambridge University Boat crew, lined up on the lawn in their Cambridge blue blazers and white flannels. 1951 had been a special year for the University rowers, who had unusually rowed two boat races against Oxford. The first was postponed when the Oxford boat sank less than four minutes into the race and the second was a huge victory for Cambridge, winning by twelve lengths, the biggest margin since 1900. The day before the royal visit the crew had just returned to England, flush with a series of victories over American university rowing teams. After lunch in King's College Hall, the royal party attended a thanksgiving service in the Chapel, primarily a celebration of the re-instalment of the ancient glass windows earlier that year. The windows had been removed from the Chapel during the war years for safekeeping. (Colthorpe, M., *Royal Cambridge*, Cambridge City Council: 1977)

April 28th

1783: On this day, the closure of a convent in Leuven, Belgium led to the sale of one of its most prized and admired paintings, the *Adoration of the Magi.* The masterpiece had been painted, supposedly in just eight days, by the acclaimed artist Peter Paul Rubens. Days after the sisters left their convent, a Brussels art connoisseur bought the painting for 8,000 florins; following his death, the painting joined the Duke of Westminster's art collection in London. When the Duke died, his executors sent it, along with other works of art, to Sotheby's auction house to pay death duties. The sale was thronging with television cameramen and press photographers, all keen to record what many considered to be the sale of the century. Paintings by Claude and Titian fetched good prices, but the real highlight of the day was the *Adoration of the Magi*, which was bought on behalf of a private collector for £275,000, the highest price ever achieved at auction for a single painting The collector later revealed himself to be property millionaire Major A.E. Allnatt, who in 1961 donated the painting to King's College Chapel in Cambridge, where it now hangs under the East Window. (*The Times* / SCTG newsletter: 2009)

April 29th

1951: This morning, the Austrian philosopher Ludwig Wittgenstein died in Cambridge. Wittgenstein had spent the last few days of his life at his doctor's house, where his last words were: 'Tell them I've had a wonderful life'. The philosopher had been working right till the end, writing the final entry in his journal less than a day before he completely lost consciousness. Wittgenstein had held the position of Professor of Philosophy at the University of Cambridge and was described by his colleague Bertrand Russell as 'the most perfect example of genius as traditionally conceived, passionate, profound, intense and dominating.' Wittgenstein's obituary in *The Times* described him as 'a philosopher with a reputation as an intellectual innovator on the highest level'. He was buried in the Ascension Burial Ground in Cambridge, near the grave of G.E. Moore, another Cambridge philosophical luminary. His tomb is a plain stone slab, simply inscribed 'Ludwig Wittgenstein 1882 – 1951'. Various small objects, from pennies and candles to cakes and pies, are regularly left on his grave by visiting devotees. A small ladder also features, recalling Wittgenstein's comments that 'he who understands me … has climbed out through them [my propositions], on them, over them. He must … throw away the ladder, after he has climbed up on it.' (*The Times* / Wittgenstein Research Archive)

April 30th

1829: On this day, William Makepeace Thackeray, an undergraduate at Trinity College, submitted his poem *Timbuctoo* to a new student magazine entitled *The Snob: A Literary and Scientific Journal, NOT Conducted by Members of the University*. 'Snob' was the current Cambridge slang for a townsman. It was Thackeray himself who, years later in his *Book of Snobs*, extended the meaning to include anyone of any social rank who displayed vanity or vulgarity, writing: 'He who meanly admires mean things is a Snob'. (Chainey, G., *A Literary History of Cambridge*, Pevensey Press: 1985)

— ◆ —

1992: Today, the Cambridge University Press Bookshop opened its doors for business at 1 Trinity Street, a very historic site, opposite the Senate House and just next to the University Church of Great St Mary's. Well remembered by many as Bowes & Bowes, books have been sold here since at least 1581, making it the oldest bookshop site in the country. From 1845 the shop was run by Daniel and Alexander Macmillan, who moved on from there to create Macmillan publishers. (*Cambridge Evening News* / Cambridge University Press)

May 1st

1505: On this day, King Henry VII granted his mother, Margaret Beaufort, a charter to found Christ's College. The book of King Henry's 'letters patent' of May 1 1505 is considered to be by far the most precious item in the College archives and has recently been described as one of the few 'absolutely outstanding examples of early Tudor manuscript production in the country', although almost certainly illuminated not by an Englishman but by one of the rather romantically named 'Dutch Masters of the Dark Eyes'. The book's opening pages have a border embellished with the Beaufort portcullis, the red rose of Lancaster and the white daisy or marguerite, the same motifs which adorn the main gateway to the college. The college rapidly became one of the largest and most influential colleges in the University and boasted the largest court in Cambridge until Thomas Nevile built the Great Court at Trinity. Christ's College has produced an eclectic mix of alumni over its five centuries, from John Milton to Charles Darwin and from Archbishop Rowan Williams to actor and comedian Sacha Baron-Cohen. (Reynolds, D., *Christ's: A Cambridge College over Five Centuries*, Macmillan: 2005)

May 2nd

2001: On this day, students thronged the First Court of Magdalene College for a glimpse of eighty-two year old Nelson Mandela, the former South African President, who arrived by helicopter in the Fellows' garden and then attended a private ceremony in the college chapel. Once the ceremonies were over, academics were surprised to see a postgraduate student perform an impromptu tribal dance, saluting Mr Mandela as a Zhosa chief. Thirty year old Jongi Klaas was one of four Mandela Magdalene scholars who had been introduced to their patron before the ceremony. 'I didn't plan to do the *Ukobonga*' he said, 'It just happened, because this was such a touching moment for me. We are from the same tribe and I wanted to salute Mr Mandela. I'll never forget it.' Mr Mandela beamed approvingly at the dance, whilst a bemused Fellow said, 'The College is five hundred years old, but I think it is safe to say that that was an unique event.' Magdalene College takes up to three South African postgraduates a year, chosen for the public service they can provide on their return home. In his acceptance speech, Mr Mandela said, 'Our country is in dire need of skilled men and women to do public service.' (*Cambridge Evening News*)

May 3rd

1867: On this day, writer and art critic John Ruskin was awarded an honorary degree from the University of Cambridge and wrote a letter to his 'dearest mother' to let her know that all had gone well. Ruskin then went on to give a detailed description of the proceedings: 'The form of admission is first that you put on a scarlet gown, furred with white: then the Latin orator takes you by the hand ... and leads you up to the middle of the Senate House, to the front of the Vice-Chancellor's seat ... There he himself stands aside, turns to the spectators and delivers a Latin laudatory speech ... some ten or fifteen minutes long; in my case, there being nothing in particular to rehearse – except that I had written books "exquisite in language and faultlessly pure in contention with evil principles" ... all said in Latin.' It is noted in *Cambridge Observed* that 'Ruskin was a notable benefactor of the Fitzwilliam Museum. On being appointed Slade Professor of Fine Art at Oxford, he gave the Cambridge institution twenty-five watercolours by his hero, J.M.W. Turner. He was not even-handed though: he gave fifty to the Ashmolean in Oxford.' (Cook, E. and Wedderbum, A., *The Works of John Ruskin*, George Allen: 1906 / Moseley, C., and Wilmer, C., *Cambridge Observed*, Colt Books: 1998)

May 4th

1932: On this day, Albert Einstein paid a visit to the Cavendish Laboratory in Cambridge. Just weeks after Cockcroft and Walton had artificially smashed the nucleus of an atom, the laboratory was buzzing with interested visitors and enquiries. Einstein was naturally taken to view the now world-famous accelerator and to meet its creators. Walton explained the operation of the machine to this 'very interested' visitor, put it through its paces and answered a few questions. In the evening there was a grand dinner at St John's College held in Einstein's honour, where Cockcroft and Walton again chatted to him along with Eddington and other scientific luminaries. Walton later said: 'He seems a very nice sort of man. I felt as if I had been highly honoured.' Einstein was also impressed, writing a few days later of his 'astonishment and admiration' at what he had seen in the Cambridge laboratory. 1932 was a turbulent year for Einstein, as he left Hitler's regime in Germany for a new life in Europe and the States. The following year, on a visit to Cromer in Norfolk, he sat for sculptor Jacob Epstein; the resulting bronze bust is now on display in the Fitzwilliam Museum in Cambridge. (Cathcart, B., *The Fly in the Cathedral*, Viking: 2004 / Fitzwilliam Museum)

May 5th

1972: On this day, the last 'smoker' (student comedy evening) was held in the Footlights' Club Room in Falcon Yard. Just six weeks later, the bulldozers moved in to demolish the old buildings and clear the way for the new Lion Yard shopping centre. The threat of demolition had been hanging over the Footlights group for some time and they had done everything to get a stay of execution, even offering the developers the accolade of honorary membership, but to no avail. Once it was known they would have to move, the club room became decidedly tatty; the carpet was full of holes and the stage curtains no longer worked. The last year was made even more unpleasant by the subletting of the rooms above to Snoopy's Discotheque, which led to fights on the stairs and the club being broken into. And so the rooms, which had hosted the likes of Clive James, Peter Cook, Jonathan Miller and John Cleese, were knocked down to make way for a shopping mall. Later the club-room re-opened in cellars next to the Cambridge Union Society, marking the start of another era which saw the emergence of actors such as Stephen Fry, Hugh Laurie and Emma Thompson. (Hewison, R., *Footlights: A Hundred Years of Cambridge Comedy*, Methuen: 1983)

May 6th

1949: On this day, the Electronic Delay Storage Automatic Calculator, better known by its acronym EDSAC, performed its first calculation. This was a defining moment in computing history: the first calculation on the world's first fully operational and practical store-program computer. EDSAC was a huge machine, taking up a whole room in the old Mathematical Laboratory on the New Museums Site in Cambridge. It had 3,000 vacuum valves arranged on twelve racks, using tubes filled with mercury as memory. Despite its large size, EDSAC could carry out just 650 instructions per second; this is far slower than the average mobile phone today. A program was fed into the machine via a sequence of holes punched into paper tape, and the result was printed out at the other end on a teleprinter two minutes and thirty-two seconds later. The life of EDSAC's creator Maurice Wilkes has spanned many decades and seen enormous advances in the world of computing. He said, modestly: 'Everyone needs a bit of luck, but if you can use the luck wisely then so much the better. My whole career has been just one stroke of luck after the other.' (*EDSAC 99*, Computer Laboratory, University of Cambridge: 1999)

May 7th

1605: On this day, Edward Lively was buried within the precincts of St Edward's Church in Cambridge. A Hebrew scholar, Lively was among the forty-seven learned men appointed by King James I to be responsible for the Authorised Version of the Bible, but died before much of the work got under way. In St Edward's Church the spirit of the Reformation lives on and the Book of Common Prayer, compiled by Thomas Cranmer, is still used for services today. (Granville Davis, P., *Church of Saint Edward, King and Martyr*, Black Bear Press)

1935: On this day, Joshua Taylor, the well-known Cambridge department store, placed an advertisement in the local paper publicising their 'six reigns of service'. This year the store's 125th anniversary coincided with the Silver Jubilee of King George V and Queen Mary, which prompted a royal theme for their advertisement, including a portrait of 'Joshua Taylor the First', whose first local store was in Ely. Fen men would visit no more than twice a year, May and October. It was then that they had their twice yearly haircut. (Payne, S., *Down Your Street*, Pevensey Press: 1983)

May 8th

1207: On this day, two years before the arrival of the first students in Cambridge, King John granted the town two important privileges: the citizens were given both the right to elect a mayor 'whom they will and what they will' and the right to pay the town's contribution to the royal exchequer directly to the King than via the Sheriff, who would have made a profit from the transaction. The first mayor, according to local historian Alison Taylor, was Hervey Dunning, who lived in, and conducted the town's affairs from, a substantial stone building which has survived to this day; now known, for some unknown reason, as the School of Pythagoras, it stands within the grounds of St John's College and is today used for meetings, lectures and recitals. The 800th anniversary of the King John charter was well celebrated in 2007; church bells rang out, there was a special exhibition at the Folk Museum and the Guildhall opened its doors to the public, giving the people of Cambridge a rare opportunity to view the ancient charters first-hand. (*Cambridge Evening News* / Curtis, G. and Bould, A., *Cambridge 800*, Folk Museum: 2007)

May 9th

1924: On this day, Lord Balfour, Chancellor of the University of Cambridge, officially opened the Dunn Biochemistry Laboratory on Tennis Court Road. The trustees of the estate of Sir William Dunn had provided over £200,000 for a new building, new equipment and an endowment for a large research programme. Dunn's new Institute made a huge impact on the history of biochemistry; between the wars, about 40 per cent of papers in the *Biochemical Journal* came from Cambridge and its students were prime candidates for chairs and directorships of biomedical institutions. The director was Sir Francis Gowland Hopkins, a Nobel laureate noted particularly for his discovery of the existence of vitamins. The laboratory fostered a strong sense of community between scientists both male and female and collaborations often progressed beyond the workplace. In the 1920s so many marriages occurred between researchers that the laboratory was nicknamed 'Hoppy's Dating Agency'. One of the most famous couples to meet there were Joseph and Dorothy Needham. One lady researcher, Marjorie Stephenson, went to work every day with her dog Judith. As many experiments conducted at the Dunn involved uric acid, Judith proved to be an important contributor to the team. (Kohler, R., Isis Vol. 69, 1978 / Department of Biochemistry)

May 10th

1894: On this day, Norwegian composer Edvard Grieg received an honorary doctorate from Cambridge University, nearly a year after the expected award which he had had to postpone because of ill health. The *Musical Times* wrote: 'Like many great composers before him, Grieg's eminence is not measured by his height and some time was spent in adapting to his stature by means of the domestic pin the doctor's gown lent to him for the ceremony.' In 1894 Grieg was at the height of his musical career and was celebrated across Europe, not least because of his incidental music for Ibsen's *Peer Gynt*. The Norwegian government had given him an annuity, allowing him to give up teaching and concentrate on composing and promoting his music through concert tours. Grieg made several visits to England and was given an honorary degree from both Oxford and Cambridge Universities. After today's ceremony in Cambridge, Grieg went straight to the post office and sent a telegram to a friend in Bergen, saying: 'Colleague, I greet thee' and was signed…Doctor Grieg. (Norris, G., *A Musical Gazeteer of Great Britain and Ireland*, David & Charles: 1981)

May 11th

1667: On this day, the funeral service of Matthew Wren, Bishop of Ely, uncle of architect Christopher Wren and benefactor of Pembroke College, took place. Despite Wren's request 'to avoid that pompe and vanity which is now too much in use' a splendid procession marked the occasion, leaving the Old Schools where his body had lain in state for two days and then moving towards Pembroke College, where he was buried. Wren had planned the event very carefully, listing the order of the mourners and what they were to wear, along with instructions to one William Dugdale to walk behind the coffin carrying a silver-gilt mitre. (Grimstone, A., *Pembroke College Cambridge*, Pembroke College: 1997)

—— ◆ ——

2007: On this day, Iraqi President Jalal Talabani visited the Cambridge University Union, amid tight security and a heavy police presence. In his speech, Mr Talabani said that he expected British and American troops would have to stay in Iraq for another year or two and sent a message of sympathy to the families of servicemen and women who had been killed there. (*Cambridge Evening News*)

May 12th

1869: On this day, the new Chapel at St John's College was consecrated and Josiah Chater observed: 'The town has been all alive today with parsons … Bells ringing all day, and not much business doing.' The consecration ceremony was attended by around 900 people, many of whom had made a day trip from London on a specially commissioned train. Opinions about the new Chapel, designed by eminent Victorian architect Sir George Gilbert Scott, were divided; William Selwyn called it a 'sermon in stones' whilst Bonney considered it be from first to last a failure. In order to clear space for the new chapel, the old chapel first had to be demolished, along with some nearby houses and much of the Master's Lodge. The extra space gained meant that there was room to expand the Hall by some 40ft, adding an extra window at the Chapel end, a work in which it was said 'Scott's flair for reproduction of the antique can nowhere have been more happily used'. Visitors to St John's College today will be challenged to see much difference between the sixteenth- and nineteenth-century windows, an enduring testament to the architect's skills. (Porter, E., *Josiah Chater's Diaries*, Phillimore: 1975 / Miller, E., *Portrait of a College*, St John's College: 1993)

May 13th

1835: On this day, Mrs Elizabeth Cook, widow of navigator Captain James Cook, died at the age of ninety-three, having outlived not only her husband but also all six of her children. Mrs Cook lies buried in St Andrew the Great church in Cambridge, close to the bodies of two of her sons, Hugh and James. Hugh had been studying at Christ's College and died of scarlet fever; his brother, Commander James Cook, died thirty-five days later and was buried in the same grave. Mrs Cook had now lost her entire family but she lived for a further forty-one years. She placed the Cook memorial tablet in the church and was herself buried in the nave. On the centenary of Mrs Cook's death in 1935, a special service was held in the church, extolling her as 'one of the world's noble band of mothers'. In 1979 another special service was held here to commemorate the bicentenary of Captain Cook's death. Captain Cook had been clubbed to death on a Hawaiian beach and burned by the natives. They did however refrain from eating him and gave him a decent burial. (*The Times*)

May 14th

1999: Cambridge University's world-famous School of Veterinary Medicine celebrated its fiftieth birthday today by inviting former colleagues from across the world to join existing staff and students for a gathering to discuss old times. The school had enjoyed a recent wave of expansion, from the 1992 opening of the cancer therapy unit to the 1995 Centre for Veterinary Science. Just ten years previously, the picture was very different; a report for the government on the number of veterinary surgeons Britain needed to train concluded that there were too many schools nationwide and that the Cambridge and Glasgow schools should close. The threat sparked an outcry in Cambridge, with townspeople and academics alike battling to keep the school open. It culminated in a petition of 200,000 names being delivered by coach to 10 Downing Street, leading eventually to a reprieve for both schools. By the time of the fiftieth anniversary in 1999, the professor of Veterinary Science was able to say, 'It's fair to say we're on a roll, with a great deal of support coming in for the work we do, from companies like Marks & Spencer, for example … the future looks bright.' (*Cambridge Evening News*)

May 15th

1999: On this day, Lord Geoffrey Howe of Aberavon, distinguished politician and the longest-serving member of Margaret Thatcher's cabinet, returned to his old college of Trinity Hall to open the new Jerwood Library. The existing library had outgrown its original location and was no longer able to meet the needs of the current college population, hence this eye-catching ultra-modern extension. The library was designed by local architect Tristan Rees-Roberts, also a college alumnus, who faced some tough challenges with the buiding's design and construction. Situated right on the River Cam, at one stage the builders had to stand in the river to get on with their job, as one part of the building actually replaced the river wall. The site was very small, just ten metres square, and there was no access road for deliveries. All materials, including a quarter of a million pounds' worth of massive oak timbers, handmade bricks and roof tiles, had to be either carried or transported on trolleys and barrows along the narrow pedestrian route of Garret Hostel Lane. And because of its position, noise restrictions on the new library were strict – they could only work between the hours of 10 a.m. and 4 p.m. (*Cambridge Evening News*)

May 16th

1491: On this day, the first stone in the tower of Great St Mary's, the University Church, was laid, thirteen years after the rebuilding of the church had begun. Dr John Keyes, founder of Caius College and historian of the University, recorded the exact date of this event, even the exact hour, which was a quarter to seven in the evening. Following the demolition of the previous church, a bell-frame, a temporary wooden structure, had been set up in the churchyard and the bells were hung on this whilst the tower was being constructed. It was recorded as early as 1515 that the bell-frame had been taken down and the bells were hung in the tower, indicating that the tower had been built by then. In 1793 Revd Dr Joseph Jowett used five bells from the tower to compose *The Cambridge Chimes*, which were later copied for Big Ben and renamed *The Westminster Chimes*. In 2009, to celebrate the 800th anniversary of the University of Cambridge, a generous gift from businessman and bell-ringer Dr Dill Faulkes led to the ancient bells being replaced by a new peal of twelve bells. (Bushell, W.D., *The Church of St Mary the Great*, Bowes & Bowes: 1948)

May 17th

1844: On this day, William Whewell, polymath, historian of science, Master of Trinity College and Vice-Chancellor of the University of Cambridge, resigned his membership of a dinner club called 'The Family' and Professor Haviland remarked: 'Well, I pity him'. Membership of The Family was open to a select, distinguished group, several of whom were Heads of Houses. Despite its exclusivity, the club had a slightly Bohemian atmosphere; the diarist Romilly wrote after his first dinner that he was 'disgusted by the introduction of pipes and spitting boxes ... most filthy', but he then philosophically remarked that 'as it is the invariable custom, one must bear it.' Menus were often exotic, sometimes including dishes such as peacock or turtle. Most dinners were apparently very pleasant occasions, but if any discipline was needed Whewell, in his capacity as Vice-Chancellor, was able to pull rank and reprimand the member concerned. One such occasion was when Prest, the owner of Stapleford Lodge, gave 'great offence to the Vice-Chancellor by observing on our smoking and by interrupting his conversation by loud talking across the table'; he was subsequently severely reprimanded. A statue of William Whewell can be seen in the antechapel of Trinity College. (Winstanley, D.A., *Early Victorian Cambridge*, CUP: 1940)

May 18th

1921: On this day, a private train brought Crown Prince Hirohito to Cambridge to receive an honorary Doctorate of Law in the Senate House. He had a full day of engagements, from viewing Japanese books in the University Library to watching rowing crews on the river, ending with dinner in Trinity College with Nobel Prize-winning physicist J.J. Thomson. Five years later Hirohito was to become Emperor of Japan. (Colthorpe, M., *Royal Cambridge*, Cambridge City Council: 1977)

———◆———

1932: On this day, *The Times* reported that two open umbrellas had been fixed to the pinnacles on the top of King's College Chapel in Cambridge. A few days later, night-climbers fastened a full-size Union flag to the top of the same building; a steeplejack had to be employed to remove it, as the shotgun owner who had removed the umbrellas refused to fire on his national flag. (Chainey, G., *A Celebration of King's College Chapel*, Pevensey Press: 1987)

May 19th

1829: On this day, the famous 'aeronaut' Mr Green made his own contribution to Cambridge's aeronautical history when, accompanied by two members of the University, he made a balloon ascent from Warwicker Yard, Newmarket Road. Henceforth, for several years, according to Gray: 'this yard each May witnessed all the excitement incident to the inflating of a balloon and its subsequent departure'. Three years later, Mr Green made his 151st ascent as part of Cambridge's coronation celebrations. (Gray, Arthur B., *Cambridge Revisited*, Heffer & Sons: 1921)

***

1939: On this day, Winston Churchill addressed a meeting in the Cambridge Corn Exchange. Alarmed at the result of a recent Cambridge Union Society debate, when 40 per cent were against conscription and 74 per cent favoured a pact with Russia, Churchill was keen to redress the balance. Votes at the end of today's 'lively' meeting showed that ten undergraduates to one were now in favour of conscription. Three days later, Hitler and Mussolini signed their so-called Pact of Steel. Just over four months later, Germany invaded Poland and the Second World War had begun. (Howarth, T.E.B., *Cambridge Between Two Wars*, Collins: 1978)

May 20th

1595: On this day, James Montagu wrote in his day-book: 'The first stone of this College [Sidney Sussex] was laid by myself on the 20th day of May 1595, in the presence of Dr Soame Dep. Vice. Chan ... and others.' Montagu later added that the stone was 'at ye corner towards ye fellowes orchard', in other words at the north-east corner of the Hall. Informed readers might question this date, as Sidney Sussex College was founded in 1596. However, there is in the college records an undated letter from Montagu to the Earl of Kent stating that foundations had been dug and that his 'next care is to conclude with Trinity College for albeit the bargan he agreed on yet the Bookes are not sealed', clearly indicating that work had begun on site some time before the formal conveyance had been delivered. Montagu, who was to become the first Master of Sidney Sussex, kept a full and careful record of all materials bought and payments made. In his day-book, still in the College's possession, are such details as loads of stone being delivered from Barrington and Haslingfield and occurrences such as a workman 'fauling from the scaffold'. (Scott-Giles, C.W., *Sidney Sussex College: A Short History*, CUP: 1951)

May 21st

1897: On this day, a poll in the Senate House to decide whether or not women should be allowed to take full degrees saw the motion defeated by 1,713 votes to 662, a resounding defeat for the women students. The poll had excited a huge amount of interest amongst both male undergraduates and also graduates, many of whom had come from London in their droves in order to register their vote of '*non placet*' (it does not please). Special trains had been laid on from London; excited undergraduates in fliers (hackney carriages) met the graduates at the station then whisked them off to the Senate House where there was a scene of general festivity; banners were strung out from Caius College and an effigy of a woman student in blue bloomers, riding a bicycle, was suspended from a nearby window. There were spectators at every window and on every available roof top. Once the result was announced, pandemonium broke out, starting with a mass demonstration and continuing into the evening with a huge bonfire in the Market Square with firecrackers thrown into the crowds. It was to be another fifty years before women were admitted to full membership of the University. (McWilliams-Tullberg, R., *Women at Cambridge*, Victor Gollancz: 1975)

May 22nd

2006: Today was the last day of the filming in Cambridge of *Elizabeth: The Golden Age*, starring Australian actress Cate Blanchett. The epicentre of the filming was sixteenth-century St John's College, converted to become Whitehall Palace in London, but its influence was felt throughout the city centre. Actors encamped in large numbers on Midsummer Common, where large tents were made available as changing rooms and canteens. For river punt chauffeurs, this was a holiday to remember as they were paid to keep away from any river scenes being filmed. Many local people were employed as extras. Particularly sought after were men with beards and pale, interesting ladies, with 'lovely, English-looking faces'. Those with darker complexions were cast as French or Spanish courtiers, for which they were paid £70 per day. Blanchett proved to be a real jet-setter since after today's filming she flew to Cannes to walk the red carpet for the premiere of her film *Babel* at the Cannes Film Festival, only to return the following day to East Anglia to film more scenes, this time in the Lady Chapel at Ely Cathedral. This high-flying activity prompted the local press to produce the headline 'Cate shows she's a Cambs Cannes girl!' (*Cambridge Evening News*)

May 23rd

1668: On this day, Samuel Pepys came to Cambridge by public coach, arriving in torrential rain. Pepys stayed at *The Rose*, which was not only one of the town's principal inns (Rose Crescent, just off the Market Place, is named after it today) but also a popular student lodging house, which he soon had cause to regret, writing: 'after supper to bed and lay very ill by reason of some drunken scholars making a noise all night.' Two days later, Pepys had a nostalgic wander round his old student haunts in Cambridge: 'I ... walked to Magdalene College; ... and there drank my bellyful of their beer, which pleased me as the best I ever drank....I walked to Chesterton to see our old walk; and there into the church, the bells ringing, and saw the place I used to sit in; and so to the ferry, and ferried over to the other side and walked with great pleasure, the river being mighty high by Barnwell Abbey; and so by Jesus College to the town, and so to our quarters and to supper; and then to bed, being very weary and sleepy, and mightily pleased with this night's walk.' (Chainey, G., *A Literary History of Cambridge*, Pevensey Press: 1985)

May 24th

1865: On this day, the 'materials' of All Saints' Church were being auctioned off to the highest bidder. The following were to be taken down and removed by the purchaser: the outer walls (very thick, containing a quantity of bricks, stone and clunch), the roof (a very handsome perpendicular one, with seven carved oak trusses and attachments to correspond), the covering (of lead, countess slate and plain tile) and the inner fittings (stout doors, lead casement windows, gas fittings, a descending stove etc …). Only twenty-five years previously the church had undergone a major campaign of restoration and repair, when many extra pews were added and the tower was practically rebuilt. Attempts to enlarge the church in 1859 led to a final decision to demolish it altogether and rebuild it in nearby Jesus Lane. The auctioning of the church was highly controversial, prompting one writer to comment in the *Cambridge Chronicle* that, 'the sale of a church by public auction … in exactly the same way as a set of fender and fire-irons would be is a decided novelty.' All that remains on the site of the church today is a memorial cross under a spreading chestnut tree in All Saints' Gardens. (Payne, S., *Down Your Street*, Pevensey Press: 1983)

May 25th

1812: King Louis XVIII, brother of the guillotined Louis XVI, was King of France in name only from 1795 and in real terms following the abdication of Napoleon in 1814. He lived in exile near Aylesbury in Buckinghamshire from 1807 to 1814. However, when he visited Cambridge, he was given a right royal welcome. The exiled King modestly registered at the Rose Inn (the site of this inn is remembered today in the name of Rose Crescent, just off the Market Place) under the name of the Comte de Lisle but when he appeared on the balcony of the inn that evening he was received with a royal salute from the local militia and the honour was repeated the following morning, which 'His Majesty spent in viewing the public buildings and colleges of the University and afterwards partook of an elegant dinner in Trinity College Hall'. In the evening the King retired with the Bishop of Bristol to Trinity Lodge and on Wednesday morning departed. His Majesty was particularly anxious to see the spot that had been honoured with the residence of Mr Pitt (William Pitt the Younger, who, following graduation from Pembroke College, became Britain's youngest ever Prime Minister). (Porter, E., *Josiah Chater's Diaries*, Phillimore: 1975)

May 26th

1910: On this day, a rather sombre looking group of university officials processed from Pembroke College to the Senate House where former US President Colonel Theodore Roosevelt was due to receive an honorary degree. Cambridge, like the rest of the country, was in mourning following the death of King Edward VII; sporting fixtures had been postponed, buildings were draped in black and neither Roosevelt nor the Public Orator who presented him were permitted to wear the usual scarlet robes. Consistently ranked by scholars as one of the greatest American Presidents, Roosevelt is popularly remembered however for something quite different: the teddy bear. During a Mississippi hunting trip, Roosevelt had famously ordered the mercy killing of wounded black bear. After a national cartoonist illustrated the President with a bear, a toy maker heard the story and asked Theodore Roosevelt if he could use his name for a toy bear, Roosevelt approved and the teddy bear was born. It was therefore not surprising that the gloom of Cambridge in mourning was broken when, at the end of today's degree ceremony, a teddy bear was lowered from the gallery and Roosevelt shook it with enthusiasm, 'prompting much laughter'. (King, Dr F., *Colonel Theodore Roosevelt, Honorary Graduand*)

May 27th

1953: On this day, Queen Salote of Tonga, accompanied by her daughter-in-law Princess Mata'aho, paid a visit to Cambridge. Their first stop was lunch in the (then) women's only college of Girton, where they were greeted by the Tongan national anthem sung in the Tongan language by college members. The afternoon visit focussed on the Leys School, which as a Methodist school had special links with Tonga, as it was Methodist missionaries who had first converted Tonga to Christianity in the 1820s. In fact the first headmaster of the Leys had a brother, Egan Moulton, who was for over forty years a missionary and teacher in Tonga and was much revered for many years. The visit obviously made a positive impression on the ladies, as Queen Salote's son sent his own sons to be educated at the Leys in Cambridge and, as King of Tonga, several times visited the school during the 1970s. Less than a week after her Cambridge visit, the statuesque figure of Queen Salote of Tonga endeared herself to the nation when despite torrential rain she insisted on riding in an open carriage to our own Queen's coronation, cheerfully waving to people lining the streets of London. (Colthorpe, M., *Royal Cambridge*, Cambridge City Council: 1977)

May 28th

1600: On this day, a Court Memorandum recorded that Henry Pepper had been involved in a 'tumultuous and disordered meeting beholding certain players and interludes at the sign of the bear,' going on to chastise him for not wearing his academic gown, having 'deformed long locks of hair and unseemly syde [= long] and great breeches undecent for a graduate or scholar of orderly carriage ... ' Tantalisingly, there is no further information about the rowdy play attended by Pepper, with its players and interludes. The 'sign of the bear' relates to the Bear Inn, situated in the centre of Cambridge opposite the Holy Trinity Church; its courtyard thoroughfare survives today as Market Passage. The keeper of the Bear Inn in 1600 was Mary Gibbons, widow of William, who had been head of the Cambridge waits (town minstrels) for several years until his death in 1595. It would appear that Mary retained legal control of the waits until her own death in 1603. William and Mary were the parents of the great composer Orlando Gibbons, who would have been about seventeen at the time of this incident and may well have then been living in the Bear, if not in residence in King's College. (Nelson, A.H., *Early Cambridge Theatres*, CUP: 1994)

May 29th

1966: On this day, the American evangelist preacher Dr Billy Graham told a packed congregation at Great St Mary's Church that in America half the hospital beds were occupied by mental patients and that even psychiatrists were going to each other for help. The service was relayed to two nearby churches, both of which were filled to overflowing. Graham concluded his sermon by asking people to open their hearts to Christ, saying: 'The world today is torn and bleeding. We need people to give help to those who are poor and diseased'. (*Cambridge Evening News*)

1981: On this day, a brand new college was officially opened in Cambridge by Her Majesty the Queen. Robinson College was founded in record time thanks to a £17m gift from local entrepreneur and philanthropist David Robinson. Famously reticent, Robinson did not attend the ceremony, but announced shortly beforehand that he would give an extra £1m to provide student scholarships. Also unveiled today was a portrait of the founder, the first public likeness of the shy millionaire for a decade. (*Cambridge Evening News*)

May 30th

1908: On this day, Sydney Cockerell wrote in his diary in capital letters: 'ELECTED DIRECTOR OF THE FITZWILLIAM' and then fondly added decades later 'a new chapter of my life lasting nearly 30 years was about to begin.' Just three weeks after his appointment, Cockerell and his wife moved into a new cottage in Cavendish Avenue and three months after that their daughter Margaret was born. Cockerell's directorship is regarded as one of the most dynamic and enriching periods in the museum's history. Pragmatic, shrewd, knowledgeable and very well connected, Cockerell was able to transform the museum from a cabinet of curiosities reserved for the privileged few into a 'Palace of the Arts', 'open to all the world'. He is however best remembered for the huge number of treasures he acquired for the museum, becoming adept at extracting loans, gifts and bequests on an unparalleled scale. Cockerell expanded the museum to house its burgeoning collections and 'humanised' the galleries by introducing a country house style. The 'new Fitzwilliam' became a model for museums elsewhere, prompting Cockerell's famous statement: 'I found it a pigsty; I turned it into a palace.' (Panayotova, S., *I Turned it into a Palace*, CUP: 2008 / Fitzwilliam Museum website)

May 31st

1921: On this day, Cambridge schoolchildren enjoyed a half-day off school, as they, along with thousands of others, welcomed the Prince of Wales, future King Edward VIII, on his visit to Cambridge. The Prince was driven first to King's College Chapel where he was taken into 'the War Memorial Chapel, which is in preparation'. Then to Emmanuel College to plant a mulberry tree and to meet the American who was to receive an honorary degree with him: Admiral William S. Sims, who had commanded the US naval forces in European waters in 1917. Their fellow lunch guests in Emmanuel College included Maynard Keynes, Ernest Rutherford and A.E. Housman. Crowds thronged round the party as they drove to the Senate House: 'never have the streets been more crowded or the enthusiasm more intense'. The two new Doctors of Law later walked, in their scarlet gowns, along Trinity Street to Trinity College, with rosettes showering down on them from upstairs windows. In Trinity there was a garden party in the Great Court for 2,500 people, followed by displays of Morris dancing and folk dancing and music from the band of the Scots guards. (Colthorpe, M., *Royal Cambridge*, Cambridge City Council: 1977)

June 1st

1881: On this day, the foundation stone of Selwyn College was officially laid. The aim of the college was to 'combine the advantages of college society and discipline with inexpensive living, so that men of slender means might afford them'. It was agreed that 'all extravagances in furniture, wine and other amenities would as far as possible be checked completely.' The college took its name from George Augustus Selwyn, first Bishop of New Zealand and later Bishop of Lichfield, a 'big, powerful, controversial, fearless man', one of the great men of his generation. Selwyn, who died in 1878, had been keen to see university education extended to many who were not able to afford it, so this college seemed a fitting tribute to his memory. Today's ceremonies and festivities began with lunch in King's College, before a procession over to the Selwyn site. The Church was represented by thirteen bishops, the State by members of both Houses of Parliament, the University by the Vice-Chancellor and by six other heads of houses and ten professors. The building was completed in record time and the college opened its doors to the first students in October 1882. (Brock, W. and Cooper, P., *Selwyn College: A History*, The Pentland Press: 1994 / *Selwyn College 1882-1973*, Selwyn College: 1973)

June 2nd

1845: On this day, Joseph Romilly, a Senior Fellow of Trinity College in Cambridge, wrote in his diary: 'A horrid report that Sir St Vincent Cotton had destroyed himself after heavy losses at the Derby. Trust there is no foundation for any part of the report: most certainly he has not committed suicide.' Vinny Cotton, alias Sir Vincent Twist, led a wild life devoted to sport and gambling. He belonged to a 'rich, rowdy, aristocratic set', often involved in brawls where his advice was 'to pitch into the big rosy men, but if you see a little lemon-faced nine-stone man, have nothing to do with him.' The reports about Twist's suicide were, as Romilly suspected, false; following massive losses on the horses, he had merely fled to Jersey in order to avoid debt. He was eventually bailed out by his mother, Lady Cotton, who continued to live at the family seat of Madingley Hall, just outside Cambridge. Nearly twenty years later, on his deathbed, Twist married his mistress, Hephzibah, in the hope that as his widow she would be socially respected. He died the next day of apoplexy and the baronetcy became extinct. (Bury, M. and Pickles, J., *Romilly's Cambridge Diary*, Cambridge Records Society: 1994 / *Dictionary of National Biography*)

June 3rd

1975: On this day, students occupied the Senate House in protest at the lack of nursery facilities for the offspring of students, academics and staff. The Nursery Action Group (NAG) had been formed in 1972 but the action today catapulted the protest on to both the national stage and the University's political agenda. Some skirmishes occurred because proctors were under pressure from the University to clear the building for an honorary degree ceremony involving General Gowon of Nigeria and they tried by force to deny access to students attempting to join the sit-in or to supply the occupants with food and water. One student was taken to hospital for a leg wound sustained when a proctor tried to pull him out of a window over spiked railings in Senate House Passage. The University did start to listen to their requests however and today was the start of one of the Cambridge University Students' Union's longest and most passionate campaigns. In 2010 Cambridge University has a dedicated Childcare Office in Trumpington Street, two day care nurseries, holiday play schemes and a regular e-newsletter to update student parents about new facilities and opportunities. (Scott, R. and Arthur, R., *Nasty forward minxes: A History of Women at Cambridge University 1897-1997*, The Hand: 1998)

June 4th

1929: On this day, a ceremony for the conferral of honorary degrees took place in the Senate House in Cambridge. One recipient was the Lord Mayor of London who became a Doctor of Law, but most eyes were focussed on Crown Prince Gustav Adolf of Sweden and his British wife, the former Lady Louise Mountbatten (her original family name was Battenberg but her father, who was Admiral of the British fleet, anglicised the family name during the First World War). A large crowd later welcomed the Crown Prince and Princess at the Arts School in Bene't Street, where the Prince gave an address on 'The Characteristics of Swedish culture'. He traced the history of Sweden from the Ice Age to modern times and described Swedish national characteristics. He spoke in 'excellent, crisp English...holding the close attention of a crowded audience for the best part of an hour.' The Crown Princess's brother was Louis Mountbatten, who had himself studied at Christ's College in Cambridge before embarking on a distinguished career both as a statesman and as Admiral of the Fleet. Mentor to Prince Charles, he was killed in 1979 by an IRA bomb near his holiday home in County Sligo, Ireland. (Colthorpe, M., *Royal Cambridge*, Cambridge City Council: 1977)

June 5th

1944: On this day, five years into the Second World War and the day before the Normandy landings, a special concert took place in King's College Chapel. The last chorus of the evening was *Dona nobis pacem* ('give us peace') which, under the circumstances, had great poignancy as the prayer soared up through the building. There was a huge interest in music during the war years, with many craving the moral and emotional support of 'serious music'. This evening's performance was a combined production by the Cambridge Philharmonic Society (CPS) and the Cambridge University Musical Society (the latter was then celebrating its centenary). The CPS had been through a 'bad patch' in 1938 but then made a remarkable wartime recovery. Recognising the morale-raising value of music, the members launched a series of concerts, enlisting the help of singers from local churches, several outlying villages and the Cambridge Co-operative Society. Despite the difficulties of black-out and of getting transport from the villages in to rehearsals, the programmes were successfully carried out and the Society was praised for its enterprise. Attending this evening's concert were many American servicemen and they went on afterwards to attend a reception in a nearby college parlour. (Knight, F., *Cambridge Music*, The Oleander Press: 1980)

June 6th

1961: On this day, gentlemen at the Leys School wore morning dress and the ladies wore hats and gloves as they prepared for a visit by Queen Elizabeth, the Queen Mother. Her Majesty arrived right on schedule at 3 p.m., opened a new building, was presented with a bouquet of flowers by the headmaster's son, Adam Barker, and watched a cricket match played between old boys and current pupils. Tea afterwards in a marquee on the headmaster's lawn included an 'enormous quantity of strawberries'. After the Queen Mother had left, it was discovered that she had left her bouquet behind. The headmaster's wife, Mrs Barker, carefully undid it and presented a flower to every boy who had met the royal visitor. She had hardly finished when the telephone rang. It was Clarence House: 'Her Majesty is most upset – she left her flowers behind – please could you send them on to her?' So Jean Barker gathered the individual flowers together, re-assembled the bouquet as best she could and took it to London herself, with an explanatory letter. She later received a charming letter saying that the Queen Mother apologised because she had guessed what had happened, 'but goodness – she had enjoyed the strawberries and cream!' (Houghton, G. and P., *Well-regulated Minds and Improper Moments*, The Leys School: 2000)

June 7th

1719: On this day, John Addenbrooke, physician and benefactor of St Catharine's College, died 'in the thirty-ninth year of his age', a time, some say, that he had predicted with uncanny accuracy to the very day and hour. Addenbrooke's name lives on, not because of a particularly distinguished medical career, but because he left in his will just over £4,000, 'to hire, fit-up, purchase or erect a building fit for a small physicall hospital for poor people'. Addenbrooke's Hospital still bears his name today. (*Dictionary of National Biography*)

1965: On this day, a banner calling for 'Peace in Vietnam' fluttered from the spires of King's College Chapel. Three students had taken seventy-five minutes to make the 147ft ascent, but faced danger from the crumbling stonework of the Chapel. The students later wrote anonymously to the Dean that unless work was carried out immediately, the safety of future Chapel climbers was in jeopardy. (Chainey, G., *A Celebration of King's College Chapel*, Pevensey Press: 1987)

June 8th

1958: On this day, the people of Cambridge woke to discover one of the most famous Cambridge student pranks of all time. An Austin Seven van had been hoisted up on to the roof of the Senate House building overnight and was firmly parked there by the time the local population started to clock in for work. The vehicle had arrived, mysteriously and undetected, overnight and even though it had taken the students just a few night-time hours to install it, it took the authorities four days to get it down again in broad daylight, and only then by using blowtorches to cut it into six separate pieces. The perpetrators, a small group of engineering undergraduates from Gonville and Caius College, maintained their anonymity for fifty years, only coming clean to mark the fiftieth anniversary of the event in 2008. By that stage they were well beyond any fear of recrimination from the college authorities and actually quite proud of their achievement; a celebratory dinner marked the anniversary and the story was covered in many national newspapers. They revealed that Hugh Montefiore, College Dean at the time, had privately suspected which students were involved and, impressed by their engineering prowess, discreetly arranged for a case of champagne to be delivered to their college rooms. (*Once A Caian...*: 2008)

June 9th

1760: On this day, the Master of Magdalene College, Dr Thomas Chapman, who had been variously described as 'an insolent coxcomb', 'Tom Forward' and a 'coarse-grained northerner with an eye for the main chance', came to a rather ignominious end, apparently as a result of his own gluttony. The poet Thomas Gray reported: 'Our friend Dr Chapman… is not expected here again in a hurry. He is gone to his grave with five fine mackerel (large and full of roe) in his belly. He ate them all at one dinner; but his fate was a turbot on Trinity Sunday, of which he left little for the company besides bones. He had not been hearty all the week, but after this sixth fish he never held up his head more, and a violent looseness carried him off. They say he made a very good end.' Other accounts say that he had died from a bout of sudden fever, but whatever the cause of his demise, he was not yet dead when lobbying to find his replacement as Master began. His legacies include *An Essay on the Roman Senate* and also some refurbishment of the college chapel. (Cunich, P., Hoyle, D., Duffy, E. and Hyam, R., *A History of Magdalene College Cambridge*, Magdalene College: 1994)

June 10th

1977: On this morning, barely twelve hours after watching firework displays in London to celebrate his wife's Silver Jubilee as Queen of England, Prince Philip landed by helicopter on St John's College playing fields in order to take up his position as Chancellor of the University of Cambridge. This was also his fifty-sixth birthday and crowds sang 'Happy Birthday' as he arrived at the Senate House; one sixteen-year-old girl gave him a surprise birthday card and present. As soon as his office was confirmed, the new Chancellor set to work immediately by granting honorary degrees, most notably to Mother Teresa of Calcutta, who as the University Orator said (here translated from the Latin), 'went alone, in poverty, to the homes of the poorest and set up a school in the midst of the slums'. Later, Mother Teresa talked in nearby Great St Mary's Church to a packed congregation, asking them 'not to give from abundance but from their love, till it hurts'. As long as Prince Philip remains Chancellor of the University, flags will fly from University buildings on 10 June, celebrating both Prince Philip's birthday and the day when he became Chancellor of the University. (Petty, M., *Cambridge Evening News*: 2002)

June 11th

1680: On this day, Alderman Samuel Newton wrote in his diary that he had caught in the River Cam near Newnham Mill a sturgeon of 'near 2 yards long measured by my Japan cane'. In 2010 fishing in central Cambridge is more restricted, requiring passes from Cambridge City Council. Recent catches have been chub, roach, carp and small, wild brown trout, but no sturgeons and nothing of such a huge size. (Waterlow, S., *In Praise of Cambridge*, Constable & Co.: 1912)

———◆———

1946: On this day, the first female speakers were welcomed to the Cambridge University Union. The debate was: 'This House views with grave disfavour the theories and practices of the Conservative Party', proposed by Lady Violet Bonham-Carter (grandmother of actress Helena Bonham-Carter), President of the Liberal Party, and opposed by Viscountess Davidson, Tory MP for Hemel Hempstead who chose, the press noticed, not to wear a hat. Bonham-Carter expressed her pride at being 'the first woman to raise her voice in your assembly in all its long and sheltered history [130 years].' (Parkinson, S., *Arena of Ambition*, Icon Books: 2009)

June 12th

2009: On this day, the world's press was out in force, eagerly seeking footage of a famously publicity-shy American citizen, one of the wealthiest men in the world. Prince Philip, in his capacity as Chancellor of the University, was in Cambridge to confer an honorary degree on one 'Gulielmum Henricum Gates', better known to the world as Bill Gates. But today the script was in Latin, and the University Orator made a fine speech about both William Gates and his wife Melinda, of the Gates Foundation which gave generously to the Computer Science Laboratory in West Cambridge and also to the foundation of the Gates Scholars, enabling the brightest of postgraduate students from around the world to come and study here at Cambridge. It must have been a challenge for the Orator to translate Gates' very modern achievements into Classical Latin, but he rose to the challenge and quoted Cicero and Plato whilst admiring the benevolence of this celebrated American couple. Other recipients of honorary degrees today included His Highness Prince Karim Al-Hussaini, the Aga Khan, and also Professor Amartya Sen, Nobel Prize-winning economist and former Master of Trinity College in Cambridge, where his portrait now hangs in the Dining Hall. (*Cambridge University Reporter*)

June 13th

1893: On this day, four foreign composers, Tchaikovsky, Saint Saëns, Bruch and Boito were awarded honorary degrees in the Cambridge University Senate House. Grieg should have been there too, but due to ill health had to postpone his award until the following year. Tchaikovsky had arrived the previous day and stayed with the eminent legal historian and professor of law Frederic William Maitland, who had invited him to be his guest at the West Lodge of Downing College. Ill at ease initially, Tchaikovsky soon found Professor Maitland and his wife Florence to be 'charming and delightful people – and Russophiles to boot'. Before the composer left Maitland's house for the ceremony in the Senate House, Florence pinned a rose in his buttonhole and took his photograph. The ceremony included an official luncheon and a reception given by the wife of the University Vice-Chancellor. Two days after returning to London, Tchaikovsky wrote to a friend: 'Cambridge … is distinguished by its manners and customs, many of which have been preserved since medieval times. Its buildings, which are reminiscent of the far distant past, made a very favourable impression.' (Poznansky, A., *Tchaikovsky: The Quest for the Inner Man*, Music Sales: 1991)

June 14th

1884: On this day, the Central Reading Room, built to the 'handsome design' of George McDonell of London, opened in the Cambridge Library. John Pink was the librarian in charge; Pink was only in his early twenties when he got the job in 1855 and continued in the post until his death in 1906. Some say that his ghost still haunts the building, which for many years served as the Cambridge Tourist Information Centre but has more recently been converted into 'Jamie's Italian', run by celebrity chef Jamie Oliver. (*Cambridge Evening News* / Pink, J., *After Fifty Years: A Retrospect of the Public Free Library Cambridge 1855-1905*: 1905)

———◆———

2010: This evening, thousands of well-wishers packed the streets of central Cambridge to welcome home soldiers of the Royal Anglian Regiment after their posting in Afghanistan. Around 200 'Vikings', many of them from Cambridgeshire, received a heroes' welcome as they marched from Shire Hall to the Guildhall. The event also remembered five comrades who did not return home from the six-month tour in Afghanistan. (*Cambridge News*)

June 15th

1891: On this day, Antonin Dvorak, Czech composer of Romantic music, conducted his Eighth Symphony and *Stabat Mater* in a concert at the Town Hall in Cambridge. Dvorak and his wife were staying at 10 Harvey Road in Cambridge as guests of the celebrated composer, conductor and writer Charles Villiers Stanford. The Czech couple were very early risers and one morning Stanford, having heard noises outside, looked out of the window and was astonished to see his guests sitting under a tree in his garden at 6 a.m. On the following day, June 16, Dvorak received an honorary doctorate in the Senate House. The degree ceremony caused him huge embarrassment: 'All the faces so grave and it seemed that nobody could speak anything but Latin. I listened to my right and I listened to my left and had no idea where to turn my ear. And when I discovered that it was me they were talking about, I wished I was anywhere but where I was, and I was ashamed that I knew no Latin.' It was to be two more years before Dvorak wrote his most popular piece of music, the *New World Symphony*. (Norris, G., *A Musical Gazeteer of Great Britain & Ireland*, David & Charles: 1981)

June 16th

1874: On this day, the Chancellor formally presented the Cavendish Laboratory to the University, in a ceremony in the Senate House. An article in the science journal *Nature* commented: 'The genius for research possessed by Prof. Clerk Maxwell [first Cavendish Professor] and the fact that it is open to all students of the University of Cambridge for researches will, if we mistake not, make this before long a building very noteworthy in English science.' In his inaugural lecture, Clerk Maxwell mapped out his plans for the future of physics in Cambridge, saying that, 'The familiar apparatus of pen, ink and paper will no longer be sufficient for us and we shall require more room than that afforded by a seat and desk, and a wider area than that of a blackboard.' This very practical, hands-on style of teaching was to have a huge impact on the University, leading to groundbreaking and internationally acclaimed research. The Cavendish Laboratory operated in Free School Lane for 100 years until it moved to its present site in West Cambridge in 1974. Today a plaque near the old gateway recognises the importance of this laboratory. (Godby, R., Jones, A. and Parker, J., *A Hundred Years of Cambridge Physics*, Cambridge University Physics Society: 1980)

June 17th

2008: On this day, at a summer garden party in the grounds of all-female college New Hall, the gathered students and staff were told that the College had received a huge donation of £30m from Ros and Steve Edwards, a former student and her husband. This gift was the largest single donation ever made in the history of the University of Cambridge. New Hall had been founded by Dame Rosemary Murray in 1954, with no permanent name and no endowment. Dame Rosemary's dream was to find someone to endow the College and today this dream became a reality; it is now known as Murray Edwards College, a combination of both names. Ros and Steve made their fortune through their business Geneva Technology, which they sold in 2001 for £700m; the couple decided to invest money in their old colleges (Steve gave a similar amount to St Edmund Hall in Oxford). Ros and Steve, who were both state-educated, were particularly pleased that a proportion of their donation would be spent both on bursaries for students from poorer backgrounds, and also outreach projects, raising the sights of pupils in disadvantaged areas, making them realise that anything, including a Cambridge education, is possible. (*Cambridge Evening News*)

June 18th

1924: On this day, over a thousand visitors flocked to the Fitzwilliam Museum, hoping to view the newly opened Marlay Galleries. The building of the galleries had been funded from the bequest of Cambridge graduate Charles Brinsley Marlay, who had been approached by the dynamic Director of the Fitzwilliam Museum Sidney Cockerell. Marlay had been keen to leave his large collection to the Fitzwilliam Museum, but Cockerell argued that money was also required 'to build a gallery to house it'. Marlay offered £50,000 for this, but the Director continued: 'What about staff?' Marlay then promised a further £30,000, plus the lease of his London house. Cockerell was content, saying: 'It was I who landed this big fish'. The opening of the galleries was carefully timed to coincide with both the twelfth anniversary of Marlay's death and the recent centenary of the foundation of the museum itself. Cockerell went on to secure more significant bequests for the museum and felt proud to have 'transformed the Fitzwilliam Museum from a cabinet of curiosities reserved for the privileged few into a "Palace of the Arts" open to all the world.' (Panayotova, S., *I Turned it into a Palace*, CUP: 2008)

June 19th

1940: In the early hours of this morning, a small Cambridge street was flattened by two huge 250 kilogram bombs, dropped by a German Heinkel 111. Three months before the Blitz on London, Liverpool and Coventry had begun, this raid on Cambridge caused the first civilian casualties of the Second World War, but reporting restrictions meant that most people were, and still are, unaware of its significance. A whole road, Vicarage Terrace, was flattened and nine people killed, but the report was given only two columns in the local paper, 'the same as wedding anniversary announcements'. The attack was a total surprise for the residents of Vicarage Terrace, even though recent news had been bad; Dunkirk had recently been evacuated and just the day before, Germans had marched into Paris. In Cambridge, the Germans' main target had been not the University but the railway yard and sidings, in order to prevent troop movements through Cambridge. As the war continued, Cambridge residents suffered further raids and there were casualties in Hills Road, Jesus Lane and Histon Road. As for Vicarage Terrace, the site was redeveloped in the 1960s and '70s and no trace of the original buildings remains. (*Cambridge News / BBC Cambridgeshire*)

June 20th

1997: On this day, a very special message was sent to Queens' College; the message needed no postage stamp as it was sent from outer space by college member Dr Michael Foale, an astronaut on the space station Mir. Dr Foale had of course plenty of time on his trip to talk to his fellow astronauts Vassily and Sasha, who apparently loved to hear tales of life in Queens' College Cambridge. Foale commented that although Mir was 'quite massive for the three of us', much space was taken up by outdated experimental equipment, so it was 'like being in a garage full of old junk'. The view from the windows was however astounding and he spent much time gazing out to admire the constellations, the Milky Way and the incredible vistas of the earth. England and even Cambridge could occasionally be seen when not covered in cloud. Dr Foale now lives in the United States but his parents still live in Cambridge. He obtained a first class degree in Physics and a doctorate in Astrophysics from the University of Cambridge; Foale made history in 1995 when he set foot outside the Discovery space shuttle and became the first Briton to walk in space. (*Cambridge Evening News / Queens' College Record*)

June 21st

1844: On this day, the second day of a visit to Cambridge by the King of Saxony, Romilly recorded in his diary how, as Deputy Librarian, he was charged with exhibiting treasures from the University Library to the royal visitor, writing: 'I had a carpet spread and a table set upon it in the New Library and a chair of state set for his German majesty. I had placed on it ... the principal book-treasures', which included Caxton's Chess of 1474, a 1483 Nuremberg Bible and a 'beautiful M.S. of Wycliffe's Bible'. The 'New Library' referred to was Cockerell's library building, later to become the Squire Law Library and currently the college library of Gonville and Caius. Romilly continued: 'It seemed to me that the K. took very little interest in any of the books' though the sight of the Nuremberg Bible did apparently 'elicit a few words'. In fact Romilly was not exactly overawed by this royal personage, having commented the previous day: 'He speaks but very little English and seems a man of few words and would excite but little interest if he were not a King' but does concede that 'he is apparently friendly and laughs heartily.' (Bury, M. and Pickles, J., *Romilly's Cambridge Diary*, Cambridge Records Society: 1994)

June 22nd

1932: On this day, a red Puss Moth aeroplane brought the Prince of Wales from Fort Belvedere, his home near Windsor, to Marshall's Airfield in Cambridge. The Prince (later King Edward VIII and, after his abdication, Duke of Windsor) was escorted to Peterhouse by an old war-time acquaintance, Field Marshall Sir William Birdwood, who had commanded the Anzacs (Australian and New Zealand Army Corps) at Gallipoli in 1915 and who now had a hopefully more peaceful posting as Master of Peterhouse in Cambridge. After lunch they drove the short distance to the Leys School, where he donned a straw hat for the sunny day and found the Leys boys in their own straw hats, blazers and white flannel trousers. There was a diving display in the swimming pool, where the Prince sat in the same place to watch as his father King George V had in 1914. He opened new squash courts and 'won the affection of the whole school, not least because of the…gift of three days added to the summer holidays and one to the Speech Day weekend.' (Colthorpe, M., *Royal Cambridge*, Cambridge City Council: 1977 / Houghton, G. and P., *Well-regulated Minds and Improper Moments*, The Leys School: 2000)

June 23rd

1993: On this day, 200 mathematicians gathered at the Isaac Newton Institute in Cambridge to listen to Andrew Wiles make what was arguably the most important mathematical announcement of the twentieth century. Wiles was born and brought up in Cambridge but later moved to the USA to become a Professor at Princeton. Rumours had been spreading that he was about to announce the proof of Fermat's Last Theorem, named after the seventeenth-century French judge who had conjectured that it was impossible to find similar triples of integers for n larger than 2. After Fermat's death, a book was found with a tantalising note in the margin: 'I have a truly marvellous demonstration of this proposition which this margin is too narrow to contain'. Wiles first read about the theorem at Milton Road Library in Cambridge when he was ten years old, launching him on a thirty-year quest to find an answer to the 300-year-old problem. It seemed therefore appropriate to Wiles that Cambridge should be the place to make his announcement, having spent the last seven years working in complete secrecy on the famous conundrum. In June 2010, Andrew Wiles was awarded an honorary doctorate from the University of Cambridge. (Singh, S., *Fermat's Last Theorem*, Fourth Estate: 1997)

June 24th

1959: On this day, Sotheby's auction house in London was crowded for the sale of eighteen paintings sent for auction by the executors of the Duke of Westminster to pay death duties. The sale was thronging with television cameramen and press photographers, all keen to record what many considered to be the sale of the century. Paintings by Claude and Titian fetched good prices, but the real highlight of the day was to be the *Adoration of the Magi* by Peter Paul Rubens, which was bought on behalf of a private collector for £275,000, the highest price ever achieved at auction for a single painting. The same private collector bought paintings by El Greco and by Frans Hals, prompting *The Times* newspaper the following day to comment: 'We may be permitted to comment that while the desire for anonymity in the world as it is today is understandable, to spend nearly £400,000 in a single morning on three pictures, one of them as world famous as the Rubens, is hardly the way to achieve it.' The collector later revealed himself to be property millionaire Major A.E. Allnatt, who donated the painting to King's College Chapel in Cambridge, where it now hangs under the East Window. (*The Times*)

June 25th

1897: On this day, around 5,000 Cambridge children gathered together on Parker's Piece where they were given a 'generous tea and pleasant evening's amusement'. This children's treat, 'the largest of its kind witnessed in Cambridge', was the culmination of five days of activities to mark the Jubilee of Queen Victoria, celebrating sixty years of her rule. The great Jubilee Day itself had been celebrated on Tuesday June 22, when there was a royal salute of sixty maroons, fired at mid-day, followed by a performance by the Suffolk Regimental Band, a flight of a thousand pigeons from Parker's Piece and then a variety of entertainment including Mlle Lilly, 'lofty trapeze artist', culminating in a 'gigantic display of fireworks' at 10.15 p.m. On June 24, over a thousand 'old folks' sat down to a dinner in two large marquees on Parker's Piece, where the menu was cold roast beef, hams, veal, salad, cheese, cake and strawberries, washed down with ale, lemonade, ginger beer and tea. The dinner was witnessed 'with evident pleasure' by the Mayor, Mr Dennis Adams, and many other leading townsmen. (Mitchell, E., *Notes on the History of Parker's Piece Cambridge*, Mitchell: 1984)

June 26th

1902: On this day, King Edward VII was due to be crowned in Westminster Abbey and Cambridge decided to celebrate by inviting 2,500 poor, elderly people to dinner on Parker's Piece. Invitations were sent to all the elderly Cambridge citizens who had previously attended Queen Victoria's coronation celebrations, but the Council could only find 250 residents who were qualified to attend. Arrangements were soon thrown into disarray however when it was announced that the King was seriously ill and needed an operation, meaning that not just the coronation but all celebrations would have to be postponed. There was a major problem; cooks from Trinity College and Trinity Hall had already baked sixty-eight large meat pies and fifty-eight gooseberry and cherry tarts. Rather than waste the food it was decided to distribute it to the intended recipients to eat in their own homes. The *Cambridge Daily News* reported: 'Several hundred of the poorest inhabitants gathered outside the Corn Exchange when the distribution began…baskets, bags and all manner of receptacles had been brought. Quite a number who had come empty-handed wrapped up quantities of fruit tarts in newspapers that could hardly have improved the semi-liquid contents.' (Woodall, S. and Inman, C., *Cambridge: Memories of Times Past*, Worth Press: 2007)

June 27th

1894: On this day, the Duke of York, the future King George V, was awarded an honorary doctorate in the Senate House; after the ceremony, the gallery gave three cheers for his new baby, born just four days previously. The baby grew up to become, briefly, Edward VIII and then, after his abdication, Duke of Windsor. That evening there was a firework display and water carnival on the Backs; college grounds were lit by 30,000 fairy lamps. (Colthorpe, M., *Royal Cambridge*, Cambridge City Council: 1977)

2000: On this day, Champagne flowed at the Sanger Centre at Hinxton near Cambridge, following a joint announcement by American President Bill Clinton and British Prime Minister Tony Blair about the sequencing of the human genome. One third of the sequencing had been done at the centre, led by Dr John Sulston, a graduate of Pembroke College. The work on the human genome was a natural progression from Crick and Watson's work in Cambridge in the 1950s on the structure of DNA. (*Cambridge Evening News*)

June 28th

1838: On this day, Queen Victoria's coronation was celebrated in Cambridge by a sit-down dinner on Parker's Piece for 15,000 poor men, women and children. There were also an estimated 17,000 spectators, bringing the total number present to an impressive 32,000. A flower-decorated rotunda had been erected to accommodate an orchestra and this was surrounded by a circular promenade for more onlookers; radiating from this, like the spokes of a wheel, were sixty long tables. The diners marched on to the Piece behind brightly coloured banners and then enjoyed a meal of cold meat and pickles, half a pound of bread each, plum puddings and beer, followed by free tobacco for the men and pipes in which to smoke it. Over a thousand joints of meat had been roasted or boiled in college kitchens and at Christ's College 1,650 puddings were made, most of them boiled in vats obtained from local breweries. At 6 p.m. Mr Green ascended with his wife in a balloon, while later there was a magnificent display of fireworks. Romilly wrote in his diary: 'The dinner...was eminently successful; the day was brilliant, & Cambridge may be proud of her fête.' (Porter, E., *Victorian Cambridge*, Dennis Dobson: 1969 / Moseley, C., and Wilmer, C., *Cambridge Observed*, Colt Books: 1998)

June 29th

1999: On this day, nine distinguished figures were awarded honorary degrees in the Senate House by HRH Prince Philip, the Duke of Edinburgh and Chancellor of the University of Cambridge. Recipients included novelist A.S. Byatt, Booker Prize-winner and graduate of Newnham College, and Colin St John Wilson, Emeritus Professor of Architecture at Cambridge and designer of the British Library at St Pancras in London. But most eyes were on the diminutive figure of the Most Revd Desmond Tutu, former Archbishop of Cape Town, anti-apartheid campaigner and winner of the Nobel Peace Prize. The University Orator had prepared a page-long speech in Latin for each of the nine recipients, with of course a translation for those more familiar with modern-day English. The Orator said of Mr Tutu: 'This is a brave man and a true model of the Church Militant'. Shielding himself from the rain, Tutu emerged from the Senate House to greet a large crowd outside. Tutu's name lives on in the jargon of the University; a 'Desmond' is the word given to a lower second pass mark (otherwise known as a Two:Two). (*Cambridge Evening News / CAM*)

June 30th

2003: Today, Roger Waters, rock guitarist and founder member of 1960s rock band Pink Floyd, was one of several prominent people who had letters published in *The Guardian* newspaper, lending support to a campaign to save Grantchester Meadows from housing development. These picturesque meadows run alongside the River Cam just outside the city of Cambridge and have a special significance for Pink Floyd fans. They were the inspiration for a song on the band's fourth album *Ummagumma*, released in 1969, a peaceful and highly atmospheric piece which pioneered electronic effects to recreate the sound of swans taking off from the water. In June 2003 Waters was living in London, missing no doubt the quiet countryside surrounding his home town of Cambridge. He wrote: 'I spent many, many happy hours fishing for roach with a bamboo rod ... in that bit of the Cam. I have powerful memories of the warmth of summer, mud oozing up between my toes. That time turned out to be creatively important to me – my work is coloured to an extent by the sound of natural history'. And the meadows, for the time being at least, were saved. (Worden, M. and Marziano, A., *A Pink Floyd Fan's Illustrated Guide to Cambridge*, Damned Publishing: 2007)

July 1st

1769: On this day, a short, witty poem was published in the *Cambridge Chronicle*, commenting on a recent petition presented by Cambridge undergraduates to the Duke of Grafton, Chancellor of the University. The students wanted to swap their current round, black caps for square caps, as worn by Doctors and Masters of Arts (said by one contemporary to resemble the headgear worn by the ancient kings of China).

> Ye learn'd of every age and climate yield,
> And to illustrious Cambridge quit the field,
> What sage Professors never could teach,
> Nor Archimedes, nor our Newton reach;
> What ancients and what moderns vainly sought,
> Cambridge with ease hath both attain'd and taught;
> This truth even envy must herself allow,
> For *all* her scholars *Square the Circle* now.

(Whibley, C., *In Cap and Gown*, Heinemann: 1898)

July 2nd

1642: On this day, at the outbreak of the English Civil War, an order was given to Sidney Sussex College to contribute £100 (a significant amount for a small college) by way of a loan to King Charles I. At the time, Cambridge was mostly Royalist in sympathy and the colleges collectively contributed large amounts to this cause. When the King went on to ask the colleges to send him their plate for what was called 'the better security and safety thereof', Sidney Sussex does not seem to have responded. Probably the college authorities realised that if they parted with their treasures there was little hope of seeing them again. They did not want to lose the Communion plate or the Harington ewer and basin; they probably had little else of value. Much of the plate sent to the King by other colleges was intercepted by Cromwell and went to fill the Parliamentary war chest. The Harington ewer has survived many more centuries, taking centre stage at a 1996 exhibition in Cambridge entitled *Colledge Goods: 400 Years of Sidney Sussex College.* (Scott-Giles, C.W., *Sidney Sussex College: A Short History*, CUP: 1951)

July 3rd

1922: On this day, the Duke of York, future King George VI, was driven from Babraham Hall, where he was staying, to Station Road corner in Cambridge. The object of his visit was to unveil the official Cambridge War Memorial, a bronze sculpture representing a private soldier returning home victorious, with flowers at his feet. The sculptor, R. Tait Mackenzie, had explained that a slight difficulty had arisen: 'Owing to an unavoidable and unforeseen delay in the casting of the statue which occurred in the last few days, it has been found impossible to have the bronze finished for the unveiling. I have therefore sent the original model from which the bronze was cast and it will be replaced by the bronze itself within the next fortnight.' Luckily no one noticed any difference between the model and the finished statue. The large crowd, acting as if it was not raining heavily, sang *O God, our help in ages past* and the Duke unveiled the memorial, telling the crowd that the men who had died 'offered their lives on the great battlefield of the war in order that our Empire might live'. (Colthorpe, M., *Royal Cambridge*, Cambridge City Council: 1977)

July 4th

1998: On this day, around 900 women, aged between sixty-seven and ninety-eight, arrived in Cambridge for what many of them referred to as 'the Senate House party'. 1998 marked the fiftieth anniversary of the awarding of degrees to women and these feisty women, many of whom had battled against the odds to receive their education, were here to be recognised and acknowledged by a University which had educated them but not given them a full degree. The first five Cambridge women students arrived at Girton College in 1869 and Newnham College followed soon after. The women took the same exams as the men, but on successful completion of their courses they were given a University certificate rather than a degree. In the nineteenth century, the University was very male dominated. Women were acceptable tea-party hostesses and made good wives, but were labelled 'nasty, forward little minxes' when they wanted equal educational rights. Women were not granted full membership of the University until 1947 and full degrees followed in 1948, but the University retained the right to limit the number of women admitted. The first woman to receive a degree was the Queen Mother, who was given an honorary degree in October 1948. (*Cambridge Evening News*)

July 5th

1847: On this day, 'a bright, brilliant, burning summer day', every shop in Cambridge closed at 10 a.m. because of a royal visit to Cambridge by Queen Victoria and her husband Prince Albert, who had recently been appointed Chancellor of the University of Cambridge. 'Turn which way you would, banners, streamers, laurels, flowers and happy faces met the eye; the churches rang out their merry peals; and everybody participated in the joyous greetings of a general holiday…Every house had a flag, some half a dozen or more…' The royal couple arrived by train, quite a novelty at the time as the railway line to Cambridge had only been completed two years previously. A previous train had brought hosts of special guests, including the other national hero, the Duke of Wellington, victor at the Battle of Waterloo. After lunch at Trinity College, the Prussian Ambassador's wife remarked on 'The Chancellor…in his beautiful dress of black and gold'. A presentation of honorary degrees in the Senate House was followed by a banquet in St Catharine's College (where the Duke of Wellington was staying), with pigeon, turtle and venison on the menu. The town celebrated with fireworks on Parker's Piece. (Colthorpe, M., *Royal Cambridge*, Cambridge City Council: 1977)

July 6th

1847: On this day, Queen Victoria and Prince Albert were guests of honour at a lunch in the Dining Hall of Trinity College. Romilly, diarist and Fellow of Trinity, was on the original guest list but his name seems to have disappeared from the final version. He commented in his diary, with more than a touch of schadenfreude: 'At this dinner and at the dinner the day before at the V.C.'s [Vice-Chancellor's], a bouquet was placed before the Queen. Her Majesty afterwards sent to Storr and Mortimer's (from whom the plate had been hired) for these two vases, as she always keeps such memorials of the public banquets at which she has been entertained and has an inscription on them to commemorate the occasion. Storr and Mortimer sent in their bill to the VC and to Trinity College: the vase at the VC's was only silver and the cost only £8.15s; that at Trinity was gold and cost above £40.' The royal visit came to an end at 3 p.m. today when the Queen and Prince left by train. Romilly recorded in his diary: 'with the Queen went the glorious weather, for a sharp rain now began falling.' (*St Catharine's College Society Magazine*)

July 7th

2006: On this day, Syd Barrett, iconic frontman of legendary rock group Pink Floyd, died in Cambridge at the age of sixty, from complications arising from diabetes. Syd had been living since 1974 in a modest, three-bedroom semi-detached house in St Margaret's Square, Cambridge, light years away from the glamorous life he had led in his 1960s heyday. Syd had been the first creative force behind Pink Floyd and was an influential song-writer, penning their early hits such as *Arnold Layne* and *See Emily Play*. His *Times* obituary said that he 'encapsulated the heady spirit of the late 1960s and the hippy dream.' Plagued by mental health problems following heavy drug usage, Syd literally walked away from his old life in London and just carried on walking to his home town of Cambridge, where he was to live in near anonymity for the next thirty years. His sister told the *Cambridge Evening News* after his death that he had loved the peace and quiet of his home area, where the only intrusions were the occasional visits from fans. He could never understand why strangers wanted his time, as the reason for his fame was always a mystery to him. (Worden, M. and Marziano, A., *A Pink Floyd Fan's Illustrated Guide to Cambridge*, Damned Publishing: 2007 / *The Times*)

July 8th

1661: On this day, a young Isaac Newton matriculated (enrolled) at Trinity College in Cambridge. Despite his mother's apprehensions (she wanted her son to stay at home and farm) Newton was encouraged in his studies by his schoolmaster in Grantham and he entered Trinity as a 'sub-sizar', in other words a student who had to supplement his income by acting as a servant either for the Fellows or for other wealthier students; in return, he was allowed to pay lower fees for attending lectures. It is not certain whether his status was a result of his mother's reluctance to spend money on education or perhaps of a desire to assist Humphrey Babington, a College Fellow, with whom he had connections from school. On his arrival in Cambridge Newton bought a notebook together with some ink; he wrote on the flyleaf 'Isaac Newton/Trin: Coll Cant/1661'. Inside are notes and exercises relating to Newton's reading, many of the notes being written in a rather crude form of 'secretary hand' that the young man practised. The 140-page bound notebook has survived and is still in Cambridge today. (Mandelbrote, S., *Footprints of the Lion: Isaac Newton at Work*, CUL: 2001)

July 9th

1835: On this, the penultimate day of festivities for the installation of Lord Camden as Chancellor of the University of Cambridge, a 'grand public breakfast' for around 2,000 people was served in the cloisters of Trinity College. Winstanley wrote: 'The Trinity cook was considered to have surpassed himself, so great was the abundance of pineapples and grapes, and so pretty the maids who handed them round. Then followed dancing and a display of fireworks and as the evening wore on, some of the party became slightly uproarious, for the champagne had not been spared. But long before the fireworks and the dancing, the Chancellor had left to attend a dinner in King's, which was provided by Gunter [a famous London catering firm] at the rate of three guineas per head.' The service was apparently abominable, with Romilly commenting in his diary: 'A dinner worse waited upon I never witnessed; without bawling and beckoning it was impossible to get anything but what was immediately before you.' But the cloud had a silver lining: the speeches took up far less time than usual, the Provost giving 'each successive toast without a word of accompaniment.' (Winstanley, D.A., *Early Victorian Cambridge*, CUP: 1940)

July 10th

1549: On this day, 'a hundred persons or more' met together with drums and proceeded to pull down the fences of an enclosure at Barnwell. Wool had become an important and lucrative export and there was not enough common pasture in Cambridge to accommodate the sheep needed. Landlords began to enclose open arable land for use as pasture, thus depriving many workers of their livelihood, at the same time changing the agricultural and social models of the Middle Ages. The Mayor and the Vice-Chancellor were united in their desire to prevent 'further mischief' and with difficulty managed to pacify the rioters. A general pardon was later obtained for the offenders, and the Duke of Somerset wrote to the Cambridge authorities recommending gentle dealing, in order that 'the difference may be tryed betwixt the ignorant and the learned, the rude and the taught.' This was in many ways a victory for the workers; they were able to preserve green, open spaces in Cambridge for the use of everyone in town, not for private profit, and we owe them a debt for 'restoring common to the commons'. And so for once, 'common' sense prevailed ... (Gray, A., *The Town of Cambridge*, Heffer & Sons: 1925)

July 11th

1916: On this day, Bertrand Russell, philosopher and political campaigner, was the subject of discussion by the governing body of Trinity College in Cambridge. Two years into the First World War, the horrors of warfare were escalating and there was no sign of a quick resolution. Bertrand Russell was a well known pacifist and had already taken two terms' leave of absence from his teaching commitments in order to address the question of how Western civilisation might be rebuilt after the First World War. More controversial however was the leaflet he wrote in support of a conscientious objector who had been sentenced to two years' hard labour 'for disobedience to the military authorities'; for this, Russell was fined £100. Today the Trinity Council agreed unanimously that 'since Mr Russell has been convicted under the Defence of the Realm Act, and his conviction has been confirmed on appeal, he be removed from his lectureship in the College'. Russell continued to get into trouble and in early 1918 was incarcerated in Brixton Prison for six months following offensive remarks about the Americans. He used his time there constructively, compiling his *Introduction to Mathematical Philosophy*. All was eventually forgiven and his lectureship was reinstated after the war. (Howarth, T.E.B., *Cambridge Between Two Wars*, Collins: 1978)

July 12th

1975: On this day, Her Royal Highness the Duchess of Kent visited the Leys School in Cambridge, the culmination of various events celebrating the school's centenary. On the actual anniversary date, February 14, the boys had celebrated with a special lunch served by the masters and the following day there had been a centenary service in King's College Chapel. But today was even more special. The Duchess of Kent entered the marquee to a magnificent fanfare from the school brass ensemble. The fanfare, which contained strains of 'On Ilkley Moor, baht at', reflecting the Duchess's Yorkshire background, was composed specially by Mr Sam Grice, Assistant Director of Music. Following the speeches, the Duchess formally opened the Kent Room, the large refurbished classroom remembered by many Leysians as the room where preparation (homework) was supervised and also early morning drill (writing 'the line'). On the steps of the King's Building the Duchess was presented by Miss Elizabeth Wiseman, daughter of the Housemaster of 'A' House, with a bouquet, and by the Chairman of the Governors, Sir Arthur Armitage, with a copy of *Partnership in Excellence*, the recently published history of the Leys School. (Houghton, G. and P., *Well-regulated Minds and Improper Moments*, The Leys School: 2000)

July 13th

2000: On this day, Prince Philip, Chancellor of the University of Cambridge, officially opened the University's new £55m Centre for Mathematical Sciences and remarked that it was better value than the Millennium Dome; unveiling the plaque to declare the department open, he said that it had cost less than the Dome and would be more useful. The Prince was also introduced to Professor Stephen Hawking, the Lucasian Professor of Mathematics, who had moved his office into the complex when it was first used in April. Architect Edward Cullinan was on hand to show Prince Philip the building's grass-covered roof (which led some journalists to make comparisons with 'Telly Tubby land') and explain its economical temperature control system. Standing on the grass roof, the group also inspected the site of the Betty and Gordon Moore Library, a circular building which was under construction next to the Centre for Mathematical Sciences. Prince Philip then went on to confer nine honorary degrees at the traditional ceremony in the University's Senate House. The witty headline in today's *Cambridge Evening News* read: 'Royal visit adds up to success at centre'. (*Cambridge Evening News*)

July 14th

1348: On this day, King Edward III launched an enquiry into the state of the King's Ditch and how best to cleanse it, following complaints from Cambridge townspeople about 'encroachments, obstructions and nuisances'. The ditch had first been constructed in 1267; running from the Mill Pool in the south, up to Park Street in the north, it served both to defend and drain the town. A section of the ditch was rediscovered in 2005 when the site for the new Grand Arcade shopping centre was being prepared. (Gray, A., *The Town of Cambridge*, Heffer & Sons: 1925 / Poole, D., *Cambridge Seven Hundred*, Wilson-Poole: 1983)

———◆———

1932: On this day, Queen Mary, wife of King George V, visited Cambridge; the visit had been kept a close secret, but passers-by quickly recognised the royal car and a crowd gathered. Following visits to Magdalene and King's Colleges, the royal visitor toured the galleries at the Fitzwilliam Museum and was photographed beneath a picture which she had presented to the museum: a view of Cambridge in about 1900, seen from near the top of the Castle mound. (Colthorpe, M., *Royal Cambridge*, Cambridge City Council: 1977)

July 15th

1965: On this day, St Swithin's Day, the weather (grey skies, with intermittent drizzle) did not bode well for the coming weeks. But the mood was happy in the chapel of Trinity Hall, where a young Research Fellow called Stephen Hawking married Jane Wilde, a friend from his childhood home of St Albans. Stephen Hawking needed a walking stick to support himself, showing early signs of an illness which would later characterise his public persona of a brilliant mind trapped in a weak, disabled body. Jane's family were conventional whilst Stephen's were academic, eccentric and opinionated. Her men-folk wore morning dress for the wedding service, whilst Stephen's father refused to do so. But all went well and after the reception in Trinity Hall Jane drove them off in their newly acquired red Mini for a blissfully peaceful week in the Suffolk countryside, based at the Bull Inn in Long Melford. The couple went on to have three children together and Jane stoically cared for her husband as his condition deteriorated. They separated in 1991, reportedly due to the pressure of fame and increasing disability. (Hawking, J., *Music to Move the Stars*, Macmillan: 1999)

July 16th

1956: On this day, the only permanent American Second World War cemetery in the British Isles was dedicated at Madingley, just outside Cambridge. The Cambridge American Cemetery is one of fourteen permanent American Second World War military cemetery memorials erected on foreign soil by the American Battle Monuments Commission. In this tranquil setting there are 3,812 headstones, arranged like the spokes of a wheel in seven rows of concentric arcs. Near the cemetery entrance is a 72ft-high flagpole, at the base of which is an inscription taken from John McCrae's poem *In Flanders Fields*: 'To you from failing hands we throw the torch – be yours to hold it high'. Next to the reflecting pools is the Wall of the Missing, where the names are inscribed of over 5,000 'missing in action, lost or buried at sea or those unknowns whose remains could not be positively identified prior to internment'. The names include Joseph Kennedy, JFK's older brother, whose plane exploded over the Suffolk coast in 1944 at the start of a secret mission, and band leader Glenn Miller who died in a plane crash over the English Channel, having set off for Paris for a concert tour from Twinwood Airfield near Bedford. (The American Battle Monuments Commission)

July 17th

2006: On this day, the funeral and cremation service of Roger 'Syd' Barrett was held in the East Chapel of Cambridge Crematorium. Syd Barrett had been, in his glittering heyday, the charismatic lead singer of super-group Pink Floyd, but for the last thirty years had led a relatively anonymous and reclusive life in a modest semi-detached house in St Margaret's Square in Cambridge. After Barrett's death the location of his house became public knowledge and it was put on the market for £300,000. The Cambridge estate agents, Cheffins, found themselves inundated with 'prospective buyers', many of whom were in fact Barrett fans in disguise. One enterprising local fan even started offering a box of soil from Syd's garden as part of a souvenir package. Barrett had spent little money during his time in Cambridge and left £1.25 million in his will. Tributes poured in after his death, but in fact Syd had not kept in touch with his old friends and band members during his later years. Today's funeral was a private family-only service, with friends from the past being politely asked to stay away. (Worden, M. and Marziano, A., *A Pink Floyd Fan's Illustrated Guide to Cambridge*, Damned Publishing: 2007)

July 18th

2009: On this day, a banner held high outside the Senate House proclaimed 'Allan Brigham MA, Roads Scholar', celebrating one honorary graduand who had an impressive portfolio career spanning Blue Badge tourist guide, local history lecturer and Cambridge road sweeper (hence the pun on the banner). Whilst honorary doctorates are awarded each year to eminent people from around the world in academia, public life, religion and music, the Honorary MA degree is awarded more rarely, and specifically for outstanding service to the University and the city. Allan works with the University Community Affairs team, acting as a 'critical friend', reminding the University of the town-gown divide and how to bridge the gap. Allan's award struck a chord with national media and soon after the ceremony he was inundated with requests for interviews. BBC Breakfast TV, the World Service, three days with a German TV crew following him around and an afternoon in a punt with David Baddiel for Radio 4 were just some of his media experiences…Having guided groups round Cambridge for years, Allan is now something of a tourist attraction in his own right and regularly gets stopped by visitors wanting to have their photograph taken next to him in his yellow street-cleaner's jacket. (*Cambridge Alumni Magazine*)

July 19th

1844: On this day, Joseph Romilly, Cambridge University Registrary (senior administrative officer), wrote in his notebook that he had been walking with his wife in Trinity College at about 6 p.m. this evening when to his 'great surprise' he was told by the College Porter that he was to dine with the judges (Alderson and Williams) that evening. It was the tradition for many years that the Judges of Assize should stay at Trinity College when visiting Cambridge. Romilly was surprised because he thought the invitation was for the following day and had already dined at 3 p.m. at home. Romilly continued: 'I hastened back to Hills Road, dressed and was in abundant time, for we did not dine until past 7. The Judges threw their 2 parties into one: the V.C. [Vice-Chancellor], Heads, Fellows of Trin. and the bar all dined together. It was a good dinner with turtle and venison.' Romilly's pleasure increased still further when he was surprised to find that the judges' servants were not at the door when he went out, thus saving him his usual tip of two shillings. Romilly summed the evening up quite simply: 'A double dinner day!' (Bury, M. and Pickles, J., *Romilly's Cambridge Diary*, Cambridge Records Society: 1994)

July 20th

1553: On this day, the Earl of Northumberland proclaimed tearfully in the Cambridge Market Place that Mary was the rightful Queen of England. Northumberland had been *de facto* ruler for the latter part of the reign of King Edward VI, after whose death he attempted to put his daughter-in-law, Lady Jane Grey, on the throne. In the meantime, Edward's half-sister Mary, a Catholic, rallied huge numbers of supporters to oppose this move and to install her as Queen of England. Northumberland, having assembled an army of 4,000 cavalry and foot soldiers, marched to Cambridge, where he was Chancellor of the University and felt on safe ground. His situation was in fact very precarious; Northumberland marched out of Cambridge on July 17, but was back the following day, his forces having been decimated by the desertion of his soldiers. There were riots in the University and the following day news reached the town that Lady Jane had been imprisoned and Mary proclaimed as Queen. Today's proclamation by Northumberland was not effective and he was arrested in Cambridge that evening. Just one month later he was executed on Tower Hill in London before 10,000 onlookers. (Porter, H.C., *Reformation and Reaction in Tudor Cambridge*, CUP: 1958)

July 21st

1798: On this day, the *Cambridge Chronicle* carried the following announcement: 'Married, at St Botolph's Church, Busick Harwood, MD, Professor of Anatomy in this University, to Miss Peschell, only daughter of Sir John Peschell, Bart ... The venerable Dr Glynn performed the office of father upon this occasion.' Gunning recalls that earlier that year, Professor Harwood had announced to him over dinner in Christ's College: 'I am going to do a devilish foolish thing. I am going to get married!' Following these remarks on the 'marriage state', 'the laugh against him became so hearty and universal that he left the party unusually early.' A third party, a Newmarket doctor, later confided in Gunning that Harwood had told him that his fiancée did not have much money but 'we are both of us great favourites with old Dr Glynn, who has plenty and no one to leave it to. It will be a devilish odd thing if we don't get a good deal of his cash.' The fiancée wrote direct to Dr Glynn, asking for his advice and approval, receiving the laconic reply that she was of an age to decide for herself. When Dr Glynn died in 1800 he left the couple a legacy of £100 each. (Gunning, H., *Reminiscences*, George Bell: 1854)

July 22nd

1997: On this day, the Queen gave her royal assent to the granting of a charter to Lucy Cavendish College, under the name and style of 'The President and Fellows of Lucy Cavendish College in the University of Cambridge.' Lucy Cavendish became the third women-only college in the University (following Newnham and New Hall) and was aimed specifically at mature students, in other words women over the age of twenty-one. 1997 was a significant year in the history of women at Cambridge. It marked not only the centenary of the defeat of the first attempt to admit women to the University but also the fiftieth anniversary of the University's approval of their final admission. The charter for Lucy Cavendish College was formally issued on November 11 1997 and a celebratory lunch was given by the College in the presence of the Duke of Edinburgh on June 23 1998. College President Lady Perry wrote that 'it marks the spirit of an era that Cambridge's newest college should be one which offers opportunity to mature women.' In 2010 there were 220 students in the College, divided equally between undergraduates and graduates. (Watson, N., *The Opportunity to be Myself*, James James, 2002)

July 23rd

1666: On this day, Samuel Pepys wrote in his diary: 'Simpson the Joyner comes and he and I with great pains contriving presses to put my books up in: they now growing numerous, and lying one upon another on my chairs, I lose the use to avoid the trouble of removing them, when I would open a book.' The presses or bookcases he mentions are those now to be seen in the Pepys Library in Cambridge. As Pepys' library grew, so did the number of bookcases, until they eventually became a set of twelve, housing exactly 3,000 books, arranged meticulously by size. One curious feature is the unusually long front bolt on the top door, devised so that Pepys, a short man, could reach it easily. He still needed steps to reach the top shelves. The bottom shelf was given doors which slid up instead of swinging outwards, perhaps because there was less danger of falling over them in a small room. Quite apart from being the earliest English examples that survive of a bookcase as a separate piece of furniture, Pepys' presses are remarkable witnesses to his ingenuity, attention to detail and insistence on neatness. (Barber, R., *Samuel Pepys Esq.*, National Portrait Gallery: 1970)

July 24th

1771: On this day, poet Thomas Gray was so overcome with nausea during dinner at Pembroke College that he had to be put to bed; some cousins came to look after him, but he died on 30 July and was buried next to his mother at Stoke Poges in Buckinghamshire. At the age of fifty-five, Gray had become quite an *éminence grise*, highly respected in the University and beyond, but emotional and health issues had dominated the last year of his life. In early 1770, Gray had met a twenty-one-year-old Swiss aristocrat called Charles Victor de Bonstetten and was 'more than merely charmed'. Bonstetten came to stay with Gray in Pembroke College, waiting on him, eating with him, reading Shakespeare and Milton with him. When, weeks later, Bonstetten had to return to mainland Europe, Gray missed him terribly, writing: 'I am grown old in the compass of less than three weeks' and his health suffered. Gout confined him to his rooms for a month and he then caught a chill whilst out walking. His one ray of hope was an invitation to visit Switzerland, but this came too late. Gray only got as far as London then had to return to Cambridge ill and feverish. (Chainey, G., *A Literary History of Cambridge*, Pevensey Press: 1985)

July 25th

1606: On this day, the directors of the Queen Anne's Company of professional actors arrived in Cambridge, with the intention of setting up and staging a play. The Mayor of Cambridge, John Edmunds, a long-time 'sparring partner' of the University, ordered carpenters to build a stage in the Guildhall for them and as a precaution ordered glass to be removed from the windows. He also gave the actors a key to the hall, so that they could come and go at will as they prepared for their performance. The University authorities were not however happy with these arrangements and summoned the actors to appear before the Vice-Chancellor's court, informing them that the University had the right to exclude all players from a five mile radius of the town centre. Under the threat of a crippling £20 fine, the actors had no choice but to up sticks and move on to Ipswich, the next town on their itinerary. It was nearly three centuries later, in 1883, that undergraduates formed their own club called 'Footlights', their first show opening with a piece called *The Lottery Ticket*. (Nelson, A.H., *Early Cambridge Theatres*, CUP: 1994 / Hewison, R., *Footlights: A Hundred Years of Cambridge Comedy*, Methuen: 1983)

July 26th

2007: On this day, the *Cambridge Evening News* had a double-page spread with the intriguing headline: 'Is there anybody out there? Fifty years of listening in on a far-from-silent universe'. The articles were celebrating the fiftieth anniversary of the Mullard Radio Astronomy Observatory, part of the Physics Department of Cambridge University. The observatory is based at Lord's Bridge, just outside Cambridge, where eight large dishes, up to thirteen metres in diameter, are dotted around the fields on either side of the main A603 road. Unlike traditional telescopes, radio astronomy is the 'study of celestial objects by means of the natural radio waves they emit', deciphering radio messages from space in a bid to discover crucial answers to universal questions. In the mid-1960s Jocelyn Bell, a graduate student, discovered pulsars here, under the direction of Antony Hewish, who went on to win the Nobel Prize for his work. Bell and Hewish labelled the first signals they heard 'LGM' for Little Green Men, thinking they could possibly be sent from an alien source. Current research at the MRAO is exploring the reasons for the universe's expansion, at an increasing rate; 'dark energy' is being held responsible for the acceleration but nobody yet knows what dark energy is. (*Cambridge Evening News*)

July 27th

1921: On this day, at 3.30 in the afternoon, a 'shocking discovery' was made when Miss Alice Lawn, an unmarried woman of fifty, was found dead in her own shop at 70 King Street in Cambridge. Her body was found at the bottom of the stairs, her head badly injured and in her mouth a gag composed of bits of paper; around her neck was a piece of string which presumably had been used to keep the gag secure. Some money had been stolen from the shop till, but the killer had missed £600 hidden in an upstairs room. Soon a labourer called Thomas Clanwaring, described as a 'man of less than average intellect', was arrested. Clanwaring was a man of lively imagination, who would regale regulars in the Rose and Crown pub with a string of tales about his life which, although entertaining, had little bearing on reality. During his questioning by police and in court the story-telling continued until it was realised that he could not possibly have walked from the Rose and Crown to Alice Lawn's shop, killed her and walked back to the pub within the time he was known to have been alone. He was found not guilty. (*Cambridge Daily News / True Crime Library*)

July 28th

1710: On this day, the German scholar and traveller Zacharias Konrad von Uffenbach cast his critical eye over Cambridge, one of several stops during his tour of England. Uffenbach wrote in his diary: 'It rained hard in the morning until about midday, when we walked about a little to view the town, which however, apart from the Colleges, is no better than a village … The inns, of which there are a couple, are very ill-appointed and dear. We had a recommendation from Baron Nimtsch to a widowed lady, Mrs Lemons, who entertained us kindly indeed, but as regards board and lodging was a bad landlady. In the afternoon … an Italian called Ferrari … took us from one College to another, and explained to us the condition of the University here, which is certainly bad. We were amazed to hear that no classes are held, and the Professors only lecture in the winter and then only three or four times; they lecture to bare walls, for no one comes to hear them. In the summer next to nothing happens, both Students and Professors being either in the country or in London.' Cambridge writer and academic M.R. James was later to describe von Uffenbach's diary as 'full of girdings and sniffings.' (Waterlow, S., *In Praise of Cambridge*, Constable & Co.: 1912)

July 29th

1845: On this day, the grand opening ceremony of the Cambridge railway took place. Josiah Chater wrote in his diary 'About ten o' clock I ... happened to meet Mr Blumson, who was going to the railway, so I went with him...I saw the Grand Train come in – it was a beautiful sight and I have no doubt it is very comfortable riding. [Later] there were grand doings at the Rail, they had a splendid dinner and there were omnibuses cutting about all day which gives life to the town. There were thousands of people there.' The dinner Chater mentions was provided by Gunter, a famous London catering firm, and was served in 'a very elegant marquee...with a boarded floor and lined throughout with scarlet and white drapery.' The station itself was decorated with flowers and flags, while on top of the building 'were numerous cannons which kept up an almost continuous popping'. The so-called Grand Train had left Shoreditch station in East London at eight that morning, filled with Directors and their friends, went on to Ely where it met up with the Norwich train then both arrived together in Cambridge in time for the grand dinner. (Porter, E., *Victorian Cambridge*, Dennis Dobson: 1969)

July 30th

1786: On this day, a youth, aged between sixteen and eighteen, was executed at Cambridge Castle for theft. The young man apparently 'behaved with decency, but testified the strongest intrepidity by taking the rope from the executioner and with amazing fortitude throwing it over his head and launching himself into eternity amidst the tears and prayers of an innumerable multitude.' The unfortunate boy's only crime had been to break into the Sun Inn and steal a silver spoon. (Gray, Arthur B., *Cambridge Revisited*, Heffer & Sons: 1921)

———•◆•———

1968: On this day, Prince Charles, whilst an undergraduate at Trinity College in Cambridge, had his first flying lesson (at Tangmere, in Sussex). He made his first solo flight six months later, later recalling his anxiety when his instructor climbed out of the plane and said: 'You're on your own mate'. Elation soon followed and Charles had a 'wonderful time', one of the rare occasions when not even his faithful detective was allowed to accompany him. (*Charles*, Pitkin Pictorials: 1969 / Regan, S., *Charles*, Magnum Books: 1978)

July 31st

1965: On this day, the University of Cambridge approved the application from Lucy Cavendish for recognition as an Approved Society. Just over two months later the new Society moved into its Silver Street rooms. *The Times* reported: 'Without tower or turrets, without chaplain or porters, without a building of its own or even a foundation grant, Britain's first graduate college for women has come quietly into being.' The college population is in fact today divided equally between undergraduate and post-graduate students, with the proviso that they are both women and mature (mature meaning over the age of twenty-one ...). One of just three women-only colleges in the University, Lucy Cavendish has, since 1970, been housed on an attractive site just off the Huntingdon Road and has an impressive list of Honorary Fellows, including actress Dame Judi Dench, HM Queen Margrethe of Denmark, author Claire Tomalin, broadcaster Anna Ford and the former Director-General of MI5 Dame Stella Rimington. Today anyone of either sex, whether mature or not, can enjoy the 'Lucy experience' by booking bed and breakfast in the college during the summer vacation. (Watson, N., *The Opportunity to be Myself*, James James: 2002 / Lucy Cavendish College website)

August 1st

1997: On this day, over 5,000 people gathered at Duxford, near Cambridge, to watch Her Majesty the Queen open the stunning American Air Museum, designed by internationally renowned architect Sir Norman Foster. The museum commemorates the role of American air power in the Second World War and much of the £13m needed to fund the project was raised by Americans, a campaign spearheaded by the actor Charlton Heston. For the museum director Ted Inman, this was the culmination of a project that began in 1978 when he arrived at the then derelict Duxford fighter base. By 1997 it was the biggest air museum in Europe, with the profile set to be raised even higher by the addition of the American Air Museum. The front of the museum consists of a huge glass wall, 90 metres wide and up to 18 metres high, divided by twenty-eight steel mullions. When, some five years later, more floor space was needed to display two extra aircraft, the entire glass wall was removed so that the building could be 'reconfigured'. The efforts were no doubt appreciated on September 27 2002, when the museum was rededicated by former US President George Bush Senior. (*Cambridge Evening News*)

August 2nd

1879: On this night and in the early hours of the following morning, severe storms, together with torrential rain, swept over East Anglia and the Home Counties. Over three inches of rain fell on Cambridge in six hours, with devastating consequences to shops, houses and businesses. The two main department stores, Robert Sayle and Eaden Lilley, suffered damage to the tune of several thousand pounds, while W.T. Palmer, a wholesale boot manufacturer at 54 Sidney Street, had over 1,000 pairs of boots and shoes ruined by flood water. The footbridge at Jesus Lock, normally standing high over the river, was now at water level and the floods reached to within 50 yards of Maids Causeway with its elegant Georgian houses. One eyewitness said: 'The lightning and thunder were awful in grandeur and the downpour of rain and hail terrible … trees were torn up, mills wrecked, cattle were killed in the field and more died from drowning…' If you go today on a punting tour on the River Cam, look out for the western pier of St John's College Bridge where two flood levels are inscribed: 3 August 1879 and just a few inches above, 14 March 1947. (Porter, E., *Victorian Cambridge*, Dennis Dobson: 1969 / Reeve, F.A., *Victorian and Edwardian Cambridge from Old Photographs*, Batsford: 1971)

August 3rd

1916: On this day, there were no grand processions for the King's visit to Cambridge, no Latin speeches and no pages to hold the train of his cloak. Two years almost to the day since the outbreak of the First World War, King George V was attired in simple army khaki. His first visit of the day was to Clare College, to inspect the work of the Staff Course taking place there; the lantern still set today in the College entrance was presented by officers of war-time courses held in Clare College. He then walked to King's College, watching an Officer Cadet Battalion training on the normally sacrosanct lawns. More training was taking place at Trinity College, this time on the grass by the river, whilst on the lawn near Queen's Road bayonet fighting was in progress. The King's final visit was to the First Eastern General Hospital (military hospital), which had grown beyond recognition since the outbreak of the war, with wards in huts spread out over several acres. The wounded men were arriving continually in hospital trains and nearly 8,000 beds were available. The King returned to London in the afternoon. (Colthorpe, M., *Royal Cambridge*, Cambridge City Council: 1977)

August 4th

1846: On this day, Josiah Chater recorded in his diary that: 'the English cholera is now raging in this town and several persons have died of it, one a waiter at the Lion. He died in a few hours.' English cholera, also known as summer, British or autumnal cholera, was characterised by severe vomiting and diarrhoea which could result in death. Alternatively, the symptoms just disappeared in a day or two, a sort of Russian roulette game for the poor sufferers. Josiah himself, at the end of July 1846, 'felt very queer' one day and thought that he had 'a slight attack of the English cholera', but after dosing himself with a blue pill and half an ounce of salts, he had recovered by the following evening. Cholera first arrived in England from the Indian subcontinent, in 1832. It was transmitted through contaminated water or food, but this link was not then understood. Many believed it was caused by 'bad air', emanating from decayed organic matter. The River Cam was badly polluted, notorious for its stench and full of unmentionable items which allegedly even caught the attention of Queen Victoria. (Porter, E., *Victorian Cambridge*, Dennis Dobson: 1969)

August 5th

1564: On this day, trumpeters sounded fanfares and crowds flocked to cheer as Queen Elizabeth I rode into Cambridge, dressed in a gown of black velvet and a hat spangled with gold, surrounded by her lords, ladies and maids of honour. The church bells of Cambridge rang out, or at least most of them did: the churchwardens at Great St Mary's were later fined 2s 2d 'for not ringing at the Queen's coming'. Queens' Lane was strewn with rushes and the walls were hung with flags and congratulatory verses. The Queen passed on horseback along the lane, past rows of kneeling students and on into King's College for the lengthy and flattering Latin welcome. Entering King's College Chapel, which her father Henry VIII had completed, she 'greatly praised it, above all other in her realm'. The choir sang 'a song of gladness' as the Queen followed them through the screen, beneath the carved initials RAS (Regina Anna Sponsa), of her mother, Queen Anne Boleyn. After Evensong came gifts: four pairs of gloves and 'six boxes of fine comfits and other conceits…which she thankfully took'. (Colthorpe, M., *Royal Cambridge*, Cambridge City Council: 1977)

August 6th

1564: This day, Sunday, was the second day of Queen Elizabeth I's famous and much documented visit to Cambridge. She had stayed the night at the Provost's Lodge in King's College, so only had a few yards to walk to King's College Chapel for the Sunday morning service, where the litany began 'incontinently'. This was followed by an hour-long sermon by Dr Andrew Perne, Master of Peterhouse, on the subject: 'Let every soul be subject unto the higher powers'. She sent him word 'that it was the first sermon that ever she heard in Latin' and that she thought 'she would never hear a better'. Queen Elizabeth returned to the Chapel that night for Evensong and again after supper for a very different purpose. At the Queen's own expense a 'great stage' had been built in the antechapel and she herself sat against the south wall, surrounded by her courtiers. There she watched a comedy in Latin, lit by torches held by Yeoman of the Guard. The University bought beards for some of the undergraduate actors, paying for 'six beards, eight shillings'. (Colthorpe, M., *Royal Cambridge*, Cambridge City Council: 1977 / Chainey, G., *A Celebration of King's College Chapel*, Pevensey Press: 1987)

August 7th

1564: Today was the third day of Queen Elizabeth I's visit to Cambridge. The entertainment provided for the Queen this afternoon was a debate in Great St Mary's, the University church. At the Queen's own expense, a 'great and ample stage' had been made, with seats all round for the packed audience and cushions for the Queen to 'lean upon'. As she entered, all the graduates kneeled and cried out: '*Vivat Regina!*' A Philosophy disputation came first: a formal debate in Latin on the subjects 'Monarchy is the best form of government' and 'Frequent changes in the law are dangerous'. Then came a disputation on Physick (Medicine). The questions discussed were: 'Is it better to have simple meals or rich ones?' and 'Is it better to eat more at dinner or at supper?' One of the main speakers was Dr John Caius, who just a few years earlier had proved such a benefactor to his old college, Gonville Hall, that it had changed its name to 'Gonville and Caius'. Later that evening, at 9 p.m., the Queen was entertained by a play called 'Dido', which had been written in Latin verse by an English author called Edward Halliwell. (Colthorpe, M., *Royal Cambridge*, Cambridge City Council: 1977)

August 8th

1564: Today was the fourth day of Queen Elizabeth I's visit to Cambridge and the royal schedule was quieter than on previous days. The Queen made the decision to stay a day longer in Cambridge than she had planned and 'if provision of beer and ale could have been made' would have stayed even longer, as 'Her Highness was so well pleased with all things'. (Colthorpe, M., *Royal Cambridge*, Cambridge City Council: 1977)

———•◆•———

1681: On this day, Provost Page of King's College in Cambridge fell down dead 'in the act of rebuking an irregular scholar' and a replacement needed to be found for him. One obvious choice was diarist Samuel Pepys, to whom a special messenger was dispatched, saying, 'I should with all joy imaginable salute you Provost'. Pepys was initially tempted, even considering donating his first year's salary to the college, but after some serious thought decided that he was not sufficiently well qualified academically for the position. Turning the post down, Pepys was elected, three years later, President of the Royal Society. (Chainey, G., *A Literary History of Cambridge*, Pevensey Press: 1985)

August 9th

1564: On this day, the fifth day of her Cambridge visit, Queen Elizabeth I 'took her progress about to the colleges, riding in state royal; all the lords and gentlemen riding before her Grace, and all the ladies following on horseback'. At Trinity, the newest college, founded by her father King Henry VIII, she was able to see how work was progressing on the new chapel, started at the expense of her half-sister Queen Mary. At Christ's College, a pair of gloves was presented to her in memory of her great-grandmother the Lady Margaret Beaufort, who had founded both Christ's and St John's Colleges. At Peterhouse a speech was made by one of the youngest undergraduates, Anthony Mildmay, 'which being a child, made a very neat and trim oration, and pronounced it very aptly and distinctly'. An evening debate ended with a request to Her Majesty to address the University in Latin. Having initially refused, Elizabeth went on to impress everyone with a 400-word speech, 'a very eloquent, sententious and comfortable oration in Latin'. The astonished and impressed audience cried out '*Vivat Regina!*' … and so Her Majesty cheerfully departed to her lodging'. (Colthorpe, M., *Royal Cambridge*, Cambridge City Council: 1977)

August 10th

1564: Today was the last day of Queen Elizabeth I's visit to Cambridge. Early this morning, many of the courtiers received honorary degrees from the University of Cambridge. A final Latin speech was made by Thomas Preston, a Fellow of King's who had already caught the Queen's eye on Monday in the philosophy debate and in 'Dido'. Putting forward her hand for him to kiss, Her Highness dubbed him 'her scholar' and handed him eight 'angels' (Tudor coins). Thomas Preston went on to become Master of Trinity Hall and his brass can still be seen in the antechapel there; the Latin inscription on the brass recalls the day when his Queen called him 'her scholar'. The Queen's final stop was at Magdalene College, where, rather than having to listen to yet another Latin speech, she asked for a written copy to take away instead. And so, as the Queen rode out of Cambridge on her way to Fenstanton to dine with the Bishop of Ely, this illustrious visit came to an end. (Colthorpe, M., *Royal Cambridge*, Cambridge City Council: 1977 / Cunich, P., Hoyle, D., Duffy, E. and Hyam, R., *A History of Magdalene College Cambridge 1428-1988*, Magdalene College Publications: 1994)

August 11th

1871: On this day, the Emperor Pedro II of Brazil was in Cambridge with his wife, part of an extended tour which took them through much of England and Scotland. The couple had arrived incognito the day before; no warning had been given of their arrival and the bell ringers of Great St Mary's Church, hastily summoned, 'struck forth a merry peal'. The couple were 'attired in English costume, in black undress, and the very best of taste, and their manners…were genial and unassuming. The appearance of the Emperor and Empress was but little different from that of cultivated English men and women'. The scholarly Emperor, who had said, 'If I were not Emperor I should like to be a school teacher', was in his element. The couple had risen very early in the morning and by 5.30 a.m. were viewing the Botanic Gardens, followed by tours of the Pitt Press in Trumpington Street and the Round Church. All this before breakfast! The party then set off for London, on their way to the Continent, declaring that they were 'highly delighted' with their visit to Cambridge. In 1889, the Emperor was forced to abdicate, Brazil became a republic and the imperial family fled to live in exile in Paris. (Colthorpe, M., *Royal Cambridge*, Cambridge City Council: 1977)

August 12th

1671: On this day, Sir Thomas Sclater, Fellow of Trinity College and Justice of the Peace, wrote in his notebook: 'This day Dr Eade and I viewed the felons' gaol and saw the iron cut off the grate about one finger and a half long and the link cuff that fastened the wooden door to the grate by a horselock. And the manacles made of hardened iron that were cut. York said that shackles were forced in the yard, and Slivet testified that he had made them.' The prisoners had apparently made their escape five nights previously. York was the keeper of the House of Correction; he also made money from running a private asylum, at a time when the only known treatment for the mentally unhinged was to lock them up in fetters and chains. The gaol and House of Correction were in the area of the Castle mound in Cambridge, today an attractive grassed hill with far-reaching views over Cambridge. In 1671 the whole area was covered in a maze of buildings, from law courts and the jury house to a fragment of the great hall of the older Edwardian castle. The most notorious building here was the gaol and the House of Correction. (Palmer, W.M., *Cambridge Castle*, Oleander Press: 1976)

August 13th

1666: On this day was born William Wotton; he was both an infant prodigy, with an extraordinary memory, and also a prodigious natural linguist who by the age of five could read Latin, Greek and Hebrew verses. He was educated by his father, who described these remarkable abilities in *An Essay on the Education of Children*. Diarist John Evelyn described him as 'so universally and solidly learned at eleven years of age, that he was looked on as a miracle.' Wotton was admitted to St Catharine's College in Cambridge when not even ten years old; at the age of sixteen he was elected to a fellowship at St John's College, at the age of twenty-one he was elected a Fellow of the Royal Society and at the age of forty-one received his Doctorate in Divinity. Despite his high-flying early career, it was later said that Wotton 'made a mark for himself without being a really distinguished man'. A great friend of Richard Bentley, Master of Trinity College, he was celebrated for 'wide learning rather than for exact scholarship'. (Jones, W., *A History of St Catharine's College*, CUP: 1936 / *Dictionary of National Biography*)

August 14th

1954: On this day, the first volume of Cambridge academic Joseph Needham's ambitious and highly influential work *Science and Civilisation in China* was published. The subtitle was *Introductory Orientations*, a mild pun, suggesting that the reader should start his enquiry by turning his mind eastwards. Although there had been considerable excitement in the run-up to the publication date, the day itself was celebrated by Joseph and his wife Dorothy in a 'quietly deliberate' style. They were staying in the small medieval French town of Amboise, the same town where Leonardo da Vinci had spent the final three years of his life. Needham had said that he wanted to spend this most memorable day beside the house and tomb of the most remembered Renaissance man who had ever lived. Dinner in the evening was accompanied by a bottle of good local white wine, a 1947 Vouvray. Needham was in constant postal contact with his Chinese collaborator and mistress Gwei-djen in Paris. Joseph Needham died in 1995 but his work still continues, now an international collaborative project coordinated by the Needham Research Institute in Sylvester Road, Cambridge. (Winchester, S., *Bomb, Book and Compass*, Penguin: 2009)

August 15th

1665: On this day, the register of St Clement's Church in Cambridge recorded a list of people who had been buried at the 'Grene and Pestehouse ffor the Parrish'. Until this date, entries for deaths had been made singly with causes given as 'of the disease' or 'of the pestilent fever', but this was the height of the plague epidemic and the citizens of Cambridge were dying in large numbers; victims were buried as soon as possible after death, many in large plague pits such as 'the Grene', which was probably Midsummer Common. One brilliant young student from Trinity College, named Isaac Newton, fled to his family home, Woolsthorpe Manor in Lincolnshire and stayed there for eighteen months, continuing his studies until the worst of the plague was over. For those left in town, life changed dramatically, with many families staying locked inside their homes for safety; victims developed large swellings in the glands and dark, blue-back blotches on the skin. Death came quickly, usually within a week. Centuries later, plans to build an underground car park on Midsummer Common, near the site of the plague burial site, were eventually abandoned and the area remains a green, attractive outdoor space. (Gray, Arthur B., *Cambridge Revisited*, Heffer & Sons: 1921)

August 16th

1475: On this day, a charter bearing the great seal of King Edward IV was witnessed in the name of Edward Prince of Wales. This charter confirmed the foundation of a house in Mill Street (Queens' Lane today) for a master and three or more fellows to study philosophy and theology; the house was to be called Catharine's Hall and Robert Woodlark, Provost of King's College, would be the first Master. A college seal was made at the same time, depicting St Catharine, crowned and standing in a canopied niche, together with the wheel and sword. The College is dedicated to St Catharine, who supposedly lived in the third century in Alexandria. Because of her Christian beliefs she was condemned to death on a breaking wheel surrounded by knives, an instrument of torture. Legend has it that the wheel broke when Catharine touched it, so she was beheaded, hence the dual symbol of wheel and sword. The Catharine wheel, from which the Catharine wheel firework gets its name, is the symbol of the College today and can be found everywhere, from the College gates to Fellows' ties and the plates in the Dining Hall. (Rich, E.E., *St Catharine's College Cambridge: A Volume of Essays to commemorate the Quincentenary of the Foundation of the College*: 1973)

August 17th

1650: On this day, Elinor Gaskin died at the impressive age of 112; she lies buried in the churchyard of St Edward's Church in Cambridge. The authorities added a little ditty to the church register, celebrating her long life:

> Elinor Gaskin said
> She lived four score years a maid
> And twenty and two years a wife
> And ten years a widow and then she left this life.

Elinor had lived through the reigns of Elizabeth I, James I and Charles I from the time when Drake sailed round the world and a king was beheaded in England by his people into the first republic established by Cromwell. The average life expectancy in England in 1650 was forty years. (Oosthuizen, S., *A Woman's Guide to Cambridge*, Woody Press: 1983)

August 18th

1988: On this day, a feast was held in the Dining Hall of Trinity College to celebrate the 100th birthday of geologist Tressilian Charles Nicholas, a College Fellow for the last seventy-six years. After dinner, the diminutive, white-haired figure stood up and talked about his long life, from his journey to school in 1898, dodging the horse-drawn traffic in central London, to comparatively recent events in the Second World War. Nicholas recalled how in the very height of battle a letter was thrust into his hands from Trinity College, advising that clocks would soon be changing to British summer time and that doctors should wear scarlet for Easter Day. Nicholas lived to be 101 and he asked for a simple memorial. As a geologist, he had been fascinated by a red-coloured stone in the cobbles outside the Great Gate of Trinity College. He recognised this as rhomb porphyry from Norway, a stone which must have been transported here by the great ice sheets some 15,000 years ago. If you look carefully on the ground, just a few feet from the entrance to Trinity College, you will see the stone, a very modest and fitting memorial, with the simple letters TCN inscribed on it. (SCTG newsletter)

August 19th

1642: On this day, it was reported at Westminster that 'Mr Oliver Cromwell had seized college plate to the estimated value of £6,000, which was being sent away from Cambridge to the army chest of the King'. Malden, in his 1902 history of Trinity Hall goes on to comment: 'Dr Eden [Master of Trinity Hall] had possibly taken the alarm and checked the dangerous loyalty of his society. Their plate was not sent, for not only the Founder's, Parker's and Barlow's cups, but other pieces of plate mentioned in 1557 are still in existence in the College and so presumably were not amongst the confiscated contributions. Or were they sent and seized, and had Eden sufficient influence to get them back again, saving them from another army chest?' Arms were also much in demand. Parliament had ordered, in July, that the county of Cambridge was to 'exercise itself in arms' and weapons were transported from London to the University. This caused some concern when townsmen starting practising with their newly found equipment 'at the windows of scholars' and University authorities had to intervene to ensure that the students did not retaliate. (Malden, H., *Trinity Hall*, Robinson & Co.: 1902)

August 20th

1815: On this day, Mary Lamb, sister of essayist Charles Lamb, wrote a rapturous letter to Wordsworth's sister-in-law Sarah Hutchinson, saying: 'In my life I never spent so many pleasant hours together as I did at Cambridge. We were walking the whole time – out of one college, into another. If you ask me which I like best ... I liked them all the best.' The brother and sister had been 'driven into Cambridge in great triumph by Hell Fire Dick', aka Richard Vaughan, driver of the Telegraph stagecoach from London. Four years later the siblings were back in Cambridge, this time lodging over Bays the hatter in Trumpington Street, later to become 11 King's Parade; its wall is now graced by a small plaque commemorating the Lambs' visit. Charles Lamb celebrated this visit with a sonnet, 'Written in Cambridge', in which he imagines himself in a doctor's cap and gown. When young, Charles Lamb had been unable to afford a university education, but he had always harboured sentimental feelings about universities and liked nothing better than to spend his holidays at either Oxford or Cambridge. (Waterlow, S., *In Praise of Cambridge*, Constable & Co.: 1912 / Chainey, G., *A Literary History of Cambridge*, Pevensey Press: 1985)

August 21st

1773: On this day, Dr Plumptre and David Hughes, the President and Senior Fellow respectively of Queens' College, approved and signed a college order declaring that 'Charles Crawford, for having been drunk and for assaulting and beating a waterman in town, and for making a riot, be banished from the Society … on or before the Monday following.' Crawford, whose insubordination 'was on a heroic scale' had arrived at Queens' College in November 1768 and had caused trouble almost from the outset, often drunk by the afternoon, assaulting innocent townspeople and writing diatribes against Christianity. The college order had little effect and Crawford remained in residence; when an attempt was made to bar his rooms against him, he hired a blacksmith to break them open again. On one occasion he even brandished a pistol at college staff but was let off thanks to a legal loophole. Winstanley relates this story at some length in his book *Unreformed Cambridge*, saying that it was 'typical of the Cambridge of the day. Crawford was certainly an abnormal character, but his University career was in many ways only an exaggeration of that of many other fellow-commoners who far too frequently were little less than licensed libertines.' (Winstanley, D.A., *Unreformed Cambridge*, CUP: 1935)

August 22nd

2001: On this day, at precisely 9.54 in the morning, a camera focussing on a coffee pot in the Trojan Room of the old Computer Laboratory of the University of Cambridge, was switched off and the pot, a German Krups model, was auctioned on eBay for £3,350. And so ended a piece of computing history, the world's first webcam, created to help people working in other parts of the building avoid pointless trips to the coffee room by providing, on the user's desktop computer, a live picture of the state of the coffee pot. The webcam was created in 1991 when, according to its creator Quentin Stafford-Fraser 'the World Wide Web was little more than a glint in CERN's eye'. The image was only updated about three times a minute, but that was fine because the pot filled rather slowly and it was only greyscale, which was also fine, 'because so was the coffee'. The images might have faded into obscurity had they not been posted on the World Wide Web, after which hundreds of thousands of people looked at the coffee pot, making it undoubtedly the most famous in the world. Sadly, according to Stafford-Fraser, this did not make the coffee any better though. (Computer Laboratory, University of Cambridge)

August 23rd

1900: On this day, a Great Eastern Railway van collided with a horse-drawn tram between Gonville Place and East Road, resulting in the first fatality on the Cambridge tramway system. The van driver, William Beer, was thrown heavily from his seat and died of internal injuries a short time after admission to Addenbrooke's Hospital. The tram driver escaped injury. Apparently the van driver had pulled to one side when he saw the tramcar approaching; the rear wheels skidded and the van swerved suddenly, causing the driver to be pitched on to the road between the van and the tram. At the inquest it was decided that Mr Beer's death was purely accidental and no blame was attached to the tram driver. It was also decided that the drivers of the GER vans should have some form of protection to secure them in position. Horse-drawn trams were used on the streets of Cambridge for thirty-four years, from 1880 to 1914, to be superseded eventually by omnibuses, whose arrival in 1907 was to sound the death knell for the trams. (Swingle, S.L., *Cambridge Street Tramways*, Oakwood Press: 1972 / Cambridge Museum of Technology)

August 24th

1876: On this day, Robert Browning, a tailor, went for a drink at the Garrick pub on the corner of King Street and got into conversation with Emma Rolfe, who was sixteen years old and had left home just a few days before. They walked across the road to Midsummer Common, where Browning attacked her so savagely with a razor that he almost decapitated her. Afterwards he could give no reason for her murder and said that it was committed on impulse. Robert Browning was hanged at Cambridge Castle the following November. The exact location of the murder was Butts Green, a corner of Midsummer Common bounded by Victoria Avenue and Maids Causeway. Men practised their archery here but there was also a gallows from which, amongst others, witches were hanged. In 1645 'a woman was hanged in Cambridge for keeping a tame frog and it was sworn to be her imp'. She was Mrs Lendale, who was said to have 'carried herself at her execution like a saint.' Very little else is known about Mrs Lendale and others who had been accused of witchcraft. (Oosthuizen, S., *A Woman's Guide to Cambridge*, Woody Press: 1983)

August 25th

1511: On this day, the Dutch scholar Desiderius Erasmus wrote to his friend Ammonio with some of his first impressions of life in Cambridge: 'The beer in this place doesn't suit me at all and the wines aren't quite satisfactory either. If you are in a position to arrange for a cask of Greek wine, the best obtainable, to be shipped to me here, you will have done what will make your friend happy. (But I'd like it to be quite *dry* wine)'. Erasmus had arrived in Cambridge by the invitation of his friend John Fisher, Chancellor of the University; a distinguished and well respected scholar, Erasmus was the first Professor of Greek in the University (in fact the first person to teach Greek here at all) and was later appointed Lady Margaret Professor of Divinity. During his two and a half years in Cambridge, Erasmus lived in Queens' College and a tower in Pump Court, overlooking Silver Street, still bears his name. As for the Greek wine, Erasmus received four casks of it during his stay, but two arrived unsealed and spoilt, which of course made him even angrier towards the 'boorish and thieving natives'. (Fowler, L. and H., *Cambridge Commemorated*, CUP: 1984 / Chainey, G., *A Literary History of Cambridge*, Pevensey Press: 1985)

August 26th

1918: On this day, Bertram Hopkinson, patent lawyer and Professor of Mechanism and Applied Mathematics in the University of Cambridge, died while flying between Martlesham Heath and London in a Bristol Fighter; he had run into bad weather and, whilst trying to find his way through thick cloud, crashed and was killed. Aged forty-four, Hopkinson died twenty years almost to the day since he had lost his father, brother and two of his sisters in a mountaineering accident (*see* August 27th). His body was brought to Cambridge and buried with military honours in St Giles Cemetery, following a service in King's College Chapel which was attended by many distinguished mourners. Hopkinson's research into explosives, guns and ammunition was crucial to the war effort and in 1916 he had opened an experimental research station at Orford Ness in Suffolk. His colleague Ewing later wrote of him: 'No worker rejoiced more in his work or accepted its call with more absolute renunciation', adding: 'Many will mourn him as a trusted friend, but only those who knew something of what he did in the war can have a right idea of the magnitude of the nation's loss'. (Hilken, T.J.N., *Engineering at Cambridge University*, CUP: 1967)

August 27th

1898: This date is recorded on a large plaque in Free School Lane, part of which reads: 'This wing of the Engineering Laboratory was erected in memory of John Hopkinson ... and of his son...who died on August 27 1898, the father aged 49 and the son 18.' John Hopkinson, a distinguished engineer, was a member of the Alpine Club and in 1898 took his wife and children to Switzerland on a mountaineering holiday. On 27 August, John set out with his son Jack and two of his three daughters to climb the rock known as *La Petite Dent de Veisivi*. The party never returned, being found the next day, all four bodies roped together in a valley 500ft below the summit. A few days before his death, Hopkinson had promised to help raise money for a new wing of the Engineering Laboratory and his widow honoured this pledge by giving £5,000 towards the building as a memorial to her husband and her son Jack, who, had he lived, would have entered the Engineering Department as an undergraduate in the following term. The plaque in Free School Lane does not mention the two daughters who were also killed. (*Engineering 125*, Department of Engineering: 2000)

August 28th

1939: On this day, at the start of the Second World War, 147 psychiatric patients were moved from the Three Counties Hospital in Bedford to the Fulbourn Hospital, near Cambridge. In anticipation of casualties from bombing raids, most of the London metropolitan asylums were emptied of psychiatric patients to free up beds. Hill End Hospital in St Albans was evacuated to Bedford, hence the need to send patients on to Cambridge. The increase in numbers at Fulbourn resulted in severe overcrowding and a drop in the standard of hygiene. By the summer of 1941, flies were 'so thick' in the sick wards that it was suggested that gauze should be used 'in protecting the faces of feeble bedridden patients'. Apparently some of the toilets were so badly blackened that it was impossible to gauge whether they were clean or not. Dysentery affected eleven patients in the summer of 1943 and tuberculosis was starting to spread; the biggest problem however was staff shortage, with many staff being recruited for the war effort. Originally opened in 1858 as the County Pauper Lunatic Asylum, the size of the facility is now vastly reduced; the original Victorian buildings now house a business park. (Clark, David H., *The Story of a Mental Hospital*, Process Press: 1996)

August 29th

1768: On this day, a nineteen-year-old Cambridge visitor, described by poet Thomas Gray as 'a genteel, lively figure', made quite an impression on the town. Crowned as King of Denmark and Norway just two years previously, King Christian VII was visiting Cambridge as part of a lengthy European tour. His Danish Majesty, wearing the ensigns of the Order of the Elephant, arrived with his entourage in eight post-chaises and coaches at the Rose Inn. The local newspaper commented: 'He converses principally in French and is extremely affable and genteel.' The King was escorted to King's College Chapel and then on to Trinity College, where he was particularly attracted to the statue of Isaac Newton. After supper at the Rose Inn, the King 'several times appeared at the balcony and seemed much pleased with the humour of the populace'. At night 'the whole Market Hill, the Shire Hall and the Conduit, all in sight of the Inn, were handsomely illuminated … and the next morning … His Majesty and his retinue proceeded on their journey to York … ordering 30 guineas to be distributed amongst the servants and other attendants'. (Colthorpe, M., *Royal Cambridge*, Cambridge City Council: 1977)

August 30th

1931: On this day, Ernest Rutherford, Director of the Cavendish Laboratory in Cambridge, celebrated his sixtieth birthday. Rutherford's Russian colleague Peter Kapitza presented him with a smart, silver propelling pencil, commenting that his fondness for blunt pencil stubs was no longer appropriate now that he had become a Lord. Just months before his sixtieth birthday, Rutherford had been offered membership of the House of Lords. He sent a telegram to his mother in New Zealand, saying, 'Now Lord Rutherford, honour more yours than mine. Love, Ernest.' This was a fitting tribute to his mother Martha, a schoolteacher, who had taught each of her twelve children the alphabet and times tables even before they started school. The registrar's writing skills were less accurate, recording the name on the birth certificate as 'Earnest' Rutherford. Rutherford came from a poor but hard-working family and was known simply as Ern. In later life, having been showered with honours, he was hailed in his homeland as 'our Kiwi Genius'. Rutherford's childhood home was demolished in 1921, but the site is marked by a memorial garden, at the centre of which is a small bronze statue of a New Zealand child stepping out into the future. (Smith, P., *Rutherford*, Educational Solutions: 2000)

August 31st

1654: On this day, diarist John Evelyn visited Cambridge and made the following observations: 'This evening to Cambridge; and went first to St John's College, well built of brick, and library, which I think is the fairest of that University ... Trinity College is said by some to be the fairest quadrangle of any university in Europe; but in truth is far inferior to that of Christ Church in Oxford ... thence ... to King's College, where I found the chapel altogether answered expectation, especially the roof all of stone, which for the flatness of its laying and carving may, I conceive, vie with any in Christendom. The contignation of the roof (which I went upon), weight, and artificial jointing of the stones is admirable. The lights are also very fair ... From this roof we could descry Ely, and the encampment of Sturbridge Fair now beginning to set up their tents and booths; also Royston, Newmarket, etc ... The market-place is very ample, and remarkable for old Hobson the pleasant carrier's beneficence of a fountain. But the whole town is situate in a low dirty unpleasant place, the streets ill-paved, the air thick and infected by the fens, nor are its churches (of which St Mary's is the best) anything considerable in compare to Oxford.' (Waterlow, S., *In Praise of Cambridge*, Constable & Co.: 1912)

September 1st

1939: On this day, following the announcement that the Germans had invaded Poland (effectively the start of the Second World War), King's College immediately sent out telegrams to holidaying members of the College Council, asking for their consent to remove the East Window of the Chapel to safety. By the end of 1941 all the ancient windows had been removed, at a cost of £50 per window. Much of the money was raised by friends of Cambridge in the USA, in particular Yale alumni. The rectangular window sections were stored in the cellars of King's College and elsewhere in Cambridge. The windows were replaced by sheets of grey tar-paper, with occasional strips of plain glass at the bottom to let in light. The West Window, a 'modern' addition dating only from 1879, remained and at last had its chance to be the star turn in the Chapel. One event which was still celebrated in those austere times, albeit with depleted numbers, was the College Quincentenary in 1941. The food-controlling authorities, usually so strict with their rationing, gave special permission for roast swan to be on the menu, no doubt the highlight of the festivities. (Wilkinson, L.P., *A Century of King's*, King's College: 1980 / Hicks, C., *The King's Glass*, Chatto & Windus: 2007)

September 2nd

1894: On this day, Yolande Lyne-Stephens died and her body was brought to lie in state overnight in Our Lady and English Martyrs, the great church she had founded in Cambridge. In the evening a funeral dirge was sung; the following day, the bishop's throne was over-hung with purple and the communion rails and pulpit were draped in black, in preparation for a Pontifical Requiem Mass. Born in Paris in 1813, Yolande had led an extraordinary life, first studying ballet at the Paris Opera and then performing at the Drury Lane Theatre in London to rapturous reviews. Thackeray later described her as 'a vision of loveliness such as mortal eyes can't see nowadays … ' She married one of her English admirers, Stephen Lyne-Stephens, who had inherited a huge fortune from his merchant father Charles, making him reputedly the wealthiest commoner in England. The couple had no children and following her husband's premature death in 1860 Yolande devoted much of her immense wealth to charitable causes, notably the building of a new Roman Catholic church in Cambridge. After her funeral service, Yolande's body was taken to Roehampton, where she was laid to rest beside her husband. (Rogers, N., *Catholics in Cambridge*, Gracewing: 2003)

September 3rd

1769: On this day, William Cole, Cambridge antiquary, wrote about the six-roomed farmhouse at Milton 'in very bad repair' which he had rented from King's College and was slowly renovating. He had managed to acquire cartloads of stones from Archbishop Rotheram's gateway to the Old University Schools, which was then being pulled down; he obtained some old book desks from the same place, together with the glass of a window, filled with the coloured emblems of York, Lancaster and the Archbishop. All these items were taken to the house in Milton. The disruption caused by the building works did not prevent Cole from inviting friends to dinner and eating 'pot luck'. On this day, he wrote: 'Mr and Mrs Bentham dined with me on beans and bacon in the great Parlour without floor and windows.' Cole's health started to deteriorate as he became lame and badly overweight. He died in Milton in 1782 and was buried in St Clement's Church in Cambridge, his grandmother's place of worship. Cole left money for the building of the church tower. When the tower was completed, almost forty years later, the words 'Deum Cole' were cut into the wall above the West door and can still be seen there today. (Palmer, W., *William Cole of Milton*, Galloway & Porter: 1935 / *Dictionary of National Biography*)

September 4th

1902: On this day, tea was provided in tents on Parker's Piece for 250 'old folk' and 6,000 children as part of the Cambridge celebrations for the coronation of King Edward VII. Over 800 gallons of tea were brewed and ginger beer and lemonade were provided. The Mayor distributed commemorative medals of the coronation. (Woodall, S. and Inman, C., *Cambridge: Memories of Times Past*, Worth Press: 2007)

———◆———

2009: On this day, a new sculpture installation was unveiled outside the Cambridge University Library, marking the seventy-fifth anniversary year of Giles Gilbert Scott's building. The sculpture looks like fourteen stacks of books, but closer inspection reveals that the leathery appearance of the books is in fact bronze. The books in the four central columns rotate independently and when correctly aligned reveal the title of the artwork *Ex Libris*. The sculptures prompted many different reactions, ranging from 'a pleasant and jolly idea' to an article in the *Guardian* by local feminist author Germaine Greer entitled 'My favourite library is being transformed into a beacon of naffness'. (Cambridge University Library / *The Guardian*)

September 5th

2005: On this day, it was announced in the *Cambridge Evening News* that Cambridge cosmologist Professor Stephen Hawking, because of his deteriorating health, was using a new gadget which enables him to communicate by blinking. The world-famous scientist, Britain's longest surviving sufferer of motor neurone disease, had for years controlled by hand the computer system which operates his now famous synthesised voice. But Hawking's hand was now getting weaker and he was pleased to move on to this new high-tech gadget, which allows him to control the computer simply by blinking his eye. The Infrared Sound Touch (IST) switch emits a very low-powered infrared beam; the reflection of the beam changes when the eye closes and the cheek muscle moves, meaning that controlling the computer is literally as easy as blinking. The switch is attached to Professor Hawking's glasses an inch from his face, so that the moving muscle can be detected. Hawking has not been able to speak naturally since a tracheotomy operation in 1985, but is very appreciative of his synthesised voice which cleverly varies his intonation and does not, in his own words, make him sound 'like a Dalek', though it does give him an American accent. (*Cambridge Evening News* / www.hawking. org.uk)

September 6th

1977: On this day, John Edensor Littlewood, one of the greatest English mathematicians of the twentieth century, died in the Evelyn Nursing Home in Cambridge, at the age of ninety-two. Littlewood, together with his close colleague Godfrey Hardy, dominated the English mathematical scene for many years. Hardy said of him: 'He was the man most likely to storm and smash a really deep and formidable problem; there was no one else who could command such a combination of insight, technique and power'. In his middle years Littlewood had suffered from a nervous illness which caused him to function at a fraction of his capacity and he spent many hours in local cinemas whiling away the hours. But in 1960 a brilliant neurologist experimented with some new drugs and cured the depression. This gave Littlewood a new lease of life in his later years and at the age of seventy-five he started to take up lecturing invitations, particularly in the United States, which he visited eight times. Littlewood is commemorated with a brass plaque in the antechapel of Trinity College. (Ed. Harman, P. and Mitton, S., *Cambridge Scientific Minds*, CUP: 2002)

September 7th

2004: On this day, the Institute of Financial Services held a dinner in St John's College, marking the occasion by unveiling a blue plaque commemorating eighteenth-century banker John Mortlock, sometimes called the 'Mr Money of Cambridge'. John Mortlock, born in Cambridge in 1755, rose to a position of enormous wealth and influence in the city. But he was also Cambridge's king of corruption, notorious for selling the city's land to his cronies and diverting cash meant for charities into his own coffers. At the age of twenty-five, Mortlock founded the first bank in Cambridge and went on to become mayor five years later. The bank was built on land in Bene't Street, where Barclays Bank now has a branch. It became the bank for Cambridge University and into its vaults went large amounts of money culled from Mortlock's nefarious schemes. Once mayor, he altered the rules of election, enabling him to hold the post thirteen times. Former Cambridge mayor John Durrant commented: 'Back in the eighteenth and early nineteenth centuries, corruption was rife – everyone was at it. Mortlock was just so much better at it than anyone else.' The blue plaque to Mortlock can be seen on the wall of Barclays Bank in Bene't Street. (*Cambridge Evening News*)

September 8th

1873: On this day, David Gregory Marshall was born in Cambridge. Marshall started an apprenticeship in the kitchens of Trinity College in 1887. His entrepreneurial spirit and business sense were quickly recognised, leading to his appointment as Steward of the University Pitt Club (today Pizza Express in Jesus Lane), where his services were described as 'quite remarkable'. In 1906 he went to Paris for the first time and was amazed at the standard of motoring compared to that in England; this was the inspiration for his motor business in Cambridge, starting originally in a stable in Brunswick Gardens, from where he provided chauffeured transport for wealthy dons and undergraduates, then moving to King Street and eventually Jesus Lane. During the First World War, the Jesus Lane garage was used for servicing and repairing vehicles for the war effort, from Rolls-Royce armoured cars to field ambulances. Joined in the business by his son Arthur, Marshall's went from strength to strength, building the first Cambridge aerodrome on their land in 1929. In 2010 the Marshall Group of Companies has nearly 4,000 employees, is still very active in the field of aerospace and has a network of sixty franchised automotive dealerships. (Marshall Group of Companies: *90th Anniversary Booklet 1909-1999*)

September 9th

2000: On this day, the inaugural meeting of the James Hilton Society was held at the Leys School in Cambridge. James Hilton had been a pupil at the Leys School and it was here, in the person of classics master William H. Balgarnie, that he found the inspiration for Charles Chipping, the hero of his classic work *Good-bye, Mr. Chips*. The story was originally commissioned by the *British Weekly* for their 1933 Christmas edition, but Hilton wrote 17,500 words instead of the requested 3,000 and it was agreed to turn it into a supplement instead. The story gained much wider fame when in 1939 it was made into a film starring Robert Donat, Greer Garson and John Mills. Hilton went on to win an Oscar for the screenplay of his next Hollywood film *Mrs Miniver*, also starring Greer Garson. Hilton's printed books have endured less well and a primary aim of the James Hilton Society, whose meeting on this day marked the 100th anniversary of the author's birth, is to persuade publishers to start reprinting his sadly neglected works. Despite apparently being a textbook in Japan, *Good-bye Mr. Chips* was still out of print in Britain in 2010. (*Cambridge Evening News*)

September 10th

1847: This day, a Friday, was one like many others for Joseph Romilly, Fellow of Trinity College and University Registrary, dealing with various enquiries and visitors and looking after his ailing sister Margaret. Today's correspondence included a letter from Lady Braybrooke at Audley End, saying that his 'lionising had given great satisfaction'. Romilly composed a letter to a Mr Maitland at Lambeth Palace who had questioned the Cambridge terminology 'salting' and 'problem' which he had found in an old college account; Maitland thought that 'salting' was a fee paid by a student on his first dining in Hall and that 'problem' was his first examination on admission (for which there was a fee). In fact 'salting' was originally a crude sixteenth-century initiation rite for freshmen, which involved drinking salt-water or salted beer. It later came to refer to the festivities of freshers' events and their cost. A 'problem' was an academic exercise in Hall whose rules were laid down in the statutes of Trinity College. Later two 'moustached Americans, agreeable gentlemanlike men' visited Romilly, researching their ancestors; they were 'much surprised at my declining any fee.' (Bury, M. and Pickles, J., *Romilly's Cambridge Diary*, Cambridge Records Society: 1994)

September 11th

1842: On this day, Joseph Romilly, Fellow of Trinity College and University Registrary, wrote in his diary that his friend Carus preached in his Sunday School. His sermon today was a thanksgiving for the abundant harvest, using Leviticus 2 about the 'green ears', which Romilly thought was 'a very happy application of the artificial mode of ripening them to education.' Today's thanksgiving was significant, as this was the first 'abundant harvest' for several years. Three years earlier, the Prime Minister Lord Melbourne had refused to sanction harvest festivals, there being no reason to celebrate. In Ireland, 1842 was the year of the great potato famine, with people dying of starvation; others fled abroad, to England and America to start new lives. Here in England, Lord Melbourne was under pressure to repeal the Corn Laws, which made the price of bread high and fostered much discontent amongst the working classes. At the end of today's much anticipated harvest festival, Romilly concluded: 'considering the wetness of the day and the deadness of this holiday time I thought the collection of more than £18 not bad … ' (Bury, M. and Pickles, J., *Romilly's Cambridge Diary*, Cambridge Records Society: 1994)

September 12th

2010: On this day, over 5,000 people came to the Imperial War Museum at Duxford near Cambridge to watch the dedication and unveiling of a memorial to Royal Anglian Regiment soldiers killed in battle. The memorial came after more than £340,000 was raised through a fund-raising campaign, launched after nine members of the regiment were killed in the 1st Battalion's 2007 tour of Afghanistan's Helmand province. The seventy-eight soldiers named on the memorial died serving their country in various battle zones, including Afghanistan, Iraq, Northern Ireland and Yemen. Hymns were sung, prayers were said and each name on the memorial was read out from a roll of honour; after the Regiment's Colonel in Chief, the Duke of Gloucester, had made a speech and the Last Post had rung out from a solo bugle player, each family was given time to lay personal tributes on the memorial before it was opened to the public. The Royal Anglian Regiment chose Duxford as the location for their memorial as the regimental museum is already located there. The Duke of Gloucester paid tribute to the fallen soldiers and said that the memorial had been 'a long time coming.' (*Peterborough Evening Telegraph*)

September 13th

1783: On this day, the following announcement appeared in the *Cambridge Chronicle*: 'To be sold, a freehold building known as the chapel of Stirbitchfair [*sic*]. The tenant draws between 7 and 8 barrels of beer during the fair. It is also convenient for laying up building materials for the fair.' The chapel in question is a little gem of Norman architecture; it is dedicated to St Mary Magdalene but is most commonly known as the Leper Chapel. The chapel was originally built in the late twelfth century at the heart of a community of lepers, following a statement from the Council of Westminster in 1175 which declared: 'lepers should never circulate amongst the healthy … these lepers would beg together, eat together and meet for divine service in their distant hospital far removed from the bounds of the town.' The lepers left as early as 1279 but live on in the chapel's name. In the twenty-first century the Leper Chapel is used for education, cultural events and worship, even serving occasionally as the highly atmospheric setting for the telling of ghost stories … (Jones, Chester H., *The Chapel of St Mary Magdalene*, CUP: 1926 / Haigh, D., *The Religious Houses of Cambridgeshire*, Cambridgeshire County Council: 1988)

September 14th

1853: On this day, Joseph Romilly was not impressed by the number of visitors descending on Cambridge. No fewer than 500 members of the Temperance Society from Kings Lynn arrived in Cambridge on an excursion train today, enjoyed a picnic lunch on Christ's Pieces and then went to visit the Fitzwilliam Museum. Romilly was able to stay somewhat aloof from this invasion as he stayed in College 'looking out passages in Aristophanes and Pindar', but his sister Lucy got caught up in the fracas. Following a calming walk in the Botanic Garden, Romilly and Lucy had dinner then went to Downing College to see 850 Sunday Scholars from Barnwell have their annual treat. Romilly professed himself 'much pleased' with the address to the children, in which it was said that 'people could not always mow without wetting [*sic*] their scythe ... so, boys and girls must sometimes sharpen their wit by good hearty play'. The children went on to sing a song about the stately homes of England, which Romilly thought was an absurd song choice for pauper children, but 'the blackbird was a very pretty song'. (Bury, M. and Pickles, J., *Romilly's Cambridge Diary*, Cambridge Records Society: 2000)

September 15th

1989: On this day, a very special wedding took place in the Chapel of Gonville and Caius College in Cambridge between two octogenarian biochemists, Professor Joseph Needham and his long-term Chinese lover and muse, Lu Gwei-djen. Both supporting themselves with sticks, both stooping and white haired they smiled broadly as they entered the chapel, she wearing a blue cheongsam with a bold peony print and he in a crumpled, elderly suit; in his younger days Needham had been described as looking like 'an unmade bed' and his style did not improve with age. At the celebration lunch in Hall, Needham said: 'It may seem rather astonishing for two octogenarians to be standing here together, but my motto is *Better late than never!*' Needham had previously been married for decades to fellow biochemist Dorothy Moyle, who accepted Gwei-djen into their marriage effectively as a second wife. The ashes of all three are scattered in the Needham Institute in Cambridge, home to the 'Science and Civilisation in China Project', started by Joseph Needham and still continuing today. Gwei-djen died of bronchial pneumonia just two years after their wedding, whereupon Needham invited three other women to marry him. All politely declined. (Winchester, S., *Bomb, Book and Compass*, Penguin: 2009)

September 16th

1849: On this day, in the early hours of the morning, fire raged through the heart of Cambridge. Josiah Chater wrote in his diary: 'There were 5 or 6 engines … most of them no better than squirts. The fire raged until 6 o'clock and burned down 8 houses and seriously damaged several more, all tradesmen's … I must confess though…that it was a glorious sight and when the chemist's was on fire, every time a bottle cracked there was an explosion superior to fireworks.' Miraculously, there was no loss of life, though many people were very close to being crushed under collapsing walls and beams. It was established that the fire had started in the house of Mr Lodge, a clothier; despite rumours that he had deliberately caused it because he was in dire financial straits there was no evidence to explain its cause. A few days later, plans began to emerge for a 'new-look' market place; Pump Lane disappeared altogether, the central block of houses in the square was never rebuilt and Hobson's Conduit was moved to its present site in Lensfield Road. This was the beginning of the market place as we know it today. (Porter, E., *Josiah Chater's Diaries*, Phillimore: 1975)

September 17th

1912: On this day, the Cambridge newspaper headlines were dramatic: 'Invaders advancing. Cambridge threatened'. There was, however, no cause for alarm; the British army's autumn manoeuvres were taking place, Cambridge was the headquarters of the army staff and 'for the first time on record the Sovereign will be present to witness the manoeuvres'. And indeed today King George V arrived by overnight train from Balmoral in Scotland and drove through cheering crowds to have breakfast in Trinity College with the Master, Dr Butler. Cambridge was transformed; there was a sentry box near the main gates of Trinity College, the Porters' Lodge had become a guardroom and dozens of special trains arrived from Salisbury Plain bringing troops. An airship caused a sensation by landing on Midsummer Common, where 'army camps' were based. Mock battles were fought between opposing camps and on the following day the King and his generals held a conference in Trinity College to discuss the lessons they had learnt from the manoeuvres. The King found time to visit his late brother Albert Victor's rooms in Nevile Court before heading back to Balmoral. The manoeuvres were over and the *New York Herald* summed up: 'magnificent, but it was not war'. (Colthorpe, M., *Royal Cambridge*, Cambridge City Council: 1977)

September 18th

1789: On this day, the annual Stourbridge Fair, one of the largest fairs in Europe, opened in Cambridge with great ceremony, causing Henry Gunning to record: 'At 11am the Vice-Chancellor, with the Bedells and ... the Proctors ... attended [the ceremony of proclaiming Stourbridge Fair] in the Senate House, where a plentiful supply of mulled wine and sherry, in black bottles, with a great variety of cakes, awaited their arrival. Strange as it may seem, the company partook of these things as heartily as if they had come without their breakfasts, or were apprehensive of going without their dinners. This important business ended, the parties proceeded to the Fair, in carriages provided for the occasion. The proclamation was read by the Registrary in the carriage with the Vice-Chancellor and repeated by the Yeoman Bedell on horseback, in three different places ... the company alighted for the dispatch of business – and of oysters ... on the table were placed several barrels of oysters, with ale and bottled porter in great profusion ... This [eating oysters] was *a very serious part* of the day's proceedings and occupied a long time'. Oyster Row is now a small street just a stone's throw from Stourbridge Common. (Gunning, H., *Reminiscences*, George Bell: 1854)

September 19th

2008: On this day, Professor Stephen Hawking unveiled a clock which he said would become 'a much loved and possibly feared addition to Cambridge's cityscape.' The gold-plated timepiece, 4ft across and topped by a grotesque mutant grasshopper called the 'chronophage' or time-eater, was created and paid for by Dr John Taylor, who studied at Corpus Christi in Cambridge in the 1950s. Taylor made his fortune by inventing a switch that enables a cordless electric kettle to connect with its base. The clock has no hands or numbers; the time is told instead by blue LED lights, which glimmer through slits on the clock face. Its time is only relative, not absolute; the time-eater sometimes stops and sometimes goes faster, just as we perceive time sometimes going faster or more slowly. The time is corrected every five minutes. Unveiling the clock, Professor Hawking said: 'Why does time go forward? Does time have a beginning and an end? Can one go sideways in time?' And as you ponder these questions, listen to the clock on the hour, when chains fall into a wooden coffin behind the clock face, reminding us all of our own mortality... (*Cambridge Evening News*)

September 20th

1961: On this day, John Roach, Domestic Bursar, was the first member of Corpus Christi College to move into new accommodation at Leckhampton; designated for Fellows and graduate students, Leckhampton House, conveniently located just off Grange Road, was acquired by the college on 26 June and was completely renovated and ready for its new occupants less than two months later. The renovation work was hampered by the previous owner's enormous walk-in safe, whose demolition employed a gang of men with pneumatic drills for over a fortnight. Seven research students from Canada arrived just after John Roach; forty years later, four of these students arranged to meet for a reunion and spent a very enjoyable and nostalgic weekend at Leckhampton with their wives in September 2001. In the early days, the house had something of the atmosphere of a pre-war country house. Breakfast was served for all nine residents every day and the Sunday teas became a highlight of the week. The accommodation was extended in 1969 with the opening of the George Thomson building, widely acclaimed as 'one of the best collegiate buildings to be erected since the war.' (Bury, M.E. and Winter, E.J., *Corpus Christi Within Living Memory*, Third Millennium: 2003)

September 21st

2008: On this day, an eminent Cambridge scientist died at the Hope Nursing Home in Cambridge. Professor Sir Brian Pippard had been both the Cavendish Professor of Physics at the University of Cambridge and the also the first President of the newly founded graduate college, Clare Hall. Pippard had first arrived as an undergraduate in Cambridge intending to be a chemist, but when the Second World War broke out his tutor said that chemists were not needed, but physicists were. Like many of the brightest wartime graduates, he was later recruited for wartime research, in particular work on radar aerials. Pippard is noted for demonstrating the presence of the Fermi surface in metals, which is useful in predicting the physical properties of solids, such as semiconductors. Described in his *Guardian* obituary as a 'mild eccentric' and 'multi-faceted', he was not only an outstanding physicist but also an innovator in science education, a science historian and a classical pianist of concert standard. Pippard created a fund to support graduate students, as his obituary concludes: 'His enormous enthusiasm for science, which has touched generations, now has a life of its own.' (*The Guardian / Cambridge News*)

September 22nd

1800: On this day, a royal charter 'passed the Great Seal' for the foundation of Downing College, the first college to be founded in Cambridge for over 200 years. Reactions were mixed; some hoped that its foundation would mark a turning point in the University, affording the opportunity to change outdated statutes and to meet the needs and requirements of a changed world. Several other colleges were however already under-subscribed and some felt that a new college would only add to 'an overstocked market'. In reality, Downing College started life poverty-stricken and with few prospects. The fortune which had been left to Downing College in 1749 by Sir George Downing (from the same family who built Downing Street in London) had been badly eroded over the years by legal wrangles between members of the Downing family and the University. It was not until March 1800 that the Lord Chancellor pronounced a final decree in favour of the foundation of the college. The development of the college buildings was therefore slow and spasmodic, the first ones being built between 1807 and 1812 to the design of William Wilkins, who in later years went on to design the National Gallery in London's Trafalgar Square. (Winstanley, D.A., *Early Victorian Cambridge*, CUP: 1940 / Downing College Handbook)

September 23rd

1992: On this day, the first *Chariots of Fire* charity race took place, in the grounds of the Perse School in Cambridge. Advertised as a 'fun event, open to all', it was a relay race, with six runners per team; each runner runs about one and a half miles, a distance achievable by anyone with a modest amount of training. A good number of teams signed up, including a team from the Coldstream Guards carrying 40lb rucksacks. Becoming a popular annual event, the race later moved to central Cambridge, starting on Queen's Green and wending its way through the streets and colleges of the historic city centre. The event name was inspired by the film *Chariots of Fire*, some of which was filmed in Cambridge. Local businessman Sir Arthur Marshall was the race's first Honorary President; he had himself taken part in the 1924 Olympic Games so was able to regale spectators with personal reminiscences of athletes such as Abrahams, Liddell and Burghley who were portrayed in the film. The race, which attracts around 2,000 runners every year, was started in 2003 by Lord David Puttnam, director of the *Chariots of Fire* film, and in 2010 by actress and comedian Jennifer Saunders. (*Chariots of Fire*, 2003)

September 24th

1828: On this day, Charles Simeon, evangelical preacher, vicar of the Holy Trinity Church in Cambridge and Fellow of King's College, marked his birthday in the same way he did every year. Whilst many would take advantage of their birthday to have a few drinks with friends and to indulge perhaps in a special cake, Simeon made a very deliberate attempt to humiliate himself in repentance and self-reproof. His diary entry for this day reads: 'I spent this day as I have for these forty-three last years, as a day of humiliation; having increasing need of such seasons every year I live.' In his notebook he wrote out twice over in large letters: 'Talk not about myself'. Simeon always remembered the lesson from his kind elderly advisor John Thornton in 1788, who reminded him of 'the three lessons which a minister has to learn, 1.Humility, 2.Humility, 3.Humility'. Charles Simeon died eight years later, in 1836; on the day of his funeral the town council closed all the shops and all university lectures were suspended, but his final resting place in King's College Chapel is marked by a suitably humble and unassuming slab, simply inscribed 'C.S. 1836'. (Hopkins, H., *Charles Simeon of Cambridge*, Hodder & Stoughton: 1977)

September 25th

1808: On this day, the Cambridge classicist Richard Porson died in London, aged forty-eight. Porson had been walking in the Strand when he collapsed in a fit and since he was paralysed, incoherent and initially unidentifiable, he was taken to a nearby workhouse. Some scraps of Greek and algebra found in his pockets alerted the authorities to his identity and he was looked after by friends until his death in his rooms at the London Institution. Porson was later buried near Isaac Newton's statue in Trinity College Chapel, during a ceremony attended by many leading academics of the day. Among Porson's many skills was an ability to write satiric verse, usually political in intent and destined for the columns of the *Morning Chronicle*. A keen drinker, he famously penned the following lines, whose wit might be lost on modern readers:

> I went to Strasburg where I got drunk
> With that most learn'd Professor Brunck:
> I went to Wortz, where I got more drunken
> With that more learn'd Professor Ruhnken.

(Whibley, C., *In Cap and Gown*, Heinemann: 1898)

September 26th

1948: On this day, Mr Brinley Newton-John, highly respected headmaster of Cambridgeshire High School for Boys and his wife Irene, daughter of Nobel Prize-winning physicist Max Born, became parents for the first time. Their daughter Olivia loved singing from an early age and later gained international fame. The Newton-John family lived at 343 Hills Road in Cambridge and Olivia later recalled a carefree childhood, especially enjoying punting on the River Cam. The family moved to Australia when Olivia was five; she went on to win talent competitions, becoming a household name when she hosted her own children's TV programme, called *Lovely Livvy.* A glittering career was just beginning and she broadened her horizons further by moving back to the UK, recording several songs with Cliff Richard and even being chosen to represent Great Britain in the Eurovision Song Contest. Most people remember Olivia however for donning super-tight black leather trousers and playing the vamp alongside John Travolta in *Grease*, one of the most successful films of all time. Now back in Australia, she recently told the *Cambridge Evening News* that she would love to return to Cambridge one day and visit her childhood haunts. The newspaper in return called Olivia 'one of Cambridge's most prized exports'. (*Cambridge Evening News*)

September 27th

2002: On this day, broadcaster and naturalist Sir David Attenborough came face-to-face with 'Megarachne', the world's largest spider, when he officially re-opened Cambridge University's Sedgwick Museum of Earth Sciences. Today marked the culmination of a huge renovation programme, with new displays, models and visitor resources. One of the most popular displays featured Megarachne, a full size model, complete with human hair on its long legs, of what was considered to be the world's largest spider, reconstructed from a 300,000,000-year-old Argentinian fossil. The spider stands proudly alongside Edwardian display cases which have been here since King Edward VII opened the museum in 1904 but which were only properly illuminated, to spectacular effect, during the recent renovations. Sir David Attenborough said: 'Displaying rocks and fossils in cases is all very well, but lighting them beautifully and then showing how they can help us to understand the complex history of our planet is something else and these new galleries do it marvellously well. I am delighted with the changes made since I was a student.' The Sedgwick Museum is open to the public throughout the year free of charge, but anyone suffering from arachnophobia should enter with extreme caution ... (Cambridge University Press Office)

September 28th

2009: On this day, illustrator Quentin Blake, a graduate of Downing College, unveiled fifteen original drawings at Addenbrooke's Hospital in Cambridge. Celebrating the 800th anniversary of the University of Cambridge, the drawings formed a mural; described as 'Cambridge's answer to the Bayeux Tapestry', it depicts some of the most distinguished people connected with the University over its 800-year history. An irritable-looking Henry VIII can be seen listening to the choir of King's College Chapel whilst Charles Darwin sits reading on top of a giant Galapagos tortoise. Poet Lord Byron is portrayed leaning on the bear that he is reputed to have kept while resident at Trinity College. Rosalind Franklin, the Cambridge scholar whose X-ray diffusion images proved vital to the discovery of the structure of DNA, also features. Two months later, when essential repair works were being carried out on the screen in front of King's College, Quentin Blake gave his permission for four of the drawings (Henry VIII, Darwin, Newton and Milton) to be reproduced and enlarged to form a massive mural, 100ft long and 26ft high to hide the scaffolding behind. For a couple of months, the mural was almost as much of a tourist attraction as the nearby King's College Chapel. (*The Times* / Cambridge University Press Office)

September 29th

1789: On this day, Francis Dawes, Senior Fellow and Bursar of Peterhouse, had organised a sumptuous dinner for several 'county families' who were in Cambridge for the annual Stourbridge Fair. Guests started to arrive, but there was no sign of Dawes. The College garden and grove were searched, to no avail; eventually someone went to the old tower in Peterhouse, where Dawes was found hanging, and 'must have been so many hours, being quite cold'. Dawes was to make national headlines over 200 years later, when his ghost allegedly returned to haunt Peterhouse, a story which features on many Cambridge ghost tours. (Gunning, H., *Reminiscences*, George Bell: 1854)

———— • ————

2004: On this day, a new £15m English Faculty building was officially opened on the University's Sidgwick Site by English alumnus, comic and broadcaster Griff Rhys Jones. Wine flowed, foot-tapping jazz was played and extracts were read from classic English novels and poems. The Faculty of English was founded in 1919 but had never, until now, had a central building of its own. (*Cambridge Evening News* / University of Cambridge Press Office)

September 30th

1900: On this day, Alan Alexander Milne was among the new students who signed the Admissions Book at Trinity College. A.A. Milne was given rooms on P staircase in Whewell's Court; thirty-nine years later, the same rooms were inherited by his son, Christopher Robin Milne. Milne had help in installing his belongings, which included some blue velvet curtains and elaborate cushions (the latter embroidered in gold thread) that his mother had made for him. Milne soon began contributing what he called 'Milnicks' to *The Granta* (Cambridge literary magazine) under the initials A.K.M. (because he collaborated for a while with his brother Kenneth). At the beginning of his second year, Milne received an unexpected invitation to take over the editorship of *Granta*, alarming his tutor, who feared that he would be distracted from his studies and might even lose the chance 'to become something respectable like an accountant'. As it was, Milne was quickly talent-spotted and recruited for *Punch* magazine, but his whole writing career was overshadowed by the huge success of his books for children, especially the stories of *Winnie the Pooh*. (Thwaite, A., *A.A. Milne*, Faber: 1990 / Chainey, G., *A Literary History of Cambridge*, Pevensey Press: 1985)

October 1st

2001: On this day, a new £7,500,000 mathematical library opened in Cambridge. The building was named the Betty and Gordon Moore Library, commemorating its donor Dr Gordon Moore, co-founder of the Intel Corporation. It was to be another two years before the Moores visited in person to open the building officially and unveil a plaque, saying in the opening speech: 'There's no other university in the world with a comparable long record. Given the opportunity to help them we are happy to.' The four-floor circular building was inspired by Thomas Jefferson's designs for the library at the University of Virginia and houses over 190,000 scientific volumes on its 9,000 metres of shelving. The library contains the Stephen Hawking archive, some of which is on display. The Hawking exhibition includes a photograph of the cosmologist in command of the *Starship Enterprise*, taken during the filming of *Star Trek*, and a letter from President Bill Clinton thanking him for delivering the White House Millennium Lecture. The star turn is however an annotated script from the *Simpsons* cartoon series, where Hawking says to Principal Skinner: 'I don't know which is the bigger disappointment, my failure to formulate a workable unified field theory ... or you.' (*Cambridge Evening News*)

October 2nd

1996: On this day, the British intelligence agency GCHQ exposed seventy-year-old Cambridge physicist Dr Theodore Hall as a senior KGB spy, in files made public only after the Americans placed them on the internet. To his neighbours in Owlstone Road in Cambridge, Dr Hall and his wife were 'that nice American couple', little realising that fifty years previously he had been MLAD, the KGB agent inside the Manhattan Project, the secret operation to develop the atomic bomb. The information leaked by Hall helped the Russians produce a bomb much faster than they would otherwise have done. The FBI identified him in 1961 as the perpetrator of what J. Edgar Hoover had described as 'the crime of the century'. Hall only escaped prosecution because any publicity would have revealed the extent to which the West was reading the KGB's messages. And so Hall emigrated to Britain and carved out a distinguished, if low key career in the Cavendish Laboratory in Cambridge. Already frail for several years from cancer and Parkinson's disease, Hall died three years after this exposure. His obituary in *The Independent* called him 'the spy who got away with it'. (*Cambridge Evening News / The Independent*)

October 3rd

1895: On this day, Ernest Rutherford, two days after arriving in Cambridge, bought a *6d* notebook, writing on the flyleaf 'E. Rutherford Cavendish Laboratory Oct 3/95'. Rutherford had recently been awarded a research scholarship from his native New Zealand; he later recalled that he was at his parents' home digging potatoes when he heard the good news about his scholarship. He threw down his spade and declared: 'That's the last potato I will ever dig!' Rutherford knew no one in Cambridge and was living on borrowed money; all he had was a scholarship, his radio-wave detector and a few letters of introduction. In his first letter home he wrote: 'It is of course a bit strange at first with all one's friends across the sea...' Rutherford had already shown an interest in X-rays, which had recently been discovered by the German researcher Röntgen. In one of his letters home, Rutherford sent his mother X-rays of a frog skeleton and a hand. These may have been the first X-rays ever seen in New Zealand, and were a source of great fascination for all. In later years, scientist Max Born was to say: 'Rutherford was the greatest scientist I have ever known, including even Einstein.' (Smith, P., *Rutherford*, Educational Solutions: 2000)

October 4th

1671: On this day, King Charles II visited Cambridge, requesting that all speeches should be 'few and short or none'. On his arrival, the King was presented with 100 twenty-shilling pieces of broad gold in a crimson coloured velvet purse with a gold fringe and gold strings. As the King processed through Cambridge, accompanied by royal trumpeters, the conduit ran with claret wine and on his departure, the University counted the cost of the day's entertainment at £1,039 5s 1d. (Colthorpe, M., *Royal Cambridge*, Cambridge City Council: 1977)

———◆———

1913: On this day, the Gaiety Theatre opened on Auckland Road in Cambridge, only to close two years later. The building was put to various uses over the years, being used as a garage by the Great Eastern Railway and more recently by Midsummer Glassmakers. The site has now been converted to housing. The Gaiety Theatre was built on the site of the old Hippodrome; described as 'a bit of flea pit', the theatre showed early Charlie Chaplin films and there is even a rumour that Chaplin himself visited at one point. (Payne, S., *Down Your Street*, Pevensey Press: 1984)

October 5th

1983: On this day, while the paint was still fresh on the walls, the first babies were delivered in the new Rosie Maternity Hospital in Cambridge. The Rosie was a 104-bed purpose-built unit, a huge improvement on the previous cramped accommodation in Mill Road, Cambridge (a building originally used as a Victorian workhouse). Despite being an NHS hospital, this vision only came to fruition thanks to a large donation from Cambridge-born millionaire and philanthropist Sir David Robinson (Robinson College is named after him). Sir David, who left school at fourteen to work in his father's bicycle shop before making a fortune in the TV rental business, donated £3m (half the total costs) to the new building. He wanted it to be named 'the Rosie' in memory of his mother, who died giving birth to her tenth child in 1922. Sir David never spoke publicly about his donation, but did impose one demanding condition: that the hospital had to be built before the end of 1983. This was a very tight schedule, reached largely thanks to the personal intervention of Prime Minister Margaret Thatcher, prompting the headline in the *Cambridge News* of 'Maggie – Rosie's champion'. (*Cambridge Evening News*)

October 6th

1943: On this day, a taxi pulled up outside Emmanuel College in Cambridge and out stepped Frank Dobie, an American academic from Austin, Texas. Dobie was to spend a year at Cambridge as guest lecturer in American history; in his spare time he jotted down comments about Cambridge University life and traditions and also scoured the dozens of American 8th Air Force bases in the area, seeking out fellow Texans. Cultural differences were apparent from the very first day at Emmanuel, when Dobie was the only Fellow at dinner not wearing a gown; on filling his pipe after dinner, he was informed that he was 'heading in the wrong direction' since smoking could not start until a toast of welcome had been recorded in the book kept in the Combination Room. Dobie later wrote a fascinating account of his Cambridge stay in wartime England, an outsider's view not only of the University system (he found the colleges' relationship with the University to be analogous to American States and the Union) but also of the reality of life in Cambridge in the 1940s, from rationing to student pranks (inebriated undergraduates once stole his Texan hat to put on the college flagpole). (Dobie, Frank J., *A Texan in England*, Hammond, Hammond & Co.: 1946)

October 7th

1689: On this day, nineteen years after his visit as the dashing young Prince of Orange, William returned to Cambridge as King William III; his title was very recent, having been ruling jointly with his English wife Queen Mary for only a few months. The King was given a lavish and jubilant welcome on Christ's Pieces. After the usual honorary degree ceremony and visit to King's College Chapel, most of the King's day was spent in Trinity College and he had the distinction of being the first monarch to visit the newly completed Wren Library. The University of Cambridge has preserved no fewer than fifty-four separate bills for payments connected with this visit and they make fascinating reading, giving clues as to the epic scale of the entertainment which had been laid on, for example: '16 dozen larks, 16s; 16 large fat geese £2.82; peacocks and pigeons ... 'Also thirteen shillings 'paid to six poor people to pull and draw all these fowls.' King William, in return, toasted the University and wished them prosperity. A few weeks later, the Vice-Chancellor of the University generously sent 74 guineas to London to be distributed as 'our gratuities to His Majesty's servants'. (Colthorpe, M., *Royal Cambridge*, Cambridge City Council: 1977)

October 8th

1890: On this day, one of the largest Roman Catholic churches in the country was consecrated in Cambridge. This huge church, built largely thanks to money gifted by a former French ballerina called Yolande Lyne-Stephens, still dominates the busy traffic junction of Lensfield Road and Hills Road. It is dedicated to Our Lady of the Assumption and the English Martyrs, since it was on the Feast of the Assumption that Mrs Lyne-Stephens decided to build the church; it was also considered important to commemorate the Catholic martyrs who died for their faith between 1535 and 1681, many of whom had been in residence at Cambridge University. Some criticised the church's neo-Gothic style but most welcomed the new building, whose spire matches the height of Ely Cathedral. The first mass in the church was attended by all the bishops of England and Wales, apart from two who were unable to come because of ill health. After the opening, Our Lady and English Martyrs (better known today by the acronym OLEM) saw a great rise in the number of Catholics in the parish and the church today still offers visitors a quiet oasis of calm just yards away from a busy road junction. (Wilkins, P., *Our Lady and the English Martyrs, Cambridge*, John Burns & Sons: 1995)

October 9th

1967: On this day, an eighteen year old Prince Charles, having achieved a grade B in history and a C in French, arrived at Trinity College in Cambridge to study archaeology and anthropology. The Prince had been driven to Cambridge in a red Mini by an equerry but arrived about fourteen minutes late, having been delayed by traffic. As he stepped from the car to be greeted by the Master, Lord Butler of Saffron Walden (known to many as RAB Butler), he found that more than a thousand sightseers had gathered outside the Great Gate of Trinity College. Someone in the crowd shouted 'Good luck!' and the Prince turned round with a smile and answered 'I shall need it!' As time went by, Charles was to be seen regularly cycling to lectures, buying food from market traders and turning up at pubs and restaurants unannounced. Years later, in a BBC documentary marking his sixtieth birthday in 2008, Prince Charles admitted that his time at Cambridge University had been tough for him, saying: 'You either had to sink or swim and that is what a lot of people never seem to understand.' (*The Times / Cambridge Evening News*)

October 10th

1662: On this day, Samuel Pepys recorded in his diary a visit to Cambridge, which began with partaking of 'a barrel of good oysters, a couple of lobsters and wine' then continued with a visit to the Regent House for the election of University officers. Four years after this diary entry, Pepys was to write an eyewitness account of the Great Fire of London as he sat in the tower of All Hallows Church near the Tower of London. The original diaries of Samuel Pepys are now kept in his old college of Magdalene. (Waterlow, S., *In Praise of Cambridge*, Constable & Co.: 1912)

———◆———

2001: On this day, a University press release welcomed to Cambridge the first of the Gates Scholars, 'some of the brightest young people in the world'. Their fees and living costs were paid by a $210 million trust set up by the Bill and Melinda Gates Foundation that will run in perpetuity and enable gifted graduate students from around the world to study at Cambridge. The benefaction was the largest single sum received by the University to date. (Cambridge University News Service)

October 11th

2006: On this day, a special congregation was held in the Senate House when HRH Prince Philip, Chancellor of the University of Cambridge, bestowed an honorary degree on the Prime Minister of India, Dr Manmohan Singh. Dr Singh had the honour of being the only recipient on this occasion and the Senate House was full of senior University academics and a large number of Indians studying in Cambridge. Dr Singh was brought up in a farming family he has described as 'very, very poor' and yet he won a Punjabi scholarship to study at Cambridge, coming to St John's College to study economics in 1955 when he was twenty-three years old. A brilliant student, he took his finals less than two years later, obtaining First Class Honours, the only first in economics to be awarded that year. He went on to take a doctorate at Oxford University, making him the most highly educated Indian Prime Minister in history. Dr Singh later said that his time at St John's College was one of the happiest periods of his life and the time when he learned the most. In his speech today, he said: 'In many important ways, the University of Cambridge made me.' (Cambridge University News Service)

October 12th

1487: On this day, John Alcock, Bishop of Ely, visited the nunnery of St Radegund in Cambridge and was not impressed by what he saw. His findings were recorded in a register where he wrote that the nunnery was 'destitute of the solace of the Prioress … the nuns unfit and disqualified to elect their future Prioress and therefore decree that in such manner of election they are justly deprived of voice.' Alcock chose Mistress Joan Fulbourne to take over the nunnery, but things were to deteriorate still further. A contemporary, John Mair, wrote that the morals of the sisterhood were 'not all that they should be' and others said that the nuns 'cast off the veil and voluntarily withdrew and that the buildings lay for some time deserted and desolate'. Bishop Alcock visited again in 1495, when it was reported that 'the buildings … of the house are dilapidated and wasted owing to the improvidence, extravagance and incontinence of the nuns … Two nuns only remain: one of them is … elsewhere, the other is of ill fame (*infamis*).' The nunnery was closed down and Alcock founded Jesus College on the site in 1496. Some of the original nunnery buildings have survived and are still in use today. (Gray, A., *A History of Jesus College*, Heinemann: 1960)

October 13th

1565: On this day, Evensong in St John's College Chapel was so controversial that in the twenty-first century it is still known simply as the 'St John's Incident'. For the last five years the College Masters (but by no means all the Fellowship) had been keen supporters of the Reformation, removing 'Popish trash' from the Chapel and even turning part of Bishop Fisher's chantry into a room for the Master. College Fellow William Fulke inflamed the situation by a series of controversial sermons, stating that if God did not take surplices away then the Devil might. Taking this to heart, a group of undergraduates gathered in the Chapel, without their surplices, on October 13 and proceeded to hiss and barrack others who were wearing them, forcing many to retreat. The Master, to the horror of some of the Fellows, openly condoned the whole incident and complimented publicly those who had rejected the surplice. The controversy led to a 'civil war' in the college, leading to the surplice incident being discussed on a national level. Eventually the issue died down, and Fulke, less confrontational in his later years, became Maser of Pembroke College in Cambridge. (Miller, E., *Portrait of a College*, St John's College: 1993 / Porter, H.C., *Reformation and Reaction in Tudor Cambridge*, CUP: 1958)

October 14th

1945: On this day, a college with a difference was 'founded'; the college was given a Master, Major George Blank, but had no official affiliation to the University of Cambridge. Bull College was the brainchild of the Provost of King's College, Dr J.T. Sheppard, who at the end of the Second World War decided to put the Bull Hotel, an old coaching inn sandwiched between St Catharine's and King's Colleges, to good use. During the war, the hotel had become the headquarters and service club of the American Red Cross in Cambridge. In October 1945, 149 American servicemen arrived to spend the Michaelmas term in Cambridge under the US Army's *Information and Education Program* and many of them were billeted in the Bull Hotel. The students recorded their time in Cambridge in a publication entitled *The Bull* and even drew up their own coat of arms. Academic studies in Bull College ranged from classics, law, history and English to education, geography and moral sciences. Shortly after this brief existence of Bull College, St Catharine's College converted the building into new student accommodation, which it remains to this day. (*The Cambridge Bull*, King's College Library)

October 15th

1827: On this day, a young Charles Darwin, having realised that medical studies in Edinburgh were not for him, enrolled at Christ's College in Cambridge with a view to becoming a clergyman. Taking a few months off for some private tutoring for his rather rusty Latin and Greek, Darwin eventually moved to Cambridge the following January, taking lodgings in Sidney Street; on the site today is Boots the Chemists, which sports a very small plaque commemorating its illustrious former resident. (Van Wyhe, J., *Darwin in Cambridge*, Christ's College: 2009)

———◆———

1946: On this day, Herbert Morrison, Labour politician and Deputy Prime Minister, took part in a packed debate in the Cambridge University Union on the subject of state control of economic affairs. The first speaker professed that the motion must have been drafted by 'an elderly and dyspeptic civil servant', being quite unaware that Morrison himself had drafted the motion's wording. Morrison's grandson, Peter Mandelson, later followed in his grandfather's footsteps to become a Labour Cabinet Minister. (Parkinson, S., *Arena of Ambition*, Icon Books: 2009)

October 16th

1987: On this day, Cambridge weatherman Peter Ashton found he had two new records following the devastating storm which had taken place during the night: at 100mph, the wind had been the fiercest ever recorded in Cambridge and the barometer reading was the lowest ever. There was huge damage to trees; 300 were lost in the city alone and nearby Anglesey Abbey lost many valuable specimens. Two lorry drivers had a very lucky escape when they were having an early breakfast at 4 a.m. in the Autostop Cafe, New Wimpole; the chimney of the building next door fell through the roof on to the table next to them. Racing history of an unusual kind was made at Newmarket when a meeting was abandoned for the first time since 1908. There were chaotic scenes at the racecourse followed by a frantic but effective clear-up operation which enabled the 'Cesarewitch' to go ahead the following day as planned. Train services were however severely disrupted, with no trains at all running between London and Cambridge; the storms had brought down overhead wires and the lines themselves were full of debris. (Ogley, B., and Reynolds, K., *Eye on the Hurricane*, Froglets Publications: 1989)

October 17th

1959: On this day, Sir Winston Churchill planted an oak tree in the grounds of what was to become Churchill College, the national and Commonwealth memorial to the world-renowned statesman. Fifty years later to the day, Sir Winston's eighty-seven-year-old daughter Lady Mary Soames planted a weeping mulberry tree nearby, using the same spade her father had used. This tree-planting launched a year of celebrations to mark the fiftieth anniversary of a college which had been conceived by Churchill as a Cambridge seat of learning dominated by science and technology students. He had been inspired by the Massachusetts Institute of Technology in the United States and wanted to create a similar institute here, whilst still incorporating a mix of non-scientists. At formal college dinners, the Master still regularly makes a toast first to the Queen and then to Sir Winston. Sir Winston Churchill was eighty-five years old when he planted the oak tree in 1959 and this was his only visit to the College. He would no doubt be proud to know that in its relatively short history, the College had seen twenty-four of its members go on to receive Nobel Prizes before its fiftieth birthday. (*Cambridge News*)

October 18th

1845: On this day, Joseph Romilly wrote in his diary: 'Thorwaldsen's statue of Lord Byron hoisted into Trinity Library thro the south window'. The statue of Lord Byron enjoys to this day a prominent position in the Wren Library at Trinity College. Lord Byron had led an exciting, dangerous and often dissolute lifestyle, leading to him being famously called 'mad, bad and dangerous to know'. After he died of fever, in Greece, a full length sculpture was crafted by Danish neo-classical sculptor Bertel Thorwaldsen, with the intention of it being placed in Poets' Corner in Westminster Abbey. The Abbey refused however to have his sculpture in their church, given his 'open profligacy' and lack of Christian beliefs. The sculpture languished for nine years in the Custom House in London before finally finding a home in Trinity College Cambridge, where he had been an undergraduate. It was not until 1969 that Byron was eventually honoured in Westminster Abbey, thanks to 'his poetic genius and mastery of the art of letter-writing'; his white marble floor memorial in Poets' Corner was given by the Poetry Society. (Bury, M. and Pickles, J., *Romilly's Cambridge Diary*, Cambridge Records Society: 1994 / Chainey, G., *A Literary History of Cambridge*, Pevensey Press: 1985 / *Westminster Abbey Official Guide*, 1977)

October 19th

1937: On this day, New Zealand scientist and Nobel laureate Lord Rutherford died in the Evelyn Nursing Home in Cambridge. Rutherford had been suffering from a strangulated hernia and was admitted to the Evelyn Nursing Home, a private hospital with full operating facilities. Because he was now a Lord, protocol demanded that the operation be performed by a titled surgeon rather than one of the perfectly competent local surgeons. The delay of eight hours was critical; his intestine stopped working and he went into a rapid decline. Rutherford's last words were about his love for his wife and his fond memories of New Zealand; he was sixty-six years old. The funeral was held six days later in Westminster Abbey, with many distinguished guests and wreaths from around the world. James Chadwick, who worked with Rutherford in Cambridge on splitting the atomic nucleus, said: 'The world mourns the death of a great scientist, but we have lost a friend, our counsellor, our staff and our leader'. An urn containing Lord Rutherford's ashes was placed in the Scientists' Corner of Westminster Abbey, near those of other great scientists, including Darwin, Faraday and Kelvin. The plaque reads simply, 'Ernest Baron Rutherford of Nelson'. (Campbell, J., *Rutherford: Scientist Supreme*, AAS Publications: 1999 / Smith, P., *Rutherford*, Educational Solutions: 2000)

October 20th

2007: On this day, a Cambridge student broke the record for the Great Court Run at Trinity College in Cambridge. This annual race, made famous in the 1980s film *Chariots of Fire*, challenges students to complete a 367 metre lap around Trinity Great Court in the time it takes the college bells to strike noon (43.6 seconds). Sam Dobin, aged nineteen, was only the third person to have completed the course on time, smashing the times of former Olympic champions Lord Burghley and Sebastian Coe. Sam, who was studying Economics at Trinity, said that beating the bells felt amazing: 'You can't hear the chimes during the race as the crowd is quite loud. I realised the crowd had gone quiet but it was only when I crossed the line and heard another chime that I thought: have I just done that?' Dobin now aims to run the 800m and 1,500m races in the London 2012 Olympic Games. A fictitious version of the Great Court Run formed a pivotal part of the 1981 film *Chariots of Fire*, which was a depiction of the story of Eric Liddle and Harold Abrahams, who ran in the 1924 Olympics in Paris. (*Cambridge Evening News*)

October 21st

1948: On this day, Queen Elizabeth, wife of King George VI (better known in later years as the Queen Mother), was granted an honorary degree in the Senate House, the first woman ever to receive a Cambridge University degree. In her honour, the flag of every college flew at full mast. Queen Elizabeth was driven from Anglesey Abbey to be welcomed by the Vice-Chancellor at Christ's College, which was in the middle of its celebrations for the quincentenary of God's House, its predecessor on the same site. But the highlight of the day was the conferral on the Queen of an honorary Doctorate of Law, watched approvingly by many women in the audience. In his speech, the University Orator recalled, in Latin, the visit of her namesake Queen Elizabeth (I) in 1564 and ended the speech with a prayer used on that occasion. Queen Elizabeth also made a speech to mark the historic occasion, telling her audience: 'The progressive emancipation of women during the past century is a story of courage and vision. To the women who will follow me in becoming members of the University, I would like to say ... the torch of learning has been handed to you.' (Colthorpe, M., *Royal Cambridge*, Cambridge City Council: 1977)

October 22nd

1934: On this day, the new University Library building was officially opened by King George V. Press reports of the time hailed the Library as 'extraordinarily impressive' and drew attention to its forty-three miles of shelving, the breadth of its holdings (ranging from priceless manuscripts to halfpenny comics) and the 'unobtrusive triumph of organisation' behind the transfer of books from the old premises to the new; almost one and a half million volumes had been transported from the old library to the new in 689 lorry loads, each drawn by a single horse. The library was designed by Giles Gilbert Scott, architect of the classic red telephone box and the Bankside power station, later to become the Tate Modern art gallery. The King and Queen were greeted at the library by the Chancellor of the University, Stanley Baldwin (who had studied at Trinity College and was soon to become Prime Minister for the third time). After the official opening ceremony, the royal couple toured the new library before emerging into the sunshine to find an excited crowd giving them cheer after cheer and hundreds of academic mortar boards raised in salute. (Colthorpe, M., *Royal Cambridge*, Cambridge City Council: 1977)

October 23rd

1876: On this day, James Stuart, Cambridge's first Professor of Mechanism and Applied Mechanics (Engineering in all but name), gave his inaugural lecture. Stuart had set up a small smithy at the back of the Jacksonian Lecture Room and employed a craftsman to produce models; one of these, the model of an ancient loom, was used in today's lecture. Recognising the importance of practical training for engineers, Stuart then persuaded the University to give him a wooden hut to serve as a workshop. This was done on condition that he furnish and equip it at his own expense. Darwin and Gladstone were among the early visitors to admire the new facility. As student numbers rose, Stuart begged for more space and in 1882 the University allotted him two cottages in Free School Lane, with a foundry in the garden of one of them. This was a cause of great concern to the Professor of Botany, over whose plants the foundry tended to smoke. Disagreements with the University led to Stuart's eventual resignation in 1890. Soon afterwards, he married Laura Colman and on the death of her father took over as Director of her family's well-known mustard company in Norwich. (Hilken, T.J.N., *Engineering at Cambridge University*, CUP: 1967 / Jackson, S., *Engineering 125*, Engineering Department: 2000)

October 24th

1805: On this day, just three days after the Battle of Trafalgar, Byron came up to Trinity College in Cambridge and quickly sorted out his priorities. Soon after his arrival Byron instructed his lawyer to order him four dozen bottles of wine, port and sherry, plus one dozen each of claret and Madeira. Quickly starting to 'admire' a college life, Byron felt that his appearance in the Hall in his state robes had been 'superb'. One month later, when the wine arrived, he wrote: 'no furniture has been got yet except what was absolutely necessary, including some decanters and wine glasses…' (Moseley, C., and Wilmer, C., *Cambridge Observed*, Colt Books: 1998)

———— •◆• ————

1958: On this day, philosopher G.E. Moore died in the Evelyn Nursing Home in Cambridge and was buried in the Ascension Burial Ground; his eminent colleague Wittgenstein would later be laid to rest nearby. Moore held that the best of lives is a life dedicated to friendship and beauty, a message taken to heart by his friends in the Bloomsbury Group, including Leonard Woolf and Maynard Keynes. (*Dictionary of National Biography*)

October 25th

1788: On this day, the newly paved and cobbled town-centre street Petty Cury was officially opened, the result of concerted efforts by both town and gown to improve the quality and safety of streets in central Cambridge. Earlier in the year, a commission of over seventy people had been established to improve conditions in the town centre, estimating that the work would take nine years. The first street lamps were soon lit and Petty Cury was the first street in Cambridge to be paved. The surveyors and others who had worked on the project paraded through the streets with a band and lighted torches, ending with dinner at the Wrestlers' Inn in Petty Cury; this inn was the finest of several on this small street and considered by some to be the town's answer to King's College Chapel. The inn was fronted with timber beams, intersected with brightly coloured plasterwork, pargetted in a design of Tudor roses with decorative borders. This building and others were demolished in 1885, their replacements standing until 1970 when the whole area was completely remodelled and pedestrianised, making way for the new Lion Yard shopping centre. (Payne, S., *Down Your Street*, Pevensey Press: 1983 / Leedham-Green, E., *A Concise History of the University of Cambridge*, CUP: 1996)

October 26th

1843: On this day, Queen Victoria, visiting Cambridge with her husband Prince Albert, experienced a 'Walter Raleigh moment' when a whole row of undergraduates threw off their gowns simultaneously and 'laid them upon the ground for Her Majesty to walk on.' Crowds had been gathering in central Cambridge since early morning, hoping to catch a glimpse of the royal visitors, who had spent the night in Trinity College. Prince Albert was due to receive an honorary doctorate and when the couple arrived at the Senate House there was 'a perfect hurricane of applause...again and again the shouts of welcome arose until one might have fancied the very walls of the building to shake'. Queen Victoria herself was less taken with the formality and Latin speeches in the Senate House than with the unusual exhibits in the nearby Geological Museum. Celebrated geologist Adam Sedgwick was there to meet them and wrote in his diary: 'I bowed as low as my anatomy would let me. The Queen seemed happy and well pleased and was mightily taken with one or two of my monsters, especially with the *plesiosaurus* and gigantic stag'. (Colthorpe, M., *Royal Cambridge*, Cambridge City Council: 1977)

October 27th

1784: On this day, Michael Lort, Fellow of Trinity College, wrote: 'Mr. Ainsly, the new Master of Downing, has been here to fix … a site for his new college … Mr Wyat, the architect, wishes much that it should be opposite to some of the colleges on the river, for then he thinks he shall not be crampt for room, and they may make four fine façades; but how will they get an access to and communications with, the town? The most promising spot seems to be that between Bishop Watson's house and the Tennis Court … The King has recommended two particulars – that it may not be a Gothic building, and that the professors be obliged to publish their lectures.' This letter was written sixteen years before the birth of Downing College; the work of its first Master was thus to establish the college, having died before the first undergraduates arrived and also before there was much in the way of buildings. Over a century later, Pettit Stevens commented: 'It may be a satisfaction that we owe the severe classical style of the Master's Lodge and the Hall to the taste of no less a personage than the King George III.' (Pettit Stevens, H.W., *Downing College*, F.E. Robinson: 1899 / Jackson, S., *Engineering 125*, Engineering Department: 2000)

October 28th

1880: On this day, the first horse-drawn trams were put into operation in Cambridge, transporting a total of 636 passengers. The trams were operated by the Cambridge Street Tramways Company and ran from the railway station via Hills Road and Regent Street to Christ's College, with diversions from Hyde Park Corner along Lensfield Road and King's Parade to Market Hill and to the depot in East Road. The horses were stabled in East Road and with just one horse pulling each tram, they were worked hard. This heavy workload took its toll and by the first week in November many of the fourteen horses were taken ill 'with sore throats, influenza, bad colds and fever feet.' With few rivals the trams were, at first, successful, but in 1896 the Cambridge Omnibus Company began a horse-bus service, which forced the Tramways Company to waste no time in purchasing vehicles to provide a similar service. In 1914 this company went into voluntary liquidation. The trams had never been known for their speedy service; it was said that if anyone was in a hurry they walked but if they had plenty of time then they would take a tram… (Porter, E., *Victorian Cambridge*, Dennis Dobson: 1969)

October 29th

1858: On this day, leading Victorian art critic John Ruskin gave a keynote speech at the Guildhall in Cambridge, part of a soirée organised for the launch of the new Cambridge School of Art in East Road. The school was the brainchild of William Beaumont, Fellow of Trinity College and vicar of St Michael's Church in Cambridge, who had a burning desire to improve, through education, the lives of the working classes. The school's location was in the suburb of Barnwell, a 'confusing rabbit warren of streets, occupied by a shifting population of travellers, the semi-criminal and the near-destitute.' Ruskin was equally passionate about education for all, having taught for the last four years at the Working Men's College in London. His speech tonight was much longer than expected and many of the ideas expressed were published two years later in the final volume of his *Modern Painters* series; it seems likely that Ruskin was trying them out tonight on a knowledgeable and (hopefully) receptive audience. The original school of art later became a polytechnic and then a university offering a wide range of subjects. In 2005 the institution was re-named Anglia Ruskin University in honour of its early patron. (Kirby, A., *Anglia Ruskin University 1858-2008*, ARU: 2008)

October 30th

2002: On this day, Baroness Margaret Thatcher opened a new wing of the Churchill Archives Centre in Cambridge. The extra space was badly needed as distinguished people, from Sir Winston Churchill to Nobel Prize-winning physicists, continued to bequeath their archives to the Centre. One of the largest archives relates to Baroness Thatcher herself, containing over a million documents in nearly 3,000 archive boxes. Thatcher never kept a diary but the archive includes many details of her role in important domestic and world events. Perhaps the most publicised item is one her iconic handbags from the mid-1980s. As a woman in a man's world there was intense curiosity and speculation about the contents of this famous lady's handbag. World leaders, including President Gorbachev, joked about its supposed contents. In July 1990, in an interview for Channel Four news, Margaret Thatcher revealed that anything she wanted to keep quiet was usually kept in her handbag, the safest place (the only *leak-proof* place) in No. 10 Downing Street. The four-storey extension unveiled by Thatcher today has a band of carved stone running its length, containing her name along with other donors, many from the USA. (Churchill Archives Centre)

October 31st

1842: On this day, George Humphrey was appointed surgeon at Addenbrooke's Hospital and immediately started giving lectures; at only twenty-two years of age, he was the youngest hospital surgeon in England. He was to revolutionise surgical practice by his anatomical teaching methods, which became known as 'Humphryology'. Together with Paget, Humphrey established Cambridge as the foremost University in the country for training doctors. (*Dictionary of National Biography*)

———•◆•———

1998: On this day, three large letters, RIP, were daubed in red paint on the sign at the entrance to the Royal Greenwich Observatory in Madingley Rise, Cambridge. Almost ten years to the day since the foundation stone had been laid for its Cambridge building, today effectively marked the end of the RGO's 323-year history as a working observatory. The name itself transferred to the old observatory at the National Maritime Museum in Greenwich, which is now used as a museum rather than as a functional observatory. The original royal observatory was commissioned in 1675 by King Charles II, who appointed John Flamsteed as the first Astronomer Royal. (*Cambridge Evening News*)

November 1st

2004: Today, all eyes on were on Prince Philip's face when he came to Cambridge to open new facilities at the University's vet school. The week before, the Prince had reportedly slipped in the bath and caught the side of his eye with his thumb, causing a very black and bruised eye. And reporters were not disappointed, as the bruise was still much in evidence, prompting the headline in the *Cambridge Evening News*: 'Prince Philip still bruised on visit'. On a more serious note, Prince Philip, in his role as Chancellor of the University of Cambridge, opened three new units at the Veterinary School: the small animal surgical unit, the farm animal medicine centre and the equine diagnostic unit. Veterinary research into treatment and diagnosis has advanced at a similar pace to its human counterpart, so that any treatment available to humans can also be offered to animals. There is much competition for places in the Vet School, but having passed all their exams, the students can graduate in the Senate House as Bachelor of Veterinary Medicine, whose academic hood is listed, with no hint of irony, as 'similar to the hood for Bachelor of Medicine, but with more fur'. (*Cambridge Evening News*)

November 2nd

1977: On this day, All Souls Day, a student club called The Jesus Old Contemptibles held an evening dinner in a room off G staircase in Jesus College, hoping to make contact with the infamous ghostly members of the Everlasting Club. The room, which at the beginning of the twentieth century had been left locked for many years, fascinated the College Master Arthur Gray to the extent that he wrote a story about it; word spread quickly amongst undergraduates and the story passed into college tradition even before its publication. According to Gray, seven young men founded, in 1738, a club called the Everlastings; the annual meetings were to be held on All Souls Night in a room in Jesus College, and they were notorious for their drunkenness and debauchery. The group quickly sobered up however when they learned that one of their members had attended a meeting, even though he had died the week before. All the other members died in mysterious circumstances, the last survivor being found dead in the club room on All Souls Day 1766. The students hoping to meet the Everlasting Club members in 1977 received no unexpected guests, so were spared the same fate as their predecessors. (Halliday, R., and Murdie, A., *The Cambridge Ghost Book*, Fern House: 2000)

November 3rd

1352: On this day, a small Cambridge church, sandwiched between Pembroke College on one side and the River Cam on the other, was dedicated by the Bishop of Ely to St Mary of Grace; in order to distinguish it from the other St Mary's in central Cambridge, it later became known as St Mary the Less, or Little St Mary's. The previous church on this site had been given, in about 1207, to the newly founded Hospital of St John the Evangelist (now St John's College), who used houses near the church to lodge some scholars. The scholars were also given the use of the church, and this was the origin of Peterhouse, the first college in the University of Cambridge. Little St Mary's Church was used by Peterhouse for services and ceremonies until 1632 when the college consecrated its own chapel. Today, the church has a thriving group of parishioners, who appreciate the high Anglican services held here; the smell of incense is evident on entering the church. Behind the church is one of the loveliest wild gardens in Cambridge, an oasis of peace and quiet in the very heart of the city. (Little St Mary's Church guide)

November 4th

1956: On this day, the Revd Mervyn Stockwood preached a controversial sermon in Great St Mary's Church on the subject of the Suez Crisis. Stockwood had already talked passionately on the subject at a rally on Parker's Piece, and the church was packed to overflowing; even the galleries were full and others were crowding outside, unable to get in. In the congregation was a young medical student called David Owen, future Labour politician and founder of the Social Democratic Party. Owen was very impressed by Stockwood's skills at oratory and described the sermon as 'unforgettable'. Even though his Suez sermon was deeply political, Stockwood made a great effort to think the issue through from both sides of the argument, a lesson which David Owen always tried to remember in his future political career. The City Council was so outraged that the university church had not supported what they felt to be the proper Tory party line that they declined to attend the traditional Remembrance Day service a week later. When the undergraduates heard of this boycott, they flocked to support Stockwood at Great St Mary's and the queues went as far as the market place. (Binns, J. and Meadows, P., *Great St Mary's*, University Press: 2000)

November 5th

1948: On this day, people across the country were letting off fireworks and lighting bonfires for the annual Guy Fawkes Night celebrations, remembering the failure of a plot by a number of Catholic conspirators (including Guy Fawkes) to blow up the Houses of Parliament on November 5 1605. For many years in Cambridge there had been a tradition of violent clashes on this night, transforming the usually tranquil city centre into a battleground between townspeople and undergraduates. By far the most serious vandalism took place on November 5 1948, as later recalled by Cambridge novelist Tom Sharpe: 'They nearly blew the windows of King's Chapel in with a bloody great bomb and overturned a car with a pregnant woman inside. I remember cycling down King's Parade with water and glass everywhere.' More damage was caused to buildings in Cambridge on this one night than during the whole of the Second World War, as crowds of youths attacked the Cambridge police station and let off smoke bombs on Market Hill and in the Baron of Beef pub. Today in Cambridge, Guy Fawkes Night is celebrated much more sedately (and safely) with a magnificent public firework display on Midsummer Common. (Weatherall, M., *From our Cambridge Correspondent*, Varsity Publications: 1995)

November 6th

1875: On this day, Mr John Death, Mayor of Cambridge, officially opened the new Corn Exchange Building in Wheeler Street. There had been significant disagreement over the building's location, with the dispute eventually being taken to the House of Lords. Even today's opening ceremony was criticised, with the *Cambridge Independent Press* blaming Mr Death for unnecessary extravagance; the town council had spent £100 on the ceremony. Worse was to come when, two days later, an inaugural concert was held, arranged by the Cambridge Musical Society; undergraduates yelled and stamped through the national anthem, police were called in and a full scale riot ensued, just the first of what came to be known as the Death Riots. From the outset, the building was used both as a corn exchange and as an entertainment venue. Events included motor shows and concerts by world-famous orchestras and bands; in the 1960s big names such as the Kinks, the Hollies and Tangerine Dream all played here. Trading in corn ceased in 1965 when a new corn exchange was built at the cattle market, but the old Corn Exchange is still today a thriving venue for the arts and entertainment. (Porter, E., *Victorian Cambridge*, Dennis Dobson: 1969 / *Cambridge Evening News*)

November 7th

1965: On this day, the sermon at Great St Mary's Church in Cambridge was given by the controversial Conservative politician Enoch Powell. Powell had been invited to talk in Cambridge by Hugh Montefiore, vicar of Great St Mary's at the time. Montefiore was keen that sermons by eminent speakers should play a key role in the church and invited some of the leading preachers and thinkers of the day, including Billy Graham, Malcolm Muggeridge, Kenneth Kaunda (President of Zambia) and Archbishop Michael Ramsey. Powell was himself a Cambridge graduate, having studied at Trinity College in the early 1930s before going on to become first a classicist, Professor of Ancient Greek at the University of Sydney and then a successful Member of Parliament, representing Wolverhampton South. His most famous speech, later to be famously dubbed 'The Rivers of Blood speech' was made by him in Birmingham just six months before this Cambridge visit. The speech warned of the alleged dangers of mass immigration and resulted in his dismissal from the Shadow Cabinet by Conservative party leader Edward Heath. (Binns, J. and Meadows, P., *Great St Mary's*, University Press: 2000 / Montefiore, H., *Sermons from Great St Mary's*, Fontana Books: 1968)

November 8th

1538: On this day, Barnwell Priory, the oldest and wealthiest religious house in Cambridge, was dissolved on the orders of King Henry VIII. Thus ended a long history, which had started in 1092 with the priory's foundation by William Picot, Sheriff of Cambridgeshire. Barnwell was one of the earliest Augustinian houses, founded not long after those at Huntingdon and Colchester, which were the first in the country. After some lean times, the priory was sufficiently comfortable and prosperous in the late twelfth century for the King to stay here on his Cambridge visits rather than in the castle; this royal tradition lasted well into the thirteenth century. According to Arthur Gray, a visitor to Cambridge at the end of the fifteenth century would have noticed that it 'contained more than the usual number of houses of religion...in the size and character of their buildings and the extent of their grounds they far surpassed anything which the colleges had yet to show'. After its dissolution, the buildings of Barnwell Priory were almost completely demolished and much of the masonry used in the construction of college buildings. (Gray, A., *The Town of Cambridge*, Heffer & Sons: 1925 / Haigh, D., *The Religious Houses of Cambridgeshire*, Cambs. County Council: 1988)

November 9th

1789: On this day, the Revd Samuel Reeve, Senior Proctor of the University of Cambridge, was found hanging from a bottle-rack in an attic room (for which he always kept the key) above the Hall of Gonville and Caius College. He had gone missing in July, following severe financial problems, and it was assumed that he had first tried to drown himself as when last seen, his clothes had been dripping wet. (Gunning, H., *Reminiscences*, George Bell: 1854)

1827: On this day, Lord Tennyson arrived at Trinity College in Cambridge to commence his studies. Having previously hardly left his home county of Lincolnshire, Tennyson went to join his older brothers who were lodging above a tobacconist's shop in Rose Crescent. Already striking in appearance, a fellow fresher described Tennyson as 'long-haired and defiant', exclaiming: 'that man must be a poet!' Lord Tennyson was to become one of the most popular poets in the English language, and the second most frequently quoted writer in the *Oxford Dictionary of Quotations*. (Chainey, G., *A Literary History of Cambridge*, Pevensey Press: 1985)

November 10th

1950: On this day, just five years after the end of the Second World War, a group of students from Gonville and Caius College came up with a novel idea of raising funds for disabled war veterans and their families. The title of 'Miss Caius' was given to a male undergraduate, wearing a bathing hat and a girl's bikini, who had to spend hours in a bath outside the college, sitting in barely tepid water laced with copious amounts of detergent; the latter apparently left him sore for weeks afterwards. The bather was just there to attract people's attention and draw them in to the toll gate beyond, where a toll was levied on any passer-by going down Senate House Passage, the rates being set on an elaborate scale which was posted on the wall. Undergraduates were penalised for such 'offences' as wearing suede shoes or bow ties and carrying books. 'Pretty girls' had to pay a penny more than 'plain women', or they could even avoid payment altogether by kissing the toll keeper! The verdict after the event was that it had been 'great fun' and it raised a substantial amount of money for charity. (Le Moignan, M., *Once a Caian …*, 2004)

November 11th

1849: On this day, a fire broke out in Michael's Church in Cambridge. Arthur Gray later wrote: 'Those were the days of manual fire engines, and street hydrants were unknown. The problem of supplying water to five engines that were quickly on the scene was solved by forming a double line of willing helpers to Trinity [College] kitchen; on one side the empty buckets were passed down to the college pump, on the other they were whirled at the rate of six miles an hour from the hands of one to the other when replenished.' Josiah Chater was there: 'I changed my clothes in order to work to better advantage, which I found a very wise plan, for in passing the buckets my feet became thoroughly wet.' It was two hours before the fire was under control; the outbreak seems to have started in the church heating system and then spread to the roof. Several buildings in Green Street were destroyed, but miraculously the church itself remained relatively intact. The celebrated architect Sir George Gilbert Scott rebuilt the roof and porch, with his son finishing off the work. Today the church houses the Michaelhouse Centre, complete with café, community centre and art gallery. (Gray, Arthur B., *Cambridge Revisited*, Heffer & Sons: 1921 / Porter, E., *Josiah Chater's Diaries*, Phillimore: 1975)

November 12th

1765: On this day, Mrs Mary Finch 'a maiden lady, sister of the late William Finch of this town' was buried at night-time in 'a grand manner' in the family vault in St Mary's Church in Cambridge. A burial by torchlight in King's College Chapel in 1800 is stated to have been the last night-time burial in Cambridge. Before then, night-time burials for distinguished people, lit only by torches, were common throughout the country. The diarist Samuel Pepys, who died in London in 1708, was also buried this way. (Bushell, W.D., *The Church of St Mary the Great*, Bowes & Bowes: 1948)

———•◆•———

1805: On this day, Lord Byron, one of the most flamboyant and dissolute undergraduates of his generation, wrote to a friend: 'this place is the *Devil*, or at least his principal residence ... I sit down to write with a head confused with dissipation, which though I hate, I cannot avoid. I have only supped at home three times since my arrival, and my table is constantly covered with invitations ... ' (Chainey, G., *A Literary History of Cambridge*, Pevensey Press: 1985)

November 13th

1844: On this day, the following Grace was passed by the Senate of the University of Cambridge: 'to allow the Chapel of St Mary, at Sturbridge, to be placed at the disposal of the Committee for providing religious instruction for the railway labourers'. The Newmarket Road chapel, often referred to as the Leper Chapel, was ready for use after years of dilapidation. A benefactor, the Revd T. Kerrich, had recently come to its rescue by funding the chapel's repair, at a cost of £84 15s 1d. The railway workers were a very recent addition to the population of Cambridge, having arrived after the 1844 Railway Act for Cambridge, which had resurrected plans for a rail link with London. Fraught with delays until now, it had taken seven years for the Northern and Eastern Railway Company to build the line from London to Bishops Stortford. Once taken over by the Eastern Counties Railway, progression was much faster and the first trains to London were in operation by the following summer. Once the railway workers had done their job, the chapel fell once again into disrepair, to be eventually restored some twenty years later under the direction of celebrated architect Sir George Gilbert Scott. (Jones, Chester H., *The Chapel of St Mary Magdalene*, CUP: 1926 / Cambridge University Railway Club)

November 14th

1843: On this day, Joseph Romilly, Cambridge University Registrary, wrote the following rather sad tale in his notebook, a sort of *Pygmalion* or *Pretty Woman* story, but with a far more tragic ending: 'Poor Charles Ingle [scholar of Trinity College, former Fellow of Peterhouse and latterly vicar of Strensall, Yorkshire] destroyed himself yesterday. He had married his housekeeper last Saturday ... He could not stand the world's censure and shot himself through the heart with a pistol which he had grasped with his left hand: he was covered up with the bedclothes and seems to have died instantaneously as the clothes were not disarranged: his face after death is said to have exhibited an awful fierceness of resolution.' His young wife, now a widow at less than thirty years old, was the sister of an innkeeper, 'interesting in appearance' and 'accomplished far above her position in life, for she played and sang with taste.' She was taught literature and 'understanding' by Ingle, with the inevitable result that 'the affections of both became irremediably entangled'. Romilly's sympathies lie however firmly with Ingle, whom he describes as having 'talents of the highest order ... and wit only second to Sidney Smith's ... he was the delight of society.' (Bury, M. and Pickles, J., *Romilly's Cambridge Diary*, Cambridge Records Society: 1994)

November 15th

1803: On this day, Edward Clarke, a tutor from Jesus College, wrote to a friend about his activities in preparation for a possible invasion by France: 'I am just come from practising the light infantry manoeuvres, over all the hedges and ditches, towards Madingley, wet, muddy and oozing at every pore… At present nothing is talked about but the drill…Yesterday we had a sort of sham fight on Parker's Piece and they all allow we do better than the town volunteers. We paraded through the streets from Clare Hall to Parker's Piece with a full band of music.' In the summer of 1803 the threat of a French invasion inspired a huge outburst of patriotic spirit throughout the nation. Cambridgeshire provided nearly 3,000 volunteers; £6,000 was raised locally for their equipment, of which £1,000 was contributed by the University of Cambridge. Clarke was later to become well known for his lectures on mineralogy, leading to his nickname of 'Stone' Clark. A contemporary wrote of him: 'I sing of a tutor renowned / Who went roving and raving for knowledge / And gathered it all the world round / And brought it in boxes to college.' (Gray, A., *A History of Jesus College*, Heinemann: 1960)

November 16th

1940: On this day, classicist A.S.F. Gow, Fellow of Trinity College, announced in his diary, '...we have a new Master ... there is much to be said for having a Humanist for a change, G.M.T. is a distinguished one, and I have no doubt that he is generally welcome'. 'GMT' was none other than the distinguished English historian G.M. Trevelyan, who threw himself into college life, helping to secure the acquisition of Newton's library for the college, tirelessly extending hospitality to visiting American dignitaries and writing *Trinity College: An Historical Sketch* in 1943. It was also during the war years, in 1944, that Trevelyan wrote his *English Social History* and although wartime restrictions on paper initially held up its production, it soon proved to be the most successful of all his books. Gow described the new Master's arrival: 'when the gates were open he [Trevelyan] made quite an impressive entry, and, at the lunch, a speech which was both audible and appropriate – and those accustomed to speeches in our Hall will welcome this innovation ... that night the undergraduates had a glass of fizz to drink the Master's health, so, though not there to see, I imagine they were content.' (Gow, A.S.F., *Letters from Cambridge*, Jonathan Cape: 1945)

November 17th

1877: On this day, Charles Darwin, author of the highly controversial and widely discussed book *Origin of Species*, was awarded an honorary doctorate in the Senate House in Cambridge. The economist Neville Keynes was there and wrote that 'the honorary degree was conferred … amidst a scene of some disorder'. Undergraduates had rigged up strings between the Senate House galleries, and swung a stuffed monkey across them, eliciting shouts and jokes about Darwin's ancestors. They also swung a large ring of iron, adorned with ribbons, from the galleries, supposed to represent the missing link. It landed eventually in the lap of one of the lady visitors, who 'pluckily cut it down and appropriated it, amidst tremendous applause'. And as for Darwin himself, Keynes wrote that he 'bore himself in a rather trying position with remarkable dignity, but I heard afterwards that his hand shook so much while he was signing the registry, that his signature was scarcely legible.' Darwin later wrote about the occasion: 'We had a grand time of it in Cambridge and I saw my old rooms in Christ's, where we spent so many happy days'. Darwin's rooms in Christ's College were refurbished and opened to the public in 2009. (Van Wyhe, J., *Darwin in Cambridge*, Christ's College: 2009)

November 18th

2009: On this day, Her Majesty the Queen had to leave the State Opening of Parliament in London very promptly in order to join her husband Prince Philip for lunch in King's College in Cambridge. Celebrating the University's 800th anniversary, the royal couple enjoyed a mouth-watering spread, for which special dishes were created, using locally-sourced ingredients such as Cambridge Bleat (a goat's cheese), Cambridge-reared Red Poll beef and local honey. It was back to business after lunch, when the royal couple attended a special ceremony in the Senate House, during which the Professor of Botany was dedicated a Regius Professor, an acknowledgment of another significant anniversary that year (200 years since the birth of naturalist Charles Darwin). Her Majesty was also invited to seal the final box in a set of archive boxes containing 800 *Letters to the Future* written by local schoolchildren and academics. And then more anniversaries – over to Ely Cathedral to celebrate the 900th anniversary of the Ely diocese and then to Marshall's of Cambridge, who were celebrating their 100th anniversary. At Marshall's, Her Majesty was presented with a specially struck gold medal, one of a limited number made and given to all employees currently working for the company. (*Cambridge News*)

November 19th

1836: On this day, the funeral of Charles Simeon in King's College Chapel was one of the most memorable that Cambridge has ever witnessed. Simeon, a highly revered preacher, priest and academic, had died six days previously, just as the bells of Great St Mary's Church were ringing out for the University sermon he was about to deliver. On the day of his funeral, the town council closed the shops, the University suspended all lectures and a congregation of 800 filled the chapel. Simeon had combined his position as Fellow of King's College with the role of vicar of Holy Trinity Church, gaining a reputation as one of the most inspirational preachers of his generation. In 1817 he began his famous conversation parties over tea on Friday afternoons, open to all undergraduates, who came to know him affectionately as 'Sims'. The large black teapot used by Simeon at these gatherings can still be seen in the Vestry of the Holy Trinity Church, along with his umbrella, reputedly one of the first in Cambridge. Simeon is commemorated in King's College Chapel by a simple legend 'C.S. 1836', inscribed on the floor about halfway between the north and south doors. (Poole, D., *Cambridge Seven Hundred*, Wilson-Poole: 1983)

November 20th

2002: On this day, press photographers and reporters outnumbered mourners at Cambridge Crematorium. Outside the chapel, twenty-five police officers kept more than sixty members of the media fenced away, as the infamous 'Moors murderer' Myra Hindley, often described in the press as 'the most evil woman in Britain', was cremated in a simple ceremony attended by just ten mourners. None of Hindley's family turned up for the service, but her former lesbian lover did attend. Hindley had died of a chest infection, aged sixty, in the Bury St Edmunds Hospital where she had been transferred from nearby Highpoint Prison. Sentenced, aged twenty-four, with her lover Ian Brady to life imprisonment, Hindley was one of the few 'lifers' to actually die in custody. In later life, Hindley was apparently a reformed character, taking an Open University degree and converting to Catholicism. Lord Longford campaigned tirelessly on her behalf, but his views were not shared by many others. One banner at the entrance to the Cambridge Crematorium today bore the simple message: 'Burn in Hell'. After Hindley's cremation, a Prison Service officer went to the back of the crematorium and quietly took possession of the ashes; she had asked her priest to dispose of them at his discretion. (*The Times*)

November 21st

1954: Tonight, a Cambridge undergraduate saw an old, stooped man in old-fashioned clothing ahead of him in Silver Street. When they were a few feet apart, the man vanished into thin air. Keen to get back to the safety of his rooms, the student climbed over the nearest wall into college; back at his desk, he wrote up the incident, which was later published by the Society of Psychical Research. The student maintained anonymity for fear of retribution for scaling the college walls after hours. (Halliday, R., and Murdie, A., *The Cambridge Ghost Book*, Fern House: 2000)

———— ◆ ————

1961: On this day, property millionaire Major Allnatt gifted Rubens' painting *The Adoration of the Magi* to King's College. The painting was placed temporarily on an easel in the antechapel, near the screen. It was to be another seven years before the massive painting was installed in its current position beneath the East window. In the meantime, the floor was levelled at the east end of the chapel, wooden panelling was removed from the walls and the painting's frame was sold (to MP Michael Heseltine). (*The Independent*)

November 22nd

1944: On this day, Sir Arthur Eddington, the Cambridge physicist who 'turned Einstein into a superstar', died of cancer in the Evelyn Nursing Home in Cambridge. Despite being one of the most prominent astrophysicists of the early twentieth century, Eddington's name has never been widely recognised outside scientific circles, though a recent television drama *Einstein and Eddington* starring actor David Tennant (better known for his role as Dr Who) certainly raised his profile. During the First World War, the young Eddington corresponded with an unknown German scientist called Albert Einstein. Einstein had come up with a ground-breaking theory which Eddington realised could unlock new ways of thinking about time and space. At a time when Britain was fiercely rejecting all things German, Eddington began to champion Einstein openly, flying in the face of both received opinion and political sensitivities. Eddington went to Africa in 1919 for the eclipse; taking photographs of stars, he wanted to show that light bends round the sun. The expedition was a success and thanks to Eddington's photographs, Einstein became an overnight celebrity. Eddington went on to write the first textbook on general relativity, interweaving the scientific text with quotes from poetry and the classics. Eddington is commemorated by a Latin plaque in the antechapel of Trinity College. (*Cambridge Evening News*)

November 23rd

2000: On this day, hundreds of people lined the streets of Cambridge in the pouring rain, waiting for a glimpse of the Queen as she visited the city with the Duke of Edinburgh. The arrival of the royal couple was greeted with a sea of flags, cheering and shouts of 'Ma'am'; during her brief walkabout, the Queen carried a see-through umbrella to protect herself from the rain. First stop was the University's Sidgwick Site, where the Queen opened the new £7.7 million Faculty of Divinity; during her tour of the new building the Queen also named the Runcie Lecture Room in honour of the late Robert Runcie, Cambridge alumnus and former Archbishop of Canterbury. Next stop was Trinity Hall, where the royal couple joined luminaries such as Terry Waite and Stephen Hawking in celebrating the 650th anniversary of the College's first royal charter. The Queen officially opened a newly refurbished room in the college's Elizabeth library building and named it the Graham Storey Room, after an outstanding scholar and college Fellow, best known for his twelve-volume edition of the letters of Charles Dickens. The Graham Storey room is now available for hire throughout the year and can be used for anything from seminars and workshops to formal dinners and weddings. (*Cambridge Evening News*)

November 24th

1898: On this day, a nineteen-year-old undergraduate wrote to his mother about the 'very exciting day' he had just had, watching at first-hand the visit to Cambridge of the great military leader Lord Kitchener. The student signed himself with his middle name, Morgan, but was later better known as the writer and novelist E.M. Forster. He wrote today from his rooms in King's College: 'The Sirdar passed so close that I could almost have touched him through the bars. Just as he drove up King's Parade, the weight of people pulling against the high iron fence…wrenched it out of its fastenings and for the length of about fifty feet fell backwards into the crowd. It is a great miracle that no one was killed … The Sirdar wore his red doctor's gown over his uniform and had his helmet on so he looked very ridiculous…This evening there was a grand bonfire in the market place…they pulled up all the … railings and posts from the backs to feed the fire…and quantities of squibs and roman candles were thrown in at the windows. We all said "How foolish" but enjoyed it very much. The chapel and the Senate House looked marvellous with the red light…' (Moseley, C., and Wilmer, C., *Cambridge Observed*, Colt Books: 1998)

November 25th

1669: On this day, Isaac Barrow, the first Lucasian Professor of Mathematics, resigned his position in favour of 'one Mr Newton'. In later years, Isaac Newton would regale his admirers with stories of how Barrow 'would frequently say that truly he himself knew something of the mathematics, still he reckoned himself but a child in comparison to his pupil Newton'. The truth was however not so straightforward. Barrow felt that his true calling was towards the Church and for centuries after his death, his reputation was largely not as the first Lucasian Professor but as a consummate and charismatic preacher. Barrow's friend Abraham Hill wrote: '[Barrow] had vowed in his ordination to serve God in the Gospel of his Son, and he could not make a Bible out of his Euclid or a pulpit out of his mathematical chair'. Barrow went on to become Master of Trinity College and initiated the building of the new college library, managing to secure the services of architect Sir Christopher Wren free of charge. (Feingold, M., *Before Newton: The Life and Times of Isaac Barrow*, CUP: 2008 / Hawking, S., Knox, C. and Noakes, P., *From Newton to Hawking*, CUP: 2007)

November 26th

1670: On this day, the nineteen-year-old Prince of Orange ('a well countenanced man with a handsome head of hair of his own') and his entourage arrived in Cambridge in three coaches, each pulled by six horses. The Prince dined with the Provost at King's College then went on to Trinity where he had no time to watch the play they had been rehearsing for him. University accounts show, rather sadly: 'For 24lbs of wax candles prepared for the comedy intended to have been acted before the Prince of Orange, £2.' (Colthorpe, M., *Royal Cambridge*, Cambridge City Council: 1977)

———— • ◆ • ————

1829: On this day, a delegation from the Cambridge Union made their first visit to the Oxford Union, for a poetic debate, Byron versus Shelley. Speakers included Arthur Hallam from Cambridge (subject of Tennyson's *In Memoriam*) and, on the Oxford side, future Prime Minister William Gladstone. One Oxford speaker later commented that the Oxford men were 'precise and orderly', whereas the Cambridge oratory 'came like a flood into a millpond', conceding nonetheless that his own team had been 'utterly routed'. (Parkinson, S., *Arena of Ambition*, Icon Books: 2009)

November 27th

1963: On this day, four guests at the University Arms Hotel in Cambridge woke to find hundreds of female fans waiting for them in the streets outside. The Beatles pop group was made up of four young men who were besieged by screaming fans wherever they went and Cambridge was no exception. The headline in the *Daily Express* this morning read 'City of learning and culture bends to the sound'. The Beatles had played the night before at the Regal (then a cinema and concert venue, now a pub). The queue for tickets had stretched all round the building and the Red Cross had dozens of helpers on hand to treat fainting and hysterical fans. After the show, while a Black Maria with headlamps blazing acted as a decoy, the 'Fab Four' were whisked quietly away in another police van, through a back gate into the University's Downing Site, along Tennis Court Road and through the back door of the University Arms Hotel. Leaving in the morning was not so easy, as the roads were blocked by hundreds of fans, causing traffic chaos as they waited for the Beatles to continue their journey to their next venue. 'Beatlemania' had well and truly hit Cambridge. (*Cambridge Evening News*)

November 28th

1855: On this day, William Whewell, newly appointed Vice-Chancellor of the University of Cambridge, was given the task of supervising the painting and gilding of the central room of the Fitzwilliam Museum; since his brief was rather uninspiring, Whewell decided he would take on extra responsibilities. He thought that some of the existing pictures of nudes were 'far too conspicuously exhibited', stating: 'the exhibition of nude figures in a public gallery is always a matter of some embarrassment ... Since in recent times we have opened the Fitzwilliam Gallery to the public indiscriminately, and to very young persons of both sexes ... such pictures ... should not be in prominent places ... '. Whewell, without any authority whatsoever, set about re-arranging the paintings, to the extent of placing one fine picture, risqué in his eyes, high up on the wall and covering it with a green curtain, to be drawn back only with the utmost discretion. Whewell was getting out of his depth and was increasingly considered to be not only a prude but also a dictator, imposing his own rather limited artistic taste on those who knew much better. The Syndicate of the Fitzwilliam Museum fought back and insisted that their own committee should in the future have the final say on the hanging and arrangement of paintings. (Winstanley, D.A., *Early Victorian Cambridge*, CUP: 1940)

November 29th

2004: On this day, a Cambridge dispute was raised to a national level as twelve leading architects, including Lord Norman Foster, Richard Rogers and Terry Farrell, wrote to the *Guardian* newspaper expressing their 'shock and dismay' at the proposed closure of the architecture department at Cambridge University. The letter was timed to coincide with a demonstration by around 2,000 students and supporters, who turned out in force today to hear speeches by local Labour MP Anne Campbell and the comedian Griff Rhys-Jones, whose son George was a student at the threatened school. University authorities wanted to close the hundred-year-old department because it was thought that the quality of the department's research had fallen below the standard expected of their distinguished institution, having been awarded only four stars rather than the usual five. In their letter, Lord Foster and the others strongly disagreed, describing the proposed closure plans as 'an act of extraordinary folly'. Just two months later, in January 2005, Cambridge's general board voted unanimously to keep the department open, albeit with a 'new academic strategy', focussing more on sustainable design; in the light of this, six of its seventeen academic staff were encouraged to take early retirement. (*The Guardian*)

November 30th

1791: On this day, Austrian composer Franz Josef Haydn wrote in his notebook about Cambridge, which he had recently passed through en route to spending three days at the home of Sir Patrick Blake in Langham, Suffolk. This was part of Haydn's hugely successful visit to England; following the death of his most important patron, Prince Nikolaus, he now had the freedom to travel and perform in England, with huge audiences flocking to his concerts. Haydn wrote: 'I passed the town of Cambridge, inspected all the Universities, which are built conveniently in a row but separately. Each University has behind it a very spacious and beautiful garden, besides a fine stone bridge, in order to afford passage over the stream which winds past. The King's Chapel is famous for the carved work of the roof, which is all of stone, but so delicate that nothing more beautiful could have been made of wood. It has endured already four hundred years, because of the firmness and peculiar whiteness of the stone. The students are dressed like those at Oxford; but it is said that they have better instructors.' (Waterlow, S., *In Praise of Cambridge*, Constable & Co.: 1912)

December 1st

1947: On the very day that he was due to receive the Copley Medal from the Royal Society, the distinguished mathematician Godfrey Hardy passed away in the Evelyn Hospital in Cambridge, his devoted sister Gertrude by his side. Hardy had shown a prodigious talent from an early age; by the time he was two he could write down numbers up to millions and later as a child he would amuse himself in church by factorising the numbers of the hymns. In the course of his Cambridge University career Hardy, together with his colleague Littlewood, produced around 100 papers of enormous influence, covering a wide range of topics in pure mathematics. One colleague observed: 'Nowadays, there are only three really great English mathematicians, Hardy, Littlewood and Hardy-Littlewood'. They were soon however joined by Ramanujan, an Indian who was so brilliant that they dubbed him 'the second Newton'. Towards the end of his life, Hardy wrote: 'I still say to myself when I am depressed, and find myself forced to listen to pompous and tiresome people, "Well, I have done one thing you could never have done, and that is to have collaborated with both Littlewood and Ramanujan on something like equal terms".' (Harman, P. and Mitton, S., *Cambridge Scientific Minds*, CUP: 2002)

December 2nd

1891: On this day, Daisy Hopkins, a seventeen-year-old prostitute, was walking the streets of Cambridge when she was arrested by University officials and taken the following morning to the Vice-Chancellor's court. Daisy wore a smart navy blue costume with gold edging and a fawn-coloured felt hat, but this outfit made less of an impression on the Vice-Chancellor than it might have done on her numerous undergraduate clients and she was sentenced to fourteen days in the Spinning House, the Cambridge gaol whose purpose was to confine women of 'ill repute'. Life in the Spinning House was grim: sixty cells, 6ft by 8ft in size, lined the narrow corridors on two floors. There was no heating and no artificial light; for washing there was a single pump in the courtyard, which served the entire gaol. The townspeople of Cambridge strongly resented the University's power to arrest prostitutes and when young Daisy Hopkins sued the University for wrongful imprisonment, her case excited interest on a national level. Just three years later an Act of Parliament abolished the Vice-Chancellor's power to send women to gaol. The much hated Spinning House was pulled down in 1901. (Parker, R., *Town and Gown*, Patrick Stephens: 1983 / *Crime Time Magazine*)

December 3rd

1946: On this day, Freddy Brittain, highly respected Fellow of Jesus College and Vice-Proctor of the University of Cambridge, wrote in his diary: 'Lunch ... then, plus the Mayor and Chief Constable, kicked off one of the three balls in the Foot-the-Ball match on Parker's Piece'. This apparently unique version of football involved three balls (coloured red, yellow and green), three goals and three referees, all on a single pitch. The novelty of the game, coupled no doubt with the announcement that the three balls would be kicked off by the Mayor, the Senior Proctor and the Chief Constable, attracted thousands of spectators and was a wonderfully light-hearted celebration. The event was filmed by Pathé News and covered by many newspapers, including *Le Figaro* and *The Montreal Daily Star*. Senior tutor Francis Bennett, enthroned on a dais, was the 'Governor' (the final arbiter in the case of any doubts or disputes). On one occasion, Bennett called two sparring players in front of him, addressed them severely in Latin and promptly invented what is now known as the 'sin-bin', ordering them to stand in the corner for two minutes. The *Cambridge Daily News* wrote that 'this venture possibly surpassed anything similar within living memory'. (Brittain, M., *The Diaries of Frederick Brittain*, Muriel Brittain: 2001 / Le Moignan, M., *Once a Caian ...*, 2008)

December 4th

1975: On this day, around 10,000 people packed into the Market Square in Cambridge hoping for a glimpse of Princess Anne, who, on her first official visit to Cambridge, was in town to open the new Lion Yard shopping centre. The concept of a shopping centre had been discussed as early as 1952, and the opening today heralded the end of many months of demolition, rebuilding, noise and dust. The Lion Hotel, together with all the buildings on the south side of Petty Cury, had been demolished along with Alexandra Street and Falcon Yard. Standing on his pedestal, surveying the new development, was the lion himself. Believed to be the original wooden carving for a cast lion which stood over the old Red Lion Brewery at Waterloo Station, he had been discovered at the Woburn Abbey Antiques Centre and refurbished at the city engineer's workshops on Mill Road. Princess Anne unveiled a plaque and signed a visitors' book before leaving for lunch at nearby Christ's College. It was then the turn of the crowds to flock into their newly opened shopping centre and admire the new shops, cafes, library and the Heidelberg roof gardens. (Petty, M., *Cambridge Evening News*)

December 5th

1914: On this day, several months into the First World War, Charles Kay Ogden, Cambridge linguist, philosopher and writer, wrote in the *Cambridge Magazine*: 'The present rumpus on the continent … has caused the decrease, or at any rate hibernation, of a large number of … various societies … but neither decrease nor hibernation has overtaken "The Heretics"; … the attendance has, all along, been hardly perceptibly diminished – in fact, even prominent members of Newnham College have been obliged to seat themselves on the floor for lack of more adequate accommodation'. Ogden himself had been judged unfit for military service following rheumatic fever as a child and so was able to throw himself wholeheartedly into the activities of the *Cambridge Magazine* and the Heretics Society, both of which he had founded two years previously, while still an undergraduate. Ogden's magazine included contributions from such literary luminaries as Siegfried Sassoon, John Masefield, Thomas Hardy and George Bernard Shaw and evolved into an 'organ of international comment on politics and the war'. The Heretics Society questioned traditional authorities, particularly religious dogmas, and attracted equally prestigious speakers, from G.K. Chesterton to Bertrand Russell, and, in later years, Virginia Woolf. (Fowler, L. and H., *Cambridge Commemorated*, CUP: 1984)

December 6th

1588: On this day, the wealthy, influential and well connected Lady Frances Sidney, Countess of Sussex, drew up her will, five years after her husband's death and four months before her own. Lady Frances specified in great detail which of her possessions should go to whom, but her greatest memorial was to be the college in Cambridge which still bears her name today, Sidney Sussex College. She left a sum of £5,000, together with all the remaining goods from her bequest, to buy land in Cambridge to found a college and to appoint a Master, ten Fellows and twenty Scholars. These were modest funds however for such an ambitious project. Dr Thomas Fuller, writing in 1655, described the college as 'so low, so lean and little at the birth thereof. Alas! What is 5000 pounds to buy the scite [*sic*], build and endow a College therewith?' But land on the site of a former Franciscan convent was acquired in the very heart of Cambridge and, crucially, Lady Frances' appointed executor was the influential John Whitgift, Archbishop of Canterbury; without Whitgift's help and influence, the foundation of the college, eight years later would not have been possible. (Beales, D.E.D. and Nisbet, H.B., *Sidney Sussex College Cambridge: Historical Essays*, Boydell and Brewer: 1996 / *Dictionary of National Biography*)

December 7th

1963: On this day, a memorial service for author, lecturer and preacher C.S. Lewis was held in the Chapel of Magdalene College in Cambridge. In 1954, Clive Staples Lewis had been elected to the new Cambridge professorship of Medieval and Renaissance English and migrated from Magdalen College Oxford to Magdalene in Cambridge (differentiated in spelling by the final 'e' of the Cambridge college). Soon after his arrival, Lewis wrote to an American friend: 'I think I shall like Magdalene better than Magdalen. It's a tiny college ... and they're all so old-fashioned and pious and gentle and conservative – unlike this leftist, atheist, cynical, hardboiled, huge Magdalen.' Although Lewis enjoyed Cambridge, he hurried home to Oxford at weekends and vacations, travelling on the train he called the 'Cantab Crawler' and it was in Oxford that he died and was buried. Most widely known because of his children's books about a magical country called Narnia, Lewis is remembered in Cambridge by a modest plaque in the antechapel of Magdalene College. His Cambridge memorial service concluded with a reading from *The Weight of Glory*, one of his most famous sermons, preached in Oxford in 1941. (Glenny, J., *C S Lewis's Cambridge*, Christian Heritage Press: 2003)

December 8th

2001: On this day, Kim Dae-Jung, President of Korea, visited Cambridge in order to receive an honorary degree from Prince Philip in the University Senate House. The President was already familiar with the city, having lived for six months in 1993 at the Pinehurst development in Grange Road whilst studying as a visiting Research Fellow at Clare Hall. Dae-Jung, or DJ as he is popularly known, had a particular research interest in German reunification and regional cooperation, which provided the basis for his famous Sunshine Policy for Peace on the Korean Peninsula. This policy, his idea of 'prodding the North forward with the promise of incentives and reducing the strain of eventual unification through economic integration', led to Kim being awarded the Nobel Peace Prize in 2000. The University of Cambridge wrote of him: 'He has devoted the major part of his life to fighting for the establishment of democracy in Korea, surviving kidnap, imprisonment and court martial'. Kim Dae-Jung died in 2009 at the age of eighty-five; a month later, in Cambridge, a memorial lecture was given by a former Ambassador to South Korea, entitled 'A Witness to Change: Three Decades of Korea-watching'. (*Daily Mail* / Cambridge University News Service)

December 9th

1856: On this day, a group of Cambridge undergraduates, founder members of the fledgling Cambridge University Football Club, drafted a set of rules that they believed would unify the sport, enabling it to be played by anyone, anywhere. These are the earliest surviving written rules of football and are kept today in the library of Shrewsbury School. The game of football had developed on the playing fields of public schools such as Eton and Harrow, also at Cambridge and Oxford Universities, but each institution had its own rules. Some allowed players to hold the ball, others let them pat it and because there were so many variations, they could not even play each other. These new rules enabled public schools, universities and working-class men to play each other, or to associate – hence the name 'Association Football'. A team from Blackheath in London objected to the rules, saying it was wrong to drop the practices of hacking and shinning. The result was the start of a breakaway, more physical game, as pioneered in 1823 by William Webb-Ellis at Rugby School; despite its title, Blackheath Football Club was the world's first rugby club not to have restricted membership. (*Cambridge Evening News*)

December 10th

1886: On this day, a sumptuous meal was served at Christ's College. The meal started with scalloped oysters and devilled lobster, before moving on to boar head and haunch of venison, finishing with mince pies and milk punch. This and other menus were handwritten in a leather-bound book which was discovered in the College in 2009. The cost of the dinners ranged from eighteen pence to ten shillings. Guests at a recent dinner in Christ's College celebrating the 200th anniversary of the birth of Charles Darwin paid £5,000 per head. (Cambridge University News Service)

1904: On this day, Lord Rayleigh, physicist and Fellow of Trinity College, was the first Cambridge academic to receive a Nobel Prize (for discovering Argon). Since 1901, Nobel Prizes have been awarded annually in Stockholm on December 10, in memory of the day when Alfred Nobel died at his home in San Remo, Italy in 1896. Between 1904 and 2010, eighty-eight prizes have been awarded to people affiliated to the University of Cambridge; Trinity College boasts thirty-two Nobel Prize winners, the most of any Cambridge college. (Nobel Prize.org / University of Cambridge)

December 11th

1791: On this day, the Revd Thomas Jones, tutor of Trinity College, gave the University sermon at Great St Mary's Church in Cambridge, quoting Exodus in an attempt to dissuade students from staging duels to settle disputes. This was a hot topic at the time, following the recent death of a student from gunshot wounds sustained at a duel. The student who had fired the lethal shot, Mr Applethwaite, was charged with murder at the Bury Assizes but was later acquitted. Strong testimony was apparently given as to his 'generally amiable conduct.' Despite a strongly worded statement from the Vice-Chancellor to the effect that any student discovered duelling would be 'proceeded against as guilty of a very high offence' and 'liable to the severest penalties', duelling at this time was not, within University circles, generally considered to be 'essential to the character of a gentleman' and such instances were few and far between. Drunken behaviour was more of an issue, with intoxication being regarded as 'the besetting sin of the University'. Drunken night-time disputes which elsewhere might have ended in a duel, were in Cambridge quickly forgotten, with parties shamelessly suffering the following morning from near total amnesia. (Gunning, H., *Reminiscences*, George Bell: 1854)

December 12th

1680: On this day, some twenty-four years before he was to build his observatory on top of the Great Gate at Trinity College, Isaac Newton recorded in his notebook that he had begun to observe a comet in the skies over Cambridge. Known as the Great Comet, it was one of the brightest comets of the seventeenth century, reputedly visible even in daytime, and was noted for its spectacularly long tail. Newton observed it carefully until it disappeared in March the following year. The comet's arrival coincided with Newton's attempts to explain the Creation in physical terms and this extraordinary phenomenon allowed him to think further about the real make-up of the heavens. The comet is given a specific mention in Newton's classic book *Principia Mathematica*, which was published in 1687. There is an illustration of the 'Great Comet', the only illustration of anything in the entire book, in a fold-out section between pages 496 and 497. The comet was also observed by Newton's friend Edmund Halley, but this was not 'Halley's Comet', which was to come a little later, in 1682. (Ed. Hawking, S., Knox, C. and Noakes, P., *From Newton to Hawking*, CUP: 2007 / Topper, D., *Quirky Sides of Scientists*, Springer: 2007)

December 13th

1688: On this day, Alderman Newton wrote of the wild scenes he had recently seen in Cambridge, part of the wave of anti-Popish riots which were sweeping the country: 'This night and several nights before there were up in arms a great many in this town, some nights 2 or 300 (many scholars among them) of the rabble…who at first under a pretence to seek for papists and such who had favoured them and to ransack their houses for arms, at last came to be very insulting and wherever they pleased, to enter men's houses and do them much mischief.' One Catholic man was made to dance naked in a ditch until he agreed to change his religion. At Sidney Sussex the chapel was attacked and vestments and other items of worship were destroyed. The college spent eleven shillings for 'mending the chamber broken by the rabble'. Just two months later, William and Mary were proclaimed King and Queen at the Market Cross and elsewhere in Cambridge with the same amount of ceremony that the fated King James had been given on his own accession just three years previously. (Beales, D.E.D., and Nisbet, H.B., *Sidney Sussex College Cambridge: Historical Essays*, Boydell and Brewer: 1996 / Gray, A., *The Town of Cambridge*, Heffer & Sons: 1925)

December 14th

1878: On this day, a large crowd gathered on Parker's Piece to watch the black flag being hoisted at the gaol in Gonville Place, marking the execution of one Robert Browning, a twenty-five-year-old Cambridge tailor who walked with sixteen-year-old Emma Rolf to Butt Green where, apparently without provocation, he attacked the girl with a razor, almost severing her head from her body. A policeman, called by horrified passers-by, found him standing by the body. On being questioned, Browning admitted: 'I know I've done it, I couldn't help it.' (Porter, E., *Josiah Chater's Diaries*, Phillimore: 1975)

1893: On this day, the Cambridge Council decided that a powerful light was needed in the centre of Parker's Piece. The gas company was unable to supply an estimate, but the Electric Supply Company offered not only to build a lamppost but also to give a year's free supply of electricity. The lamp-post has had the words 'Reality Checkpoint' daubed on it since the early 1970s, when passing hippies would decorate it with ribbons and flowers. (Mitchell, E., *Notes on the History of Parker's Piece Cambridge*, Mitchell: 1984)

December 15th

1792: On this day, the Mayor summoned a meeting in Cambridge Town Hall with the aim of forming an association for 'preserving Liberty and Property against Republicans and Levellers'. A few days later, the town's publicans issued a joint declaration that they would immediately give notice to the magistrates 'should it come to their knowledge that any persons in talk or by circulation of seditious books or pamphlets were endeavouring to excite riot or enflame the minds of the populace.' Just three years after the French Revolution, these were turbulent times; the Levellers were rebels and revolutionaries, the name resurrected from the seventeenth-century group of Christian radicals who had conflicted with Charles I and his claim to govern Britain on the divine right of kings. They represented the aspirations of working people and they spoke for those who experienced the hardships of poverty and deprivation. Much of the opposition to the 'Republicans and Levellers' was directed towards Thomas Payne and his controversial and influential work *The Rights of Man* and on the last day of 1792 Payne's effigy was burned on the Market Hill in Cambridge. (Gray, A., *The Town of Cambridge*, Heffer & Sons: 1925)

December 16th

1882: On this day, the wife of John Hobbs gave birth to her son John Berry at their home in Brewhouse Lane, Cambridge, little knowing that one day this little baby would become one of the most successful and popular cricketers of all time. Sir Jack Hobbs, as he was later known, was the oldest son in a working-class family of twelve. He left St Matthew's School early in order to work as a baker's errand boy, taking home two shillings and sixpence each week. Despite his long working hours, Jack practised at six o'clock each morning on Parker's Piece, a place he was later to describe as 'probably the finest and most famous public cricket ground in the world.' He started his professional cricketing career with Cambridgeshire then moved to Surrey, where he played for thirty years, scoring his last first-class century at the age of fifty-three. The Hobbs Memorial Gates at the Oval cricket ground in London are dedicated to him. In Cambridge, Hobbs Pavilion on Parker's Piece has been named in his memory; on the roof of this building, now a restaurant, is a weather vane in the shape of a cricketer by the stumps, bat in hand. (*Cambridge Evening News*)

December 17th

1546: On this day, the charter of Trinity College was sealed, marking its foundation by King Henry VIII, whose statue now adorns the front gate of the college. King Henry granted to the college the estates of thirty-six dissolved religious houses, no doubt to the huge relief of members of the University, who had feared that colleges might also be destroyed, along with monastic foundations; an Act of 1544, just two years previously, had given the King the power to dissolve any college at either Cambridge or Oxford and to appropriate its possessions. It was thanks to this Act of Parliament that the three previous establishments on the site, Michaelhouse, King's Hall and Physwick Hostel, had been dissolved, making way for the foundation of Trinity College. It was said that Henry VIII named his college Trinity not just because it was dedicated to God, one in three persons, but also because he himself had created a new college out of three former ones. The foundation of Trinity College was one of the last acts of Henry VIII's life, as he died just a month later, in January 1547. (Porter, H.C., *Reformation and Reaction in Tudor Cambridge*, CUP: 1958 / Anon., *The King's Scholars and King's Hall*, published privately: 1917)

December 18th

1967: On this day, in the early hours of the morning, several fire engines and thirty firemen turned out to deal with a fire at the Turks Head Grill, a Berni Inn steak house in Trinity Street. The fire had been burning for several hours on the top floor but was not discovered until it burst through the roof at four in the morning. At exactly the same time, a fire was raging in another Berni Inn steak house in St Albans, and detectives from two police forces worked together to see if there was a link between the two incidents. Trinity Street was closed for several hours and eyewitnesses said they could see the fire from more than half a mile away. The bar had to remain closed over the festive period, a terrible blow for the manager, but the lower floors were littered with debris and soaked with water from the hoses. Residents and workers at the nearby Blue Boar Hotel were amongst the first to spot the fire, and a nineteen-year-old employee took the initiative and got a very early morning coffee supply organised for all helping. In 2010 the building houses Jigsaw clothes shop. (Baker, E., *A History of Firefighting in Cambridgeshire*, Jeremy Mills: 2006 / *Cambridge Evening News*)

December 19th

1627: On this day, John Harvard paid his fee of ten shillings and was admitted, at the relatively late age of twenty, to Emmanuel College in Cambridge. Little is known about this young man, but his name lives on in Harvard University, one of the most prestigious universities in the world. John lost his father (a butcher in Southwark) and four brothers and sisters in the plague of 1625. It is not known what he looked like; his portrait in the Victorian stained-glass window in the College Chapel was modelled on the face of poet John Milton, but with longer hair. Just five years after his graduation, Harvard crossed the Atlantic with other graduates who were seeking a freer climate for their Puritan views. On his early death in 1638 he bequeathed his library of some 400 volumes and half of his estate to a college which had recently been founded by another Emmanuel graduate, Thomas Shepard. The grateful college community declared that it should forever bear Harvard's name. Still today there are annual student exchange programmes between Harvard University and Emmanuel College Cambridge. (Emmanuel College website)

December 20th

1532: On this day, Thomas Brakyn MP visited Thomas Cromwell on behalf of the Mayor of Cambridge, thanking him for 'the service they owe him and for his favour in their causes'. The letter was accompanied by a gift of fish: twenty pikes and ten tenches. Brakyn knew that Cromwell, who had gained the confidence of King Henry VIII and had risen to be his Chief Minister, was very susceptible to flattery and lavish gifts. The main objective of this manoeuvring was to secure complete control of Sturbridge Fair, which had now reached such proportions that more business was done there in its two weeks' duration than in a whole year in the market place. Brakyn himself had a vested interest as he was the foremost fishmonger in Cambridge, having built up a lucrative business by rather dubious means. As official purveyor of pikes to King Henry VIII, Brakyn would buy fish at a discounted price, saying that it was 'for the king' and then sell it on to all and sundry at an elevated price. One of his less successful rivals reckoned that Brakyn had defrauded the king of nearly £400 over a period of thirteen years. Heads have rolled for less. (Parker, R., *Town and Gown*, Patrick Stephens: 1983)

December 21st

1904: On this day, Bessie Jones died at the age of eighty-four; for eighty-two of those years she had been deaf, dumb and blind. In St Paul's Church, Hills Road, Cambridge, a stained-glass window commemorates Bessie's life, showing scenes of Jesus healing the deaf, dumb and blind and in the centre, a representation of one of the most famous pre-Raphaelite paintings, Holman Hunt's *The Light of the World*. Born Elizabeth Jones, Bessie was the oldest daughter of renowned Cambridge dentist John Jones, later to be appointed 'Dentist in Ordinary to the Queen'. Her disabilities probably resulted from a severe attack of measles at the age of two, and her life was to become an inspiration to many as an example of how it is possible to adapt to physical handicaps and live a full life. Despite her blindness, she was able to produce beautifully stitched needlework, and made a purse which was presented to Queen Victoria on the occasion of Prince Albert's installation as Chancellor of the University of Cambridge in 1847. Dr Whewell, Master of Trinity College, was fascinated by Bessie's ability and made a study of her life. (Brook, S., *Ely Ensign*)

December 22nd

1987: On this day, biochemist Dorothy Needham died at her home in Grange Road, Cambridge, aged ninety-two. For the past nine years she had bee suffering from Alzheimer's disease, so even though she had lived just long enough to be told that her husband's institute (the Needham Research Institute) had opened its doors, it is doubtful that she ever really understood. Sharing with her husband an 'unshakable commitment to Christianity and socialism', Dorothy Needham was a quite remarkable woman in her own right. She was a Fellow of no fewer than three Cambridge colleges: Lucy Cavendish (which she was instrumental in establishing), Girton (where she had studied as an undergraduate) and Gonville and Caius (where her husband was Master for eleven years). In their later years, the Needhams only rarely dined in Gonville and Caius. When confused, Dorothy had to be led to her place by a steward, while her wheelchair-bound husband would be hauled up from the kitchens to the Hall in a dumb-waiter. The College is more wheelchair-friendly today, as one of its most eminent fellows is the severy disabled cosmologist Professor Stephen Hawking. (Winchester, S., *Bomb, Book and Compass*, Penguin: 2009 / *Dictionary of National Biography*)

December 23rd

1930: On this day, at 7.25 p.m., as eminent physicist Ernest Rutherford was getting ready for dinner in Trinity College, a nurse arrived with the dreadful news that his daughter Eileen, his only child, had died. Twenty-nine year old Eileen had recently given birth at home to her fourth child; all had gone well with the delivery, so this sudden death, following an embolism, was quite unexpected. The following day Rutherford telegraphed his wife May, who was staying with relatives in her native New Zealand: 'It is a sad ending for Eileen's adventure but it may be called in a sense a happy end for I was always afraid of her becoming an invalid. If her lung trouble had flashed out again, it would have been a bad complication ...' Eileen was buried under a cypress tree in the churchyard at Ashmore, near her family's holiday home. On New Year's Day 1931, barely a week after Eileen's death, Rutherford's name was in the newspapers for a different reason; he had been elevated to the peerage and would be known from now on as Lord Rutherford. (Oliphant, M., *Rutherford: Recollections of the Cambridge Days*, Elsevier: 1972 / Campbell, J., *Rutherford: Scientist Supreme*, AAS Publications: 1999)

December 24th

1918: On this day, a new Christmas Eve service of lessons and carols, designed and planned by College Dean Eric Milner-White, took place in King's College Chapel; no one then could have realised that it would become the most widely known and best-loved of Cambridge traditions. Milner-White had just finished serving as a First World War army chaplain. His inspiration for the Christmas Eve service came from the Bishop of Truro, who had 'arranged from ancient sources a little service for Christmas Eve – nine carols and nine tiny little lessons which were read by various officers of the church, beginning with a chorister and ending with the Bishop.' In King's College, the service was adapted to exemplify the links between the College and Eton, both founded by King Henry VI, and between the town and the University of Cambridge. The Festival of Nine Lessons and Carols has been celebrated every Christmas Eve since 1918 and broadcast on the radio almost every year since 1928. A pre-recorded television version, entitled *Carols from King's*, has been broadcast since 1954. The first verse of *Once in Royal David's City*, sung unaccompanied by one young chorister, signals to listeners around the world that Christmas has finally begun. (*BBC Music Magazine*)

December 25th

1801: On this day, Samuel Chilcott visited the library at Sidney Sussex College in Cambridge and signed out four volumes of Johnson's *Works*. As James Basker wrote: 'One needn't be a Dickensian sentimentalist to find pathos in a lonely don trying to divert himself with the works of Johnson on Christmas Day.' If lonely Samuel Chilcott had been living in Cambridge in the early twenty-first century, he could have availed himself of the 'Christmas College', not a college in the traditional Cambridge sense, but in fact a society of the University which, unlike most other student societies, was at its most active during the Christmas vacation. The club was founded for all those members of the University, a surprising number in fact, who found themselves in Cambridge over Christmas with nowhere else to go. Their publicity shouted: 'When everything else shuts down – this society comes alive!' But not for long, as the society de-registered when the organisers forgot to file returns, so in the meantime perhaps Johnson's works might regain their festive appeal ... (Beales, D.E.D. and Nisbet, H.B., *Sidney Sussex College Cambridge: Historical Essays*, Boydell and Brewer: 1996 / Christmas College)

December 26th

1643: On this day, the fervent Suffolk Puritan William Dowsing, having been appointed 'commissioner for removing the monuments of idolatry and superstition from all of the churches in the eastern association', arrived at King's College Chapel in Cambridge. A few months earlier, Parliament had decreed the abolition from churches of stone altars, altar steps, crucifixes and all pictures of the Trinity, Virgin Mary and saints. This edict resulted in a widespread destruction of stained glass and at the spearhead of this destruction was William Dowsing himself. On his arrival at King's College, he wrote in one of his notebooks: 'Steps to be taken and 1 thousand Superstitious Pictures ye layder of Christ & theves to goe upon many crosses, and Jesus write on them'. This is generally taken to be a threat to the glass, in particular the East window, with its scenes from the Crucifixion. Miraculously, despite Dowsing's detailed intentions, the glass in King's College Chapel was not harmed; there has never been a satisfactory explanation for this. Various legends arose about the glass being taken down and hidden, but these rumours have never been substantiated. (Chainey, G., *A Celebration of King's College Chapel*, Pevensey Press: 1987)

December 27th

1664: On this day, Trinity College undergraduate Isaac Newton noted down detailed observations of the comet which was moving through the night skies over Cambridge. Newton's notebook has survived; dated on the fly leaf 'Isaac Newton/Trin: Coll Cant/1661' it is probably the one that he bought, together with some ink, on his arrival in Cambridge. Newton observed the comet over several days at the beginning of December and then again between 1 and 23 January 1665. The notes include a diagram to illustrate the relative position of the comet with reference to the location of the stars, though his descriptions of the comet are not always very clear. He was however obviously excited to see for the first time 'a Comet whose rays were round her, yet her tayle extended it selfe a little towards [the] east'. Through his reading of Descartes, Newton was also aware of contemporary ideas that the appearance of the comet's tail might simply be an optical phenomenon. It was however to be another sixteen years before he made detailed observations of the so-called Great Comet, later building an observatory above the Great Gate of Trinity. (Mandelbrote, S., *Footprints of the Lion: Isaac Newton at Work*, CUL: 2001)

December 28th

2002: On this day, renowned Cambridge cosmologist Professor Stephen Hawking took a tumble from his wheelchair and broke his hip whilst out with a nurse on the cobbled streets of Cambridge. Hawking was taken to Addenbrooke's Hospital where doctors were able to pin the hip, but because he suffers from motor neurone disease and has had a tracheotomy, he had to remain conscious throughout the operation and was given instead an epidural painkiller injection into his spine. Hawking later commented that the equipment used to pin the hip sounded like a Black and Decker drill. Hawking had apparently been driving his wheelchair much too fast, taking a corner at speed, and he was thrown out against a wall. Just over a week later, Hawking had recovered sufficiently to attend a symposium in Cambridge to mark his sixtieth birthday, attended by visitors from around the world. Hawking, Britain's longest surviving sufferer of motor neurone disease, was also determined not to miss a birthday party in his honour, attended by 250 friends, colleagues and close family. A Marilyn Monroe lookalike sang him *Happy Birthday* which delighted him, and his oldest son, Robert, made a speech. (*Cambridge Evening News*)

December 29th

1643: On this day, William Dowsing, Puritan iconoclast, charged by Parliament to destroy 'idolatrous images' in East Anglian churches and chapels, was in Cambridge. In just one highly charged day, Dowsing visited several Cambridge colleges and churches, leaving a trail of destruction behind him. Trinity College at least was well prepared. Seven years previously, Trinity had been singled out, in a report to William Laud, as a place 'ripe for improvement', for example: 'Divine service was slackly attended, the men of the choir were 'ignorant and unskilful' whilst the day choristers 'never could sing a note'. The layout of the Chapel and the style of worship were also said to be unsatisfactory. Reforms were quickly carried out, no doubt spurred on by a visit from Laud himself, and about £500 was spent on renovations and refurbishment of the Chapel, including new altar cloths and painted hangings. In March 1642, King Charles I visited and 'seemed very well to approve all their ornaments'; just months later, under a new parliamentary regime, the college removed to safety all the new, valuable additions to the college. Little remained for Dowsing to remove or destroy: just four cherubims and some steps 'to be levelled'. (Cooper, T., *The Journal of William Dowsing*, Boydell Press: 2001)

December 30th

1643: On this day, William Dowsing visited two Cambridge colleges and two churches, seeking out 'idolatrous images' that he and his men, Puritan iconoclasts, could destroy. Their first visit, to Sidney Sussex College, was brief and unproductive, the college already being a well-known centre of Puritanism, where Oliver Cromwell himself had studied. The chapel here contained 'none of the aids to devotion associated with the Laudian movement'; no surprise then that Dowsing found 'there was nothing to be mended'. Magdalene College fared less well, having been 'little influenced by events in other colleges'. Dowsing wrote afterwards in his diary: 'We brake downe about 40 superstitious pictures, Joseph and Mary stood to be espoused in the windows'. Today little is known about the glass destroyed by Dowsing in Magdalene, though some armorial glass seems to have outlived his visit. The east window, which presumably held the 'superstitious' glass in question, was bricked up in 1754, then exposed, replaced and reglazed in the nineteenth century. The old glass in the windows today was almost certainly imported, having been part of the collection amassed by Thomas Kerrich, late eighteenth-century antiquary and President of the College. (Cooper, T., *The Journal of William Dowsing*, Boydell Press: 2001)

December 31st

1914: On this day, a long-standing Cambridge New Year's Eve tradition ended as, for the last time, the Deck family set up rockets in the open space in front of King's College. For three generations the Deck family had marked the end of the dying year by firing a rocket at the first stroke of midnight and, as the vibration of the twelfth stroke stopped, letting off another to welcome in the New Year. The tradition was started by Arthur Deck, who was nicknamed Guy Fawkes by his friends because of his pyrotechnical inclinations. The Decks ran a chemist's shop at 9 King's Parade, which counted amongst its customers HRH the Prince of Wales, later King Edward VII. According to Arthur Gray, the crowd that gathered to watch this ceremony would be gradually hushed to expectant silence as the clock's hands crept towards the stroke of twelve, then break out into 'loud huzzas and mutual congratulations' as the second rocket showered overhead and the bells of Great St Mary's 'burst out into a brief but joyous peal.' (Gray, Arthur B., *Cambridge Revisited*, Heffer & Sons: 1921 / Reeve, F., *Cambridge from Old Photographs*, Batsford: 1971)